Manliness and Militarism

Manliness and Militarism:

Educating Young Boys in Ontario for War

Mark Moss

OXFORD
UNIVERSITY PRESS

OXFORD

UNIVERSITY PRESS

70 Wynford Drive, Don Mills, Ontario M3C 1J9
www.oupcan.com

Oxford University Press is a department of the University of Oxford.
It furthers the University's objective of excellence in research, scholarship,
and education by publishing worldwide in

Oxford   New York

*Athens   Auckland   Bangkok   Bogotá   Buenos Aires   Cape Town
Chennai   Dar es Salaam   Delhi   Florence   Hong Kong   Istanbul
Karachi   Kolkata   Kuala Lumpur   Madrid   Melbourne   Mexico City
Mumbai   Nairobi   Paris   São Paulo   Singapore   Taipei   Tokyo
Toronto   Warsaw*

with associated companies in
Berlin   Ibadan

Oxford is a trade mark of Oxford University Press
in the UK and in certain other countries

Published in Canada by Oxford University Press

Copyright © Oxford University Press Canada 2001

The moral rights of the author have been asserted

Database right Oxford University Press (maker)

First published 2001

Canadian Cataloguing in Publication Data

Moss, Mark Howard, 1962–
Manliness and militarism : educating young boys in Ontario for war

(The Canadian social history series)
Includes bibliographical references and index.
ISBN 0–19–541594–9

1. Military socialization—Ontario—History. 2. Militarism—Ontario—History.
3. Masculinity—Ontario—History. 4. Boys—Ontario—Attitudes.
5. World War, 1914–1918—Public opinion. 6. Public opinion—Ontario—History.
I. Title.   II. Series.

U21.5.M67 2001   306.2'7'09713   C00–933069–0

1 2 3 4 — 04 03 02 01

This book is printed on permanent (acid-free) paper ∞.
Printed in Canada

Contents

For my children, Jesse and Becca.

Preface

This book examines the efforts made in the decades preceding 1914 to prepare the boys of Ontario for war through a double emphasis on manliness and militarism. It is not an investigation of the causes of war, nor is it a military history of World War I. It makes no attempt to cast light on the whole of Ontario society in the period between 1867 and 1914. Rather, its investigation is confined to the most obvious and accessible group: the middle classes.

Young boys and men living in Ontario in the period under examination were exposed to a variety of influences that had enormously powerful effects both in forming their attitudes towards war and in persuading them that enlisting was not only right and proper but the only thing to do. Collectively, they had very little choice. Although there are many ways of approaching this subject, I have chosen to explore the forces and structures that made the ideals of manliness and militarism so persuasive. Consequently, the theoretical foundations I have found most relevant have to do with socialization and social control. Among the most interesting revelations I came to in researching this work were the cultural similarities between Ontario, Britain, and the American eastern seaboard. The parallels were most striking in the areas of book culture, attitudes towards manliness and the military, and the rearing of boys. For this reason many British and American studies on the culture of war and manliness proved extremely useful in explaining events in Ontario.

Parts of this work first appeared in *Popular Culture Review* 6, 1 (Feb. 1995). My research and writing were initially guided by David Levine, my thesis supervisor at the Ontario Institute for Studies in

Education/University of Toronto. His knowledge, experience, guidance, and time were all so forthcoming that it is safe to say that this work would never have materialized without his help. For all his contributions, I thank him. Jim Moran, my colleague and friend at Seneca College, also helped in many ways. He took the time to read many drafts and his thoughtful and sagacious advice is very much appreciated. Many people have aided me in many different ways: at Seneca, David Phillips, Henry Decock, and Tracey Pinkney; at Oxford, Len Husband, Richard Tallman, and Phyllis Wilson; and series editor Gregory S. Kealey. My wife, Ellen Feinman, provided me with the time to finish this work and to her I owe a special thanks.

1

Introduction

It seemed useless to carry on peace work in an atmosphere charged with talk of imperialism, patriotism, heroism and loyalty. The military craze has been carried on to such an extent that those who did not bow down as hero-worshippers were looked upon as disloyal.[1]

The above comment was made during the Boer War, by a superintendent of the Dominion Woman's Christian Temperance Union. It captures with perfect clarity the sentiments unleashed with the short South African War, which was fought from 1899 to 1901 and included only a small Canadian contingent. Yet the deluge of passion and enthusiasm for this war was remarkable in a number of ways. It seemed to express a feeling in Canada, and especially Ontario, that war, or at least the chance for the adventure of war, was a desirable thing. As well, it rallied Canadians around a particular set of ideals centred on the British experience. Anyone who was foolish enough to voice dissent to those ideals ran the risk of being labelled a traitor to the British Empire. And that was not something that most were willing to attempt. So vocal was the support for Britain and Canada during the South African War that even the most die-hard pacifists were leery of stepping too far out of line. The support and passion for war that affected the country between 1899 and 1901 would only increase in the years leading up to the Great War of 1914.

Dramatic reminders of that war and those who fought it are still present. Walking down University Avenue in Toronto, one cannot help being struck by the number of monuments to the war dead of Canada. From Queen's Park at the north end to Queen Street at the south, memorials dot the park and line the street. Similar monuments can be found in most of the province's small towns, where they serve as focal points for inhabitants and visitors alike. Bruce McCall writes, in his 1997 memoir, that the principal landmark of Simcoe, Ontario, was, and remains today, the Carillon Tower, 'a limestone rectangle erected in 1925 to commemorate the local fallen of Vimy, the Somme, Passchendaele, and Ypres with bronze plaques, and twenty-three bells, eternally tinged with mourning, pealing the hours.[2] Like McCall, many Ontarians grew up with the memory of a war monument as a seminal feature of civic life. It was, for McCall and others, a significant link to the past, to a time when boys did not ask why, but simply went and did their duty without questioning the powers that be. Why did they not question or, more accurately, why did they not question aloud? Had they done so, perhaps there would not be so many memorials.

War monuments have been a part of Ontario's symbolic geography since 1812, but they multiplied greatly following the wars in the Crimea (1853–6) and, in particular, South Africa. Commemorating those who gave their lives in the service of their country, cenotaphs, sculptures, and memorial gardens are located in places of privilege, usually near the city halls, for all to see, reminders even now of the sacrifices made out of patriotic loyalty.

Whether on University Avenue in Toronto or in a rural cemetery, many World War I monuments list, in beautifully engraved Gothic script, the names of those who died. Why are there so many names? Why did so many want to serve? What was happening in the province of Ontario in the years before 1914 to provoke such support for a European war? What forces were employed to teach young boys and young men that war was noble and glorious? Some answers to these questions are suggested in the following pages.

In the course of the Great War 205,808 volunteers came from the province of Ontario—almost half of all the men who volunteered to serve in the Canadian Expeditionary Force (CEF). By 1918, 231,191 men or 43 per cent of overall Canadian enlistments were from Ontario; 68,000 Ontarians were among the killed, wounded, or missing.[3]

For the 'Sons of the Empire', the Great War was the culmination of a long tradition not only of Canadian patriotism but of love for English Canada's mother country, Britain. This patriotism was supplemented by a vast array of role models, codes of conduct, and manufactured traditions that young men had to respect if they wished to be seen as upright, steadfast, and manly. The pressures to conform in this way came from numerous sources: the family, the church, the school, the various levels of government, the playing field, the press, even the toy shop. The common thread linking these agencies together was the conscious decision to teach impressionable young men what it meant to be a proud representative of Ontario, a good citizen of Canada, a patriot of the Empire, and a manly warrior. There could be no better way to demonstrate such loyalty than to fight for one's country.[4]

Young men have been persuaded to go to war for many reasons. One could dwell at length on motives such as the desire to preserve the past, or solidarity with comrades. Yet the most commonly cited motives in 1914 were patriotism and the desire for adventure. As one member of the Canadian Expeditionary Force put it: 'When war's alarm sounded in Canada, like many thousands of young men, the spirit of adventure was strong within me and here was an opportunity, as I thought, to kill two birds with the same stone'—'gratify my love of adventure and serve the Empire at one and the same time.'[5]

The strong ties that bound the citizens of Ontario to Britain made it relatively easy for them to view conflicts overseas as 'domestic' and relevant to their own lives. George Sterling Ryerson explained the traditional view of Ontario's British connection in 1924:

> They are not a warlike people, but the spirit of the United Empire Loyalists, of the old soldiers of 1812 and of the Napoleonic wars who had settled in Canada and laid the foundation of British Canada, is still strong. It is too much to say that Canadians all think Imperially, but there is a large and substantial element of the population, irrespective of creed or political affiliation, who regard the empire as a great entity, something to love, and if necessary, to die for. Hence, when a call to arms comes it meets with an immediate and whole-hearted response.[6]

Many felt it was their duty to volunteer. The origins of this sense of duty are the main subject of this work. But can duty alone explain why so many young men flocked to join up with the CEF in 1914? Peer pressure was undoubtedly one factor, as was the prospect of regular pay. Some politically informed young men had more complex reasons, such as moral outrage at Germany's actions, or the idealistic hope of rescuing Belgium.[7] Also important, however, was a value system that prized martial qualities and made boys want to be manly men. This work seeks to demonstrate how traditions were harnessed to the loyalties of young men for the purpose of making them into warriors for the Canadian nation.

In virtually all accounts of World War I, Britain's declaration of war on Germany in August 1914 was greeted in Ontario—as elsewhere—with enthusiasm, even euphoria.[8] Whether the cheers that broke out were 'for King, Britain and Victory' or for the prospect of war itself is impossible to tell. In any event, support ruled the day. According to Leslie M. Frost, in the small town of Orillia a stunned silence was followed by a burst of 'unbound enthusiasm . . . mark[ing] Orillia's determination to stand behind the empire and the old flag. Canada was one of the lion's cubs. With the rest of the family she would stand with the Motherland. The bands played, the men marched, the crowds cheered and Orillia responded to the challenge of war.' Similarly in Sudbury, Hamilton, and Toronto, most Ontarians welcomed the conflict.[9]

From Confederation onward, governments had sought to mould Canadians into patriotic and nationalistic citizens.[10] Much of the apparatus put in place in the years after 1867 had been intended to gear the new nation towards the production of such upstanding citizens. In the last years of the nineteenth century and the opening decade of the twentieth, education took on an importance that it had never held before. Suddenly, the government was extremely interested in the education system as a method of producing solid citizens. At all levels of involvement—federal, provincial, and municipal—through the school systems, welfare agencies, and medical associations, the government began to exert an influence in the lives of its citizens that would not have been possible without the developments associated with an increasingly modern society. This has led some commentators to suggest that it was at this point in time that the state began to exert an influence harmonious with social control and socialization.

Official government agencies were closely involved in the rearing of children through institutions such as the libraries, the schools, children's aid societies, and the courts. At the same time, a variety of nonofficial organizations such as the YMCA and the Boy Scouts stepped up their efforts to influence how children would be reared and to guarantee the production of patriotic citizens. Their efforts were buttressed by those of ministers, social workers, journalists, and writers who sought to instil in little citizens a specific set of ideals. Quite often, the ideals that these various organizations advocated merged. In the area of reading, for example, the school system, the library, and the YMCA complemented each other by pushing for books that would be morally uplifting and would enshrine a set of expectations that would guarantee patriotic and loyal citizens. The same message was reinforced over and over again at school, on the playing field, in civic celebrations, and—just to make sure—in the reading material made available to young people.

The term 'education' encompasses more than what went on in and around the schools. While pedagogy in the traditional sense was vital, ancillary forms of education began to play a growing role. After 1867, the 'ever-increasing close control of the school system maximized the possibility that the content of formal education would reflect the ideologies of those controlling the system.' Directly or indirectly, those in control of young people tried to educate them according to their own ideas of society's needs. Schooling is a particularly important consideration in this book because its main goal was to make pupils into citizens.[11] Specifically, much of the work is concerned with the processes of socialization, moral training, and character formation that were put in place to produce manly boys for manly deeds.

No specific class analysis is undertaken here. For the most part, the focus is on the middle classes, though in certain places direct reference is made to the working classes, and sometimes specific examples are drawn from the upper classes. Avenues of dissent were few and far between. Members of the working class were more likely than others to be suspicious of militarism and resented intrusions by the government and its agencies into arenas that involved 'character formation'. These individuals or, more accurately, their representatives were quite suspicious of the imperial sentiment and 'jingoistic' fever of the dominant classes.[12]

This work assumes a social control and a socialization framework. Despite the ongoing debates in regard to these approaches, especially the former, this work assumes the relevance of both to the elaboration of its themes.

Much of the material discussed in this book reflects a deliberate and conscious attempt by representatives from the middle and upper-middle classes to shape, mould, and control the behaviour of the majority of the population. The concept of 'hegemony' might well be applied here. Nevertheless, this very successful attempt to manage the population in both formal and informal ways in no way nullified working-class attempts to make its own set of rules or to fashion its own versions and variations of a particular activity. Contemporary literature is usually written and published from a middle- and upper-middle-class viewpoint. Secondary source descriptions employed here on any number of issues also have a tendency to focus on the traditional, middle-class approach.

The opinion-makers and information purveyors as well as the 'character moulders' who all influenced and affected the political, social, and cultural life of the province of Ontario have been understood to be representative of a dominant homogeneous 'class'. In effect, there was a tendency for them to take a stance on many of the progressive and major ideas that governed the life of the province. This is not to say that they all agreed all the time and that there weren't pockets of dissent, but, rather, that the main ideas stemmed from a similarity of time and place. This similarity is one of the reasons why socialization was so uniform and so successful in this province.

At its most fundamental level, socialization is the 'process by which one becomes a functioning member of a group'. A more complex definition suggests that it is 'the developmental processes whereby each person acquires the knowledge, skills, beliefs, values, attitudes, and dispositions which allow him or her to function as a more or less effective, though not inevitably compliant, member of society. Through these developmental processes the individual learns how to live with others, even though values, beliefs and patterns of behaviour may vary from one generation to the next.'[13] But how does an organization, political group, or society know if the process of socialization has succeeded, given the intricacies of modern society?

Socialization becomes problematic when there are competing agents of socialization, each with its own agenda. This inevitably leads to conflicts and inconsistencies in experience. Yet when a society is dominated by a strong, vocal, and well-organized élite that controls the traditional agencies of socialization—such as the church, the media, and the schools—there is little room for conflicting messages. Ontario was dominated by an Anglo-Protestant élite that virtually ruled all the discourse of the province. Until the last decades of the nineteenth century it faced little or no organized competition. With the rise of women's groups and labour voices that broke with tradition, things began to change, albeit not very much.

The dominant ideas and values of manliness and militarism had permeated virtually every facet of society since Confederation. To be sure, there were voices of dissent from working-class, labour, feminist, and Francophone residents of Ontario, but, in general, young boys were exposed to enthusiastic support for war and war culture. Working-class antagonism towards militarism and imperial sentiment originated from the displacements brought about as a consequence of modernization. Whether on the farm or in the factory, imperial zeal was something of which to be wary. On the farm, imperialism would pull sons away from working the land, while in the factory, imperialism would embroil those most hard-pressed in society to engage in matters not of their making and of benefit only to those oppressing them. This line of thinking was not articulated by the new urban masses but, rather, by those who sought to give voice and coherence to working-class concerns.

In the last quarter of the nineteenth century, aided by advances in technology, literacy, and transportation, the labour press became an important forum for the discussion and dissemination of working-class concerns. Labour journalists increasingly defined the agenda for situations and issues affecting the working class. The journalists for the labour press began to mark out new territory for a readership that had almost nothing in common with the dominant classes. The labour press served as an 'educational forum for working people'. Labour journalists did not see anything of merit in the militaristic flavour of the province. To counteract this mood, they embraced a pacifist stand in their articles and spoke out and wrote against closer imperial ties. The point here is that those writing and editing these journals and newspapers had one coherent position on the subjects of imperialism and militarism, while those reading or those to whom the articles were addressed may not have possessed the same sentiments.

Labour journalists were opposed to war and militarism for a number of tangible, class-derived reasons. Suspicion of nationalism, the close links of military and capitalist enthusiasts, and deflection from working-class problems are three main reasons behind the labour journalists' suspicion of militarism. Labour journalists consistently opposed anything related to the militarization of society. Military instruction in the schools, for example, was anathema to them. Yet the dominant ideals of the period 1867–1914 were too powerful to reject, despite valiant efforts of those like the labour journalists.[14]

The church's power declined slowly and a host of 'secular' organizations and agents voiced the same messages through different channels. The YMCA, the libraries, the Boy Scouts, and the schools, professional organizations, volunteer groups, and patriotic institutions all stepped in to pick up the slack. For example, what young boys read was often whatever was available, and what was available was decided by opinion and decision-makers who held similar attitudes to those who controlled the province.

Children's literature, as R. Gordon Kelly, has observed, is 'one of the few elements of child-rearing behaviour that remains accessible for research long after its intended function as entertainment and instruction has ceased'. What is contained in the adventure story or the journals for boys comes from a specific point of view and is oriented around a governing set of principles. The fact that children's literature is written by adults with their own intentions further cements this idea. The same situation is applicable to the schools. The schools worked by the dictum that getting the child as early as possible made it less likely that the child's opinions or 'orientations' would change as an adult.[15] Morals, character, manliness, patriotism, and militarism were all enshrined in the curriculum, both formal and informal, in order to rear a specific kind of adult. All the knowledge, beliefs, attitudes, and dispositions that were acquired by a young person in school, and buttressed through reading and participation in sports, would no doubt lead to a process that stressed certain specific ways to behave and act in society at large.

Political socialization differs slightly from the generalized conceptions of socialization. On the one hand it is 'the deliberate inculcation of political information, values and practices by instructional agents who have been formally charged with this responsibility'. Yet a more generous and broader definition of political socialization includes the impact of virtually every kind of 'political learning', 'deliberate and unplanned, at every stage of the life cycle, including not only explicitly political learning but also nominal nonpolitical behaviour, such as the learning of politically relevant social attitudes and the acquisition of politically relevant personality characteristics'. When it comes to militarism and patriotism, this kind of socialization takes on added importance. It becomes relevant in the eyes and mind of a child as he is bombarded constantly with images of specific political ideals. If both in and outside of the school he is reading subjects that reinforce each other, then he is being groomed consciously and subliminally to be a certain kind of person who is learning what is acceptable and appropriate. Even non-official agents have an impact on the child's development, especially if they hold similar opinions to the government. This kind of 'massive indoctrination' is surely effective, particularly when there is little in the way of alternatives. The period under examination here offered few alternatives and in all realms—leisure, schooling, sports—conveyed a uniform inculcation of specific social, political and institutional loyalties. What gives this form of political socialization added weight is the fact that it is an ongoing process, affecting the child continually throughout his formative years and well into adulthood.

Children are particularly susceptible to political opinions and are capable of making specific identifications while holding patriotic opinions at a very early age. Given the lack of alternatives, the ideal of commitment to the nation is extremely effective during the school years and 'is not only formative, but in good measure enduring'. Political indoctrination and education, in virtually any form, serves to promote the acceptance of the 'prevailing social order and its values; adaptation to its economic, political and military requirements; acceptance of a world view; ignorance of alternative social orders'. The media, schools, sports groups, and youth groups fostered a particular acceptance of patriotism, imperialism, manliness, and militarism, which, in effect, served to mirror the concerns of both official and élite culture.[16]

One of the main features of modern societies is the fact that the state has increasingly taken control over various mechanisms previously left to the individual or the family. The concept of social control occupies a pivotal role in the following chapters, for it is more than just a hallmark of modernism. The concept of social control provides a useful framework for analysing the structures that induced people, especially young boys, to 'behave willingly and *voluntarily* in ways that the guardians of law and order deemed conductive to law and order'. A basic premise of social control is that those with the power in society—a small, powerful, and dominant élite—are interested in the maintenance of this power but, more to the point, attempt to 'control' those without it. This is partially accomplished by expanding the agencies of socialization, and further, by governing the rules and structures of socialization. Those who create laws, as F.M.L. Thompson has observed, are affecting conduct and expressing their own biases and fears regarding 'the consequences of law breaking'. In late Victorian and Edwardian society lawmakers were codifying their views of society and of how it should be run and controlled. Another way of stating this is that social control is not necessarily used to defend certain interests; rather it originates as a 'broadly based corrective to "generally" perceived threats of social disequilibrium and disorder'. The explicit regulation of leisure time and the constrictions and rules around the playing of sports were subject to this same kind of social control.[17]

The creation of 'rational recreation' in the form of libraries and clubs, youth organizations, and parks was an overt attempt by middle- and upper-class social controllers 'to shape the tastes and habits of the working classes'. A discussion of this attempt leads to an analysis of how the pre-modern community adapted to the forces of modernization—industrialism, communication, and transportation—that radically altered its traditional social needs. Given the changing nature of society, no longer were the time-honoured, rural, and folk methods of community capable of governing the modern society that was emerging. To make matters more confusing, as immigration increased, Old World ideas continued to influence communities in their pre-modern ways. This flew in the face of the pace of modernity.[18]

Economic, industrial, and communications transformations caused those in power to respond to what they perceived to be a chaotic disruption in society. Perceiving a crisis that would affect and alter all realms of society, including the behaviour of the 'lower or dangerous classes', members of the middle and upper middle classes sought to 'instil' a variety of controls on those they feared most. According to John A. Mayer:

> Members of the middle and upper classes who sensed this breakdown most acutely instituted a series of reform measures designed to impose social controls upon the lower classes; these reforms would control the behaviours of the lower classes towards the desired ends of self-discipline, industry, punctuality, thrift—in other words, towards what has come to be called middle-class morality.

Mayer suggests that the acceptance of this 'modernity' thesis is the reason for the consistent employment of the social control paradigm. At the same time, he is quick to recognize that this 'middle-class' interpretation and application, utilized in numerous studies on welfare, reform, and education and in political surveys, has a major drawback.

The problem with the concept of middle- and upper-class agencies controlling the 'behaviour' of lower, working, or immigrant classes is that it is theoretically incapable of recognizing the success of the control, its motivations, and the reactions and responses of those who were to be controlled. What Mayer indicates to be even more problematic is the fact that historians writing in the 1970s and 1980s were using the idea of social control from the sociological standpoint of controlling deviant behaviour. Immigrants and the working classes who were the recipients of certain controls in various ways were different from those who imposed them, but as Mayer suggests, they were not clinically deviant. A further complication is added when considering the vibrancy of ethnic communities. How successful are social control mechanisms and agencies given the robustness of certain ethnic groups at retaining their culture and traditions?[19]

This last point can be partially addressed by looking at the attempts of the state, the schools, and various groups to Canadianize their charges through aspects of education designed to patronize them. Yet the use of the sociological definition of social control

remains problematic. To rectify this, Mayer employs Morris Janowitz's reworking of the term to encompass a broader and more relevant explanation especially for historians. Janowitz expands social
control's relevance by suggesting that it should be seen as a dominant
group's attempts to apply self-regulation in order to achieve a harmonious outcome in a functioning society. This takes the concept away
from coercion and puts the emphasis on shared ideals. There are,
then, two separate (but not unrelated) ways to see or define social
control: as a form of coercion and as a form of self-regulation. The
latter definition still involves attempts to change or influence
behaviour, but (and this is especially applicable for the themes discussed here) it relies on 'persuasion, rhetoric, symbolism, operational
rewards and (non-forceful) punishments'. Taking this a step further,
Mayer uses the term 'associative social control' for situations that
involve a person's willing and free desire to have his or her behaviour
and ideals shaped. Mayer factors in the importance of psychological
rewards in this category and feels this category would be extremely
relevant to the needs of ethnic communities.[20]

The main concern with the concept of social control is that despite
Janowitz's expansion, there is little allowance for the 'agency' factor
in the historical process. Since the publication of E.P. Thompson's
massive work, *The Making of the English Working Class*, an attempt
to account for the interaction of structure and agency has been constant in historiography and social history. The ability of individuals to
make their own history is a major focus of Thompson's work as is his
concept of agency. If we forget that individuals, regardless of their
origins, are capable actors in their history, who are aware of what they
are doing, and if we view all of society as one homogeneous mass
dominated by institutions, great men, or structures, then central components of past experiences are nullified or, at the least, relegated to
the fringes. No matter how these 'invisibles' have been marginalized,
they have had some impact on the structures that have been employed
to control them.[21]

The economic, political, and social 'structures' that have been
used to control individuals are understood, according to Anthony
Giddens, as 'rules and resources implicated in the form of collectivi-
ties of social systems, reproduced across space and time'. The actions
of members in a particular institution give rise to the structures that
serve as forums for the exercise of power. What gives structures so
much authority is the fact that they are historically charged and transformed over time by people and practice, and, in turn, they affect and
alter those they control. Whereas individuals can and do alter their

conditions, they are too affected by structures. 'Societies or social formation are prior to the existence of individuals and shape their characteristic attitudes and modes of conduct.'[22]

In their work on the American Play Movement, Stephen Hardy and Alan G. Ingham suggest that many historians, especially play historians, have neglected 'to grasp' the fact that everyone is an agent 'in the production and reproduction of the structures through which we make history'. What is significant about their comment in regard to this work is that while individuals are capable actors in the creation of their history, the structures or conditions that they must work under and in are not, to paraphrase Marx, of their own choosing. The individuals who formed the schools, the clubs, the libraries, and the rules and regulations that governed the province possessed a 'wider range of resources and capabilities within the structures they created'. What is significant for this view is the way they 'used their power to manipulate structures'.[23]

Power relationships prove a very interesting and useful area for illustration given the themes of this work. Closely related to agency and structure and social control is the idea of hegemony. A significant feature of a modern, consumer-oriented, increasingly urban society is the ability of a dominant group to exercise a certain amount of power with the consent of the lower groups.

One of the significant features of hegemony, as defined by Antonio Gramsci, is that it helps to unify and clarify the other framework suggested above. The general thrust of hegemony is defined in Gramsci's essay 'The Formation of the Intellectuals'. Here Gramsci states two significant definitions of hegemony, one cultural and one political, although there is a great deal of interchange between the two:

(1) The 'spontaneous' consent given by the great masses of the population to the general direction imposed on social life by the dominant fundamental group; this consent is 'historically' caused by the prestige (and consequent confidence) which the dominant group enjoys because of its position and function in the world of production.

(2) The apparatus of state coercive power which 'legally' enforces discipline on those groups who do not 'consent' either actively or passively. This apparatus is, however, constituted for the whole of society in anticipation of moments of crisis of command and direction when spontaneous consent has failed.[24]

As with the concept of social control, there are a number of discrepancies in the first definition of hegemony. As T.J. Jackson Lears has asked, 'What components of a dominant culture require the consent of subordinates?' Jackson Lears suggests that Gramsci was talking about values, perceptions, norms, and sentiments that support and define the institutions of power. Consent, incidently, was often a Marcusian commitment to the established order. And yet the working class was not completely domesticated. Like E.P. Thompson's 'subjects', they were conscious of their place and could act up at any time. The problem as Gramsci states it, and as Jackson Lears comments on it, is the fact that most do not act up even though they might feel a mixture of 'resignation and resistance'.[25]

This mixture is fostered, encouraged, and perpetuated through a variety of spheres—public, private, cultural, and economic—that make hegemony much more fluid and difficult to challenge. The almost ephemeral character of these spheres, and their 'continuous creation', leads to fragmentation and changes in alliances depending on the time. People may share in a kind of 'half-conscious complicity in their own victimization'. What is significant and controversial here is the fact that traditionally powerless individuals may have unwittingly played a part in the perpetuation of their powerlessness. Specifically in the arena of culture, hegemony did not have to depend on brainwashing, but rather 'on the tendency of public discourse to make some forms of experience readily available to consciousness while ignoring or suppressing others'. As 'abstractions', the values, mores, and ideals of the dominant culture were a part of working or non-middle-class culture, but when they got too close they could be reworked and even ignored.[26]

Keith Walden even goes so far as to suggest that the dominant ideals of the culture of the age could be found in store windows. Official Anglo-Protestant Ontario culture could weave its way into the unsuspecting minds of passersby, reaffirming the 'social order' and radically redefining notions of education:

> Stocking windows with seasonal goods indicated, perhaps especially to city people, that human culture was linked to a regular, predictable progression in nature. Hunting windows and cleaning windows defined gender role expectations; Christmas confectionary windows reinforced ideas about the nature of children and childhood; patriotic windows with flags, bunting, and pictures of the king and queen buttressed concepts of nation and race. Besides delineating traditional categories, windows provided more general reassurances about the actuality of order.[27]

The dominant political ideology in Canada, and specifically Ontario, at this time—and one that merged easily with militarism, manliness, patriotism, and nationalism—was imperialism. Imperialism separated settlers of British heritage from all others. Canada was dominated by Anglophones seeking to reconstruct the values and culture of their original society.

From approximately 1867 onward, Canadian imperialists agitated for closer ties to Britain, the mother country, and the role they sought for Canada was not always a passive one: they desired a large role in the workings of the Empire. Prestige and influence were equated with closer relations with Britain and the Empire. Through imperial unification, Canada could join the ranks of the great nations and achieve 'a great national destiny'. The most active proponents of imperialism were, by and large, members of the country's Protestant élite such as the Presbyterian Reverend George Grant, principal of Queen's University.[28]

By 1881 in Ontario, the most British of provinces, approximately 83 per cent of the population were Protestant. An informal alliance between the Methodists, Anglicans, Presbyterians, and Baptists, both spiritual and state-oriented, made for easy accommodation on many issues. By the last few decades of the nineteenth century, Protestantism in English Canada was facing many challenges from a growing population of immigrants from other religious traditions. The Protestant denominations were also being affected by changes that were moving Ontario towards an urban, modern, industrial, and more secular culture. This new environment, with its factories, schools, and mass media, was much more open to secular notions than had been the case in previous generations. As A.B. McKillop has commented, a new focus had to be found for Anglo-Protestantism so that it could continue to speak to its constituency but, at the same time, move beyond the spectrum of orthodox theology, rigid moralism, and dated traditions.[29]

As English Canada moved towards secularization, a strong moral dimension prevailed. The fact that, even in small-town Ontario, not everyone attended church simply presented new challenges and prompted new solutions, which rescued Christianity by changing it into a form of 'social religion'. A kind of 'non-denominational Protestantism', to use Susan Houston's term, was to step in and 'provide a common faith on which to rest the shared loyalty basic to national consciousness'.[30]

In this context, then, the separation of church and state is almost irrelevant. The institutions of the state were run by people who shared similar fundamental convictions. Protestant culture thus enjoyed an authority that permeated all levels of Ontario society and shaped its very consciousness.[31] Whether the imperialism was intellectual or purely material, its purveyors shared the same heritage. Imperialism was unique to English Canada; it had no appeal whatever to French-speaking Canadians.[32] As Douglas L. Cole has put it, 'Imperialists were imperialists in large measure because they were acutely conscious of ethnic ties and ethnic differentiation.' Imperialism was by definition confined to those of British background.[33]

One may speculate that the appeal of imperialism had much to do with the comfort of tradition at a time of marked change. The forces of modernization, in particular industrialization and urbanization, were pushing Ontario society away from its rural roots and traditional small-town ways and bringing change in almost every area of life, from the search to find work in the city to the reduction of manual labour to the increasing levels of immigration. Fearing that the modern age would render them superfluous, many men from all classes tried desperately to hang on to their traditional roles of bread-winners, providers, and citizen-soldiers.[34] Hence it became vital to the leaders in late nineteenth- and early twentieth-century society to promote any form of training that would protect their cherished positions, privileged access, and time-honoured power. In this process, of course, the upbringing of children was of special importance.

In a climate where the most 'important watchwords' were 'discipline, efficiency, and development',[35] men sought to revive a manliness that appeared to be vulnerable. Opportunities to recapture a particular ideal of what real men were about could take many diverse forms: getting back to nature, participating in sports, reading adventure novels, cheering for sports teams, or bonding at the pub—any of these might serve to revive the essential male spirit that was threatened by the forces of modernization.[36] The ultimate forum for the exercise of masculinity, however, was war. At a time when there was no actual war to fight, suitable substitutes would have to be found to develop the skills and hone the character traits that would be required for combat sometime in the future.

Not surprisingly, this culture of manliness was extended downward to young boys who seemed the most at risk of not growing up to be manly men. Many organizations, from the Boy Scouts to the cadets, were created in response to worries about manliness. Most of these, as David Macleod has observed, had a middle-class viewpoint and were orchestrated along lines that reflected middle-class concerns and values. There was a generalized concern, among middle-class reformers, that the crowded and dirty conditions of the new urban environment were taking their toll on Ontario's youth. The unhealthy living conditions in cities were seen as contributing to the decline of manly virtues. To reverse the downward trend, camps and youth groups stressed outdoor activity, fresh air, and the strenuous, character-building qualities of nature.[37]

Contributing to concerns about manliness was the fact that so many women were now involved in the teaching of young boys. For many men, and some women, this development represented a further step in the erosion of the traditional methods by which boys were taught to become suitably manly men. And, as the new world of work took fathers away from the home and into the office or factory, some observers felt that boys simply would not receive the masculine guidance that had been a staple of farm life and pre-industrial society. Many were concerned about the dominance of the female influence and the impact that this was having on boys. It was felt that men must not only rescue their sons from the influence of women but also find new outlets and avenues to recapture their own manhood as well as their sons'. An often recommended corrective was physical exercise and vigorous participation in sports and games. Not only were these active masculine endeavours, but they would aid in teaching responsibility, teamwork, honour, and patriotism. After 1870, sports and games increasingly came to be seen as having both character-building and military value.[38]

The poor physical condition of Canada's youth, especially in the cities, was a major cause of concern. Some felt that city living was sapping the vigour of Canada's youth and beginning to threaten the overall quality of its citizens. Among them was R. Tait Mackenzie, who warned that modern conditions had

> done away with the time when hard outdoor work for the young laid a foundation of physical strength which would last through a maturity of less healthful conditions. And unless some means were found to combat such a position, there would ultimately come a reduction in the national physique which would react upon the progress of the people.[39]

Such concerns were first highlighted during the Boer War, and suggested that much more had to be done to increase the health and strength of Canada's youth. It was felt that a more modern approach was required: mothers had to be trained in the new scientific child-rearing methods; schools had to encourage drill, obedience, loyalty, and the right values. Supervision that did not come from the home or the school would have to be improvised elsewhere. Organizations such as the Boy Scouts and the cadets offered to fill this void.

Canadians were fortunate to live in a climate that encouraged 'physical vigour', 'pristine morality', 'energy, strength, self-reliance, health and purity'. Sports of all kinds could be used to develop not only the physical abilities required of a warrior but the qualities of character that seemed to be in decline among Canada's young people. Lacrosse, ice hockey, baseball, soccer, rugby, cricket—all were capable of instilling habits of teamwork and loyalty. Another manly pursuit actively promoted as a remedy for the perceived weakening of the nation's young men was hunting, which—in addition to developing courage and skill with a gun—offered the actual experience of killing.[40]

Children came to be looked at in a new light during this period. Like flowers, they required special cultivation; nothing should be left to chance. With the proper character-building nutrients they could mature into adults with the values required to make appropriate contributions to their society. The spectre of delinquency hung darkly over those who failed at this task.[41] Parents who wanted their boys to be manly should encourage them in that direction. Fathers working outside the home should make sure that their sons' toys provided the right kind of stimulation; toy soldiers and games of strategy were ideal. It was equally important to make sure that young boys had the right kinds of reading material, especially in fiction, where patriotic adventure novels by writers like Henty and Kipling were highly recommended. In many cases, especially among the middle class, there was a fear that their boys were 'growing up weak'. This appears to have reflected the fathers' anxiety that they themselves were unmanly.[42]

Men of the period were supposed to exercise firm self-control, not show their emotions. Proper deportment and decorum were all-important. Heroic examples abounded, from military heroes to business tycoons. The definitive illustration was US President Theodore Roosevelt. Master of all he attempted, as sportsman, cowboy, warrior, statesman, or historian, Teddy Roosevelt was the embodiment of manly character—a living, breathing testament to the 'all conquering powers of white manhood'.[43] To alleviate the growing concerns about their masculinity, men and boys of this period embraced every opportunity to display their manliness. It became common to demonstrate one's worth, to perform as a male for oneself and for others. The pressures of boyhood accelerated; no longer was it a carefree and tranquil time. For example, defending oneself against taunts and teasing became a much more serious concern at this juncture in history. Fear of being labelled a sissy was enough to provoke a boy into a fight to prove who he was and demonstrate his toughness. According to one historian, the First World War served much the same purpose, transforming boys into men who had tested their mettle.[44]

Love of country dovetailed neatly with the character traits—service, obedience, hard work, team effort—that had served the British Empire so well. Ontario's Lieutenant-Governor summed up the importance of patriotism and loyalty in an 1892 speech commemorating General Isaac Brock, the hero of the War of 1812. The Queen's representative said that young boys must be instructed 'in the patriotic spirit' if they were to succeed in emulating 'the deeds of their forefathers'.[45] The boys who grew up in the 1890s would become the young men who flocked overseas in such large numbers in 1914. The reasons behind their enthusiasm are the subject of this book.

No examination of the period 1867–1914 can confine itself within rigid chronological or national boundaries. Synthesis is as important here as the recognition of diversity. As Peter Gay points out, he uses the term 'Victorian' throughout his multi-volume *Bourgeois Experience* 'as a synonym for "nineteenth-century"': Victorians, according to Gay and others, existed before Queen Victoria ascended the throne and lasted until the outbreak of hostilities in 1914. As well, another factor that must be considered is that the traditional attribution of Victorian traits to Great Britain does not take into account the fact that these ideals had appeal to many other nations. As Steven Mintz notes, 'Victorianism has generally been treated as an exclusively English phenomenon. But during the nineteenth century, there was a constant flow of ideas among England, Scotland and America.'[46] Both Gay's and Mintz's comments apply equally well to Ontario culture, which had many links with American as well as British culture.

This double influence must be recognized as a significant factor in the province's social and cultural life. Still in its adolescence, Canada was not without external models on which to pattern its national character. With Britain there were long 'constitutional, military, economic and social ties', and with the United States there was an increasing closeness in regard to 'economic, social and geographic' matters. For the average citizen the closest bonds to either the United States or Britain were emotional. The fact that the United States was so large, so close, and so powerful inspired both admiration and fear in Ontario.[47] For those in positions of intellectual, political, and artistic power, this general emotional dualism led to attempts to find a common ground. A.B. McKillop sums up this situation with direct reference to English Canada's intellectual élite:

> Caught historically between a British Heritage, which many of them conceived to contain the best elements of Western civilization, and an American neighbour, which advanced ineluctably

towards modernity in its modes of thought and action, Anglo-Canadians in the Victorian Era sought to establish and to preserve in Canada a broad moral code that would constitute the core of a way of life reconciling belief and inquiry, tradition and innovation, concern and freedom.[48]

The idea of a national character had been debated and discussed in depth since the 1830s. By 1860 a 'Canadian Type' was being identified —one that immigrants were expected to emulate. Although a full-fledged definition was as problematic then as it is today, two factors have remained consistent obstacles in defining a Canadian: the fact that this was a British colony, and the fact that the country is situated so close to the United States. As early as 1824, it was noted that, in contrast to other British colonies, Canada was 'almost wholly inhab-ited by natives of Great Britain and their decendants.' Consequently, Canadians 'possessed "the same moral and political sentiments and cherished the same domestic and national feelings as their fathers and their ancient kindred."' As strong as that historical connection was, however, it was subject to threats, both real and imagined, from the United States. The threats seem to have been greatest in the socio-cultural realm. The influence of American ideas, via magazines and books, only increased as the nineteenth century closed and the twen-tieth began. In 1887, Sara Jeannette Duncan wrote that 'more Ameri-can than British writers were familiar to Canadians.' She also noted that 'Canadian writing displayed American characteristics' and that while those of British ancestry will gravitate towards British books, 'the mass of Canadians prefer American writing.'[49]

Regardless of how many individual Canadians drew their heritage and culture from Britain, the American influence on Canadian thoughts and ideas was strong. Many Canadian collective traditions and the myths of land, notions of progress, and individualism were, as Allan Smith has noted, 'cast largely in terms of ideas drawn from the South.' Canadians gravitated towards American heroes, American mythology, and American news, literature, and culture. What was popular in the US was often just as popular in Canada. Whether the reason was the obvious geographical proximity of the US or the easy flow of people and ideas across the border, many American events were of great interest to Canadians.[50] Popular American attitudes, especially in the areas of sports, literature, child-rearing, and of course, war, were extremely relevant to people in Canada, especially in Ontario. Thus experiences such as the US Civil War had a lasting impact on Canadians. As Smith writes:

The exposure of Canadian to the memoirs, biographies and histories which were issued in such quantity after 1865 ensured that after its termination they would continue to feel a strong sense of involvement in the Civil War. Its heroes, indeed, occasionally assumed the same status in Canada as they had attained in the United States. The sentiments which led the *British American Magazine* to characterize Stonewall Jackson 'as a moral hero' who belonged 'to the world as an example through all time,' were still in evidence thirty years later when a Canadian trade journal commented on the authorized life of Lincoln, then in preparation. The book, it said, ought to sell very well in Canada 'as in no land is the name of Lincoln more revered than here.'[51]

The growing influence of American cultural products upon Canadian motivations, actions, and ideas, therefore, cannot be dismissed. It must be considered as a force equal to, if rarely overshadowing, the British influence.

The historical background outlined in Chapters 2 and 3 establishes the content for this book. After a wide-ranging general analysis of the movements, themes, and ideas pervasive at the time, the remaining chapters focus on examining the specific elements that shaped the lives of young Ontario males in the direction of militarism, patriotism, and manliness. Chapter 4 looks at one of the major sources of influence at this time, literature. It examines why certain writers were read in Ontario from the time of Confederation until World War I, the importance of the adventure novel, and the influence of boys' magazines. Chapter 5 discusses the politics of schooling, including the curricular emphasis on drill and physical culture and the deliberate inculcation of the concept of Empire. Boys' culture, from toy soldiers to the Boy Scouts, from hunting to sports heroes, is the focus of Chapters 6 and 7.

With virtually every facet of society teaching boys that the warrior was the ultimate masculine ideal, there could be little mistake about the message. Canada had to prove its worth to its citizens, to Britain, and to the world. In volunteering so many of its youth, Canada passed its own test of nationhood.

2

Historical Context:
Imperialism and Militarism

For I believe in Britain's Empire, and
In Canada, its true and loyal son,
Who yet shall rise to greatness, and shall stand
At England's shoulder helping her to guard
True liberty throughout a faithless world.

Charles Mair, 'Tecumseh' (1886)

Both manliness and militarism wove their way into the fabric of Ontario society in the last quarter of the nineteenth century and the first decade and a half of the twentieth. Intertwined with the various 'isms' and ideologies characteristic of an emerging society, they were arguably the dominant themes of the province's social, political, and cultural discourse.

'The cult of manliness' was one of 'the principal features of Victorian Canada'. This cult had its origins in the social vision according to which the prospective tamers of the land—all descendants of British stock, of course—required both a certain 'temper' and a specific 'code of conduct'. The 'Victorian British Canadian' produced by this code—'a highly masculine, athletic, outdoor man, independent of mind and trained in the habit of authority'—was 'a dominant stereotype' of the age.[1] Farmer or factory worker, rural dweller or city inhabitant, man or boy, no male could escape the pressure to be manly.

As the nineteenth century drew to a close, however, the traditional association of masculinity with the land and the outdoor life was weakening, and a new definition was required. In essence, men now had to be able to adjust, to withstand the changes affecting their world. 'Men had to be "manly" and women very female.'[2] As urbanization eclipsed the traditional rural life and civilization encroached on wilderness, understandings of manliness had to evolve as well. The reborn cult of manliness was never far from the minds of men or boys in the late Victorian era.

In the same period Canada's military situation was changing. Since the 1850s, Britain had been seeking to reduce its staggering defence commitments, especially in its colonies. One reason was economic, but another reflected a general opinion that self-governing colonies and those moving towards independence should take a greater share of their own defence responsibilities.[3]

Although the American Civil War, in the early 1860s, compelled the British to strengthen their defences in North America, the gesture was essentially hollow. That the Americans could quickly overrun any British force was obvious both to British politicians and to the Canadian public. Together, the threat of an American invasion and Britain's weariness with its defence commitment led to only one conclusion: Canada should have its own army. Most Canadians did not embrace the idea of a standing army. Whether they feared diverting energies and resources that Britain had previously supplied, felt ambivalent about the new country's own independent role, or simply preferred a citizen army, most residents of British North America were not eager to begin the task of organizing a purely Canadian defence force. The first Militia Act, hammered out amid controversy and political apprehension in 1868, created what Desmond Morton has described as 'no more than a modest auxiliary for the British regular garrison which really defended Canada'. Thirty-six years later, a revised Act led to the creation of a true 'national army, commanded by Canadians and standing on its own in North America'. From one extreme, Canada moved to the other.[4]

From the late 1860s until the eve of World War I, the federal government had to sell the idea of a standing army to the populace—as Stephen Harris puts it, 'to somehow shake Canadians out of their lethargy and convince them to reform their military institutions.'[5] The success of that campaign would take all Canadians into a new era of militarism.

To prove the worth of Ontario's boys and men would require some kind of dynamic action. The ultimate demonstration of manhood, of course, would be to fight in a war. In the meantime, the connection between manliness and militarism was strengthened, creating a climate in which there was little to distinguish between the two.

Patriotic Imperialism

A standing army on Canadian soil was not something that appealed to most Victorian Canadians. Yet from Confederation onward, the image of the militia had developed a mystique that grew with the number of citizen soldiers. From the Riel Rebellions through the Boer War, Canadians generally believed that the average male citizen could do a more than adequate job against a professional army. This belief reflected the changing national character, growing patriotism, and increasing awareness of imperial ties, all of which helped to generate sympathy for militarism. In the Edwardian years patriotism blossomed among English-speaking Canadians from the middle class, and their fervour increased each year until World War I. By 1913, 55,000 militiamen were training at a cost of almost $11 million per year.[6]

The influence of British culture on Ontario was immense. So powerful was the tie that in 1910 Wilfrid Laurier had said that when Britain was at war, Canada was at war. In short, 'the society saw itself more as English Canadian than Ontarian.'[7] Thus when the actual fighting began there was much sympathy for Britain, even though Canada was thousands of miles from the action. Strong bonds united the two countries; attitudes and homefront conditions were quite similar. 'The enthusiasm and intense patriotism of a large segment of the population showed that Ontario still considered itself to be a very British province, steadfast in its loyalty to the King and to the Motherland.' The Empire 'inspired the utmost loyalty and devotion', and 'no public utterance was complete without laudatory reference to the Empire. Loyalty to the Mother Country was as fundamental as the religious attitudes of the day.'[8] Patriotism and nationalism were integral components of the province's character. As Gwynne Dyer and Tina Viljoen put it, 'It was the fantasy world of the *Boy's Own Annual*: the great majority of English Canadians were convinced that any war Britain got involved in would be just and very many believed that war, or at least militarism, was a positive moral good.' The citizens of Ontario did not need to be convinced that the British cause was just: during the Boer War, that sentiment was explicit. Everything Britain did was right, glorious, and honest, and this belief only strengthened in the years leading up to the Great War.[9]

British writers such as Rudyard Kipling sang Canada's praises as the devoted and 'dutiful imperial daughter'. Influential Anglo-Canadians such as George Parkin, the poet Wilfred Campbell, and the engineer Sir Sandford Fleming wrote and spoke at length about the benefits of Canada's place in the Empire.[10] With so many so devoted to Mother Britain, Canadians received the messages they wanted to hear from both sides of the Atlantic.

A significant factor in this respect was the prominence of British settlers among the upper ranks of Canadian society. According to Patrick A. Dunae, 'between the end of the Napoleonic Wars and the outbreak of the First World War, an army of British public school boys, retired military officers, university graduates and aristocrats invaded Canada. . . . Collectively the well born, well-educated British settlers were known as "gentlemen emigrants".' Culturally, politically, socially, and athletically, they did more than any other group to shape Canada's character. Information from one source suggests that the Dominion claimed 18 per cent, or approximately 45,000, of Britain's 'high-class migrants' during the last quarter of the nineteenth century. During the Edwardian years, Canada's share of these 'gentlemen emigrants' increased from 23 per cent in 1906 to almost 40 per cent in 1913.[11] Members of this group were among the first to join the Expeditionary Force, and 'former Brits' in general made up a substantial number of recruits in the first contingent, setting an example that others gladly followed.

Britons who immigrated to Canada and Ontario in the years preceding World War I had a firm understanding of who they were and where their loyalties lay. They considered their attachment to England to be supreme and unswerving, and the rise of imperialism played an important role in solidifying that bond: 'imperialism was Edwardian England's nationalism and English identity in Canada was an overseas manifestation of that ideology.'[12] As Eric Hobsbawm has pointed out, however, 'the very act of democratizing politics, i.e., of turning subjects into citizens, tends to produce a populist consciousness which seen in some lights is hard to distinguish from a national, even a chauvinist patriotism—for if "the country" is in some way "mine", then it is more readily seen as preferable to those foreigners, especially if these lack the rights and freedoms of the true citizen.'[13] Imposing the values of the dominant culture on new immigrants also serves to remind the population as a whole of the foundations of their society.[14] The use of myths and symbols to convey the ideas behind a newly created state has proven to be enormously effective. The idea of settlers intensely loyal to Britain originated in the influx of settlers arriving in British North America during and after the American War of Independence. This 'Loyalist myth' was employed in Ontario and Canada both to create a unified sense of national identity and to pull the young nation together under the umbrella of British traditions.[15]

When Britain began to expand and consolidate its colonial holdings throughout the world, especially after 1870, this 'new imperialism' only reinforced Britain's belief in its superiority. The so-called Anglo-Saxon mission to civilize and extend Britain's influence had an enormous impact on the Canadian psyche. The new imperialism gave Canadians of British/English descent, especially in Ontario, a feeling of connection to a glorious destiny that was extremely appealing, for it conferred on them a kind of privilege. At the same time, the new imperialism became a pretext for the pursuit of militaristic activities by manly men. Britain's successes, particularly in exploration and war, were glorified in every way possible, and Canadians of British origin gained confidence and pride in Britain's achievements. According to Robert Craig Brown and Ramsay Cook, 'their sense of national identity could even find expression in it.' The greatest honour for Canada would be to fight alongside Mother Britain in war, but until that time came, various surrogates would have to suffice.[16]

Militarism

There was a strong current of militarism in pre-World War I Edwardian Britain, and a similar feeling was pervasive in Ontario. Indeed, interest in war and the military seems to have grown every year. The militarization of society found its most concrete expressions in Ontario. According to Alan R. Young, 'the enthusiasm and attendant rhetoric when Canada went to war in 1914 matched responses in Britain'; one of the reasons 'was a shared literary heritage of romance and neo-chivalric values imbibed from childhood which encouraged a misleading view of the realities of war.'[17]

This viewpoint did not spring to life suddenly. Over a period of many years, traces of militarism were interspersed with other ideologies and manifested themselves in a variety of ways. Desmond Morton and J.L. Granatstein write that 'for a few pre-war years, militarism had been in fashion in Canada, as a conservative response to urbanization, industrialization and immigration.' The formation of drill and rifle associations in Ontario and its predecessor, Canada West, was also an indication of militaristic interest. Egerton Ryerson was an enthusiastic supporter of drill and felt that familiarity with the 'rudiments of the arts of war' was a prerequisite for citizenship. The American Civil War had aroused an interest in things military among individuals from many different walks of life, and after the Boer War that interest became so intense that a number of organizations, among them the Canadian Military Institute and the

Canadian Defence League, were created to give voice to the militarist viewpoint.[18]

Militarism has been defined in various ways. Perhaps the most concise definition is Brian Bond's: 'excessive permeation of civil society with the military outlook and behaviour values'.[19] According to the *Oxford English Dictionary*, militarism is 'the spirit and tendencies of the professional soldier; the prevalence of military sentiment and ideals among a people; the tendency to regard military efficiency as the paramount interest of the state'. C.B. Otley defines militarism as the 'doctrine and practice of exalting war and the armed forces over other social functions and institutions of the state. . . . the encroaching of military forms, personnel and practices upon civilian institutions of social order.' Volker R. Berghahn contends that although the term 'militarism' was known throughout Europe by 1869, it was Herbert Spencer, in his *Principles of Sociology*, who advanced the 'first systematic analysis of militarism', which he described as 'an examination of the *militant type of society*'. The historian Carl Berger, on the other hand, defines militarism simply as the 'exaltation of martial values'.[20]

As if the deeds and actions of 'the army' could not be contained, militaristic elements appear to have seeped into civilian society at all levels, 'exerting a decisive influence' on institutions and agencies in every environment and most aspects of civil popular culture. Universal conscription, the publicizing of wars and battles, military tactics in sports and games, the constant comparison of sport to war, and the general elevation of the army in the eyes of the public all contributed to a militarization of civil society. At the extreme there were those for whom the army was a secular church, complete with vows, uniform dress, and codes of conduct. Yet even seemingly innocuous policies, such as the one dressing employees of the railways in uniforms, served to transmit military values to society.[21] In children's wear, sailor suits modelled on the ones worn by the young Prince of Wales, the future King Edward, became extremely popular beginning in the 1880s, and by 1892 the Eaton's catalogue was offering boys' overcoats in a military style.[22] Even the most popular sheet music was martial and patriotic. There were back-to-nature movements, fitness programs, adventure stories with military heroes, and youth groups with paramilitary themes. Newspaper editorials advocating the introduction of military drill in the schools argued that the nation's security depended on a populace prepared for whatever challenge should arise: drill was the 'nucleus of a great army', and without it the country would be vulnerable. National histories were rewritten to emphasize military valour. Mock battles were described in one news-paper as having 'All the Pomp and Magnificence of Glorious War'. The most popular spectacles at the massive Industrial Exhibition held annually in Toronto (later Canadian National Exhibition, or CNE) were re-enactments of famous battles. From the 'Siege of Sebastopol' to the 'Battle of Tel-el-Kebir', troops stormed, forts exploded, and whenever possible the Union Jack was flown. As a reporter for the *Globe* noted, these spectacles were 'splendid representation(s)' of war scenes. Between 1886 and 1903, 13 major and elaborate re-creations of battles were played out to the tenor of British success, to which the audiences responded enthusiastically. In sum, 'positive attitudes to warfare' were ingrained in many of the social, cultural, and intellec-tual fads of the time.[23]

Rites of Passage

It is not surprising, therefore, that the response to World War I was so fervent. Given the forces bombarding Ontario youth, what young man would not have jumped at the chance to demonstrate his man-liness in the great adventure? Then, as always, war was a rite of pas-sage, and—given the chance—most young men wanted to pass the test. Together, the 'ingrained warrior ethic that is the heritage of every young human male'[24] and the need to prove one's 'manliness' were an extremely potent, possibly explosive, combination.

One of the most lucid explorations of this combination is Ray Raphael's examination of the role played by war in the coming of age and socialization of young men. 'In most cultures', he writes, 'boys must repudiate their prior vulnerability and aspire to a matrix of per-sonality traits more appropriate to manhood: strength, endurance, courage, confidence and self-reliance.'[25] One way for a society to help a young man 'deny his childish past' and create a new identity is through structured initiation rites in which the boy must overcome formidable obstacles. Indeed, Raphael suggests that the initiation rite is 'a crucial stage in the process of socialization'. For such a rite to have the desired effect, however, the boy and his culture must have specifically defined notions of manhood. 'How can a youth be initi-ated into manhood', asks Raphael, 'when he has no clear concept of what manhood entails?'[26] This is an important question.

From the late 1870s to 1914, a great deal of energy was expended on defining the manly ideal. Of course, the notion of a masculine ideal was nothing new, but by the late nineteenth century interest in the subject had become unusually intense. The new era stood in marked contrast to traditional cultures where, as Raphael puts it, 'the image of manhood is clear: men are hunters and warriors, providers and protectors.'[27]

Traditionally, it was in war that young males displayed their prowess, virility, chivalry, and manliness. Warriors were vital to their societies, and thus wielded enormous power and influence. Fears that the comforts and conveniences of modernity would make boys soft help to account for the popularity of adventure stories, beginning in the 1880s, as well as for the increased fascination with surrogate warfare in the form of sports. Sports and athletics, team competition, and contests of endurance become increasingly important in societies that are driven by factories and automation. Demonstrations of strength, speed, and power come to define manliness for men in cultures that restrict natural displays of men's abilities. And these contests, whether in hunting or athletics, seek to re-enact the classic struggle to survive. When one searches for a reason to explain the mania for sports and games, and the general culture of manliness in the years surveyed here, a large part of the answer has to do with the fact that modern society limits natural demonstrations of manliness. As a result, artificial arenas must be manufactured.[28]

Manliness

In the eighteenth century, 'manly' meant the opposite of 'boyish' or 'childish'. By the early to middle Victorian period, the term had come to be used as the opposite of 'feminine' or 'effeminate'. Just prior to the American Civil War, manliness was linked to living an exemplary life, close to God and dedicated to the pursuit of spiritual or moral betterment. After the Civil War 'manly' underwent another shift in meaning. Now it often described a male who had distinguished himself in battle with honour and character—'a stronger, a tougher, less thoughtful man'. This shift put more emphasis on 'character traits, attitudes, and appearances' than on deeds. The word retained a strong moral dimension; as one definition put it in the 1890s, 'manly' referred to the 'proper characteristics of a man; independent of spirit or bearing; strong and brave'. Heroic or admirable men were described not as 'masculine' but as 'manly'. At the end of the nineteenth century, 'manly' came to be used more frequently because it conveyed how men wanted to be perceived. To be manly meant not to be womanly—in effect, a definite 'negation of all that was soft, feminine or sentimental'.[29]

During the mid-Victorian period, 'manliness' was most commonly used to mean courage and independence, but by the end of the century it had come to refer to a wide range of virtues: honour, fair play, forthrightness, vigorous physical activity, chivalry, courage, ambition, toughness, pluck, sacrifice and self-reliance, decisiveness, determination. Comprising everything that Victorians thought desirable in the male, manliness was 'the ultimate masculine quality, the attribute of the ideal male'.[30] The Pandora's box of character traits that was 'manliness' was to have a profound effect on a whole generation of boys.[31]

In his fascinating *Nationalism and Sexuality*, George L. Mosse suggests that 'manliness was not just a matter of courage, it was a pattern of manners and morals. Masculine comportment and a manly figure exemplified the transcendence of the so-called lower passions.' The double emphasis on character and decorum reflects the historic roots of the manly ideal:

> Manliness as an outward symbol of the inner spirit had roots in the ideals of Knighthood, whose symbols were employed in daily speech, defining male attitudes towards women as well as in the popular culture surrounding modern wars. Chivalry in battle was a sign of national superiority. But above all, manliness was based upon the Greek revival which accompanied and complemented the onslaught of respectability and the rise of modern nationalism.[32]

Manliness became increasingly closely identified with the defining images and ideals of the nation. Among those ideals, according to Mosse, were 'spiritual and material vitality, being part of the team, [and] loyalty to group and country'.[33] Courage, physical strength, and military discipline became paramount dimensions of manliness in the years after 1870.[34]

The emphasis on manliness during this period is closely allied with the ideas of nationhood and the changes that most new nations were facing. Manliness was supposed to 'safeguard the existing order against the perils of modernity, but it was also regarded as an indispensable attribute of those who wanted change.'[35] As a consequence of the changing nature of society, the gradual yet profound shift from agriculture to industry, from rural life to city/town life, there was increased pressure on men to meet traditional male role demands: those of husband, provider, capitalist, and even warrior. Many men were confined to the factory, the store, and the office, away from the home for many hours during the day. Not only were they cut off from the manly activities that were central to farm life, but this new reorientation limited their ability to supervise the rearing of their sons. Within a generation, men were more isolated and less involved in life at home, and this brought the influence of women to the fore.[36] As with sports and athletics, men now sought alternative ways to recapture what they felt they had lost. Linking the notion of an ideal manliness with the nation seemed to be of great appeal to many. The search for a pure Canadian type was often invoked in terms of manly attributes and came into vogue at the end of the nineteenth century as a way to recapture what was perceived to have been lost.

In harmony with the emerging modern society, manliness moved outdoors; in essence, it became closely tied to the increasingly visual nature of North American society, the harsh climate, clean air, vitality, one more dependent on image and action than the sedentary nature of office life. Demonstrations of manliness could take any number of forms, from overt (the successful sportsman or businessman) to subdued (the 'strong silent type', the good soldier, the dutiful citizen). Especially—though not exclusively—in the realm of sports, the demonstration of masculinity was often motivated by fear of being perceived as too feminine.[37]

Sports, manliness, and militarism have been associated for centuries. In ancient Greece, which the Victorians and Edwardians revered, equal prominence was given to the athlete and the warrior.[38] There was little to differentiate the training for each. According to Allen Guttman, 'The confluence of military and athletic motives guaranteed that masculinity for most Greeks meant active physicality.' In one race in the ancient Olympic Games, runners wore armour that linked the athlete to the warrior and served to remind those watching that the two 'were one and the same person'. In the same way the mock battles and jousts of medieval knights combined the warrior and the athlete.[39]

As sports became more organized, less free, and arguably more competitive and professional, the focus of play also changed. The increasing commodification of sporting activity at the end of the nineteenth century made the idea of losing take on a new connotation of effeminacy. To balance this connotation, it became important to stress the manly qualities of 'guts' and giving one's best. 'Not quitting' and 'never backing down', especially in combative sports, became vital for both winners and losers. For the loser it meant 'symbolically maintaining the integrity of masculine identity in a losing cause'. When these conditions of manliness were stressed, winners and losers alike could emerge from a contest 'with their masculine pride fully intact';[40] one could lose and still be respected, still be thought of as a manly competitor.

Ministers increasingly used the pulpit to preach the connection between manliness and high moral standing.[41] Christian manliness was first explicitly articulated by the Religious Tract Society and Thomas Hughes, author of the extraordinarily influential novel *Tom Brown's School Days*, but it reflected the influences of Charles Kingsley, Thomas Arnold, and Thomas Carlyle. After 1850, 'muscular Christianity' and 'manly Christianity', the complementary philosophies of Hughes and Kingsley respectively, came to represent a force capable of guiding man's moral nature.[42]

Tom Brown stressed the qualities of fair play, courage, honesty, and team spirit. For Arnold, 'Christian manliness' referred to the Christianization of a man's character 'through moral endeavours with a muscular or physical dimension'.[43] Manliness in this context meant not just following orders, but doing what was morally proper: 'an inner response to the spirit of Christianity'.[44]

The actual term 'Christian manliness' was the title of a work published by the Religious Tract Society in 1867. According to Norman Vance, it was a 'common Victorian preacher's catch-phrase. It represented a strategy for commending Christian virtue by linking it with more interesting secular notions of moral and physical prowess. "Manliness" in this context generously embraced all that was best and most vigorous in man.' This version of manliness was closely related to the military as well as patriotic qualities, and was directly linked to chivalry.[45]

Chivalry was an important component because it allowed men to reach back in time and draw inspiration and power from the knightly code. Chivalry was highly regarded in Victorian culture. The story of the *Birkenhead*, a ship that sank off the coast of South Africa in 1852, became a watershed in ideas of chivalry and manliness. After evacuating all the women and children, the 438 extremely disciplined British troops went down with the ship. This ultimate test of will became required reading for a part of the 1896 Ontario teachers' entrance examination, and it was endlessly retold as an example of heroism and military discipline.[46] Whether in the actions of Captain Scott and his ill-fated party at the South Pole or in the composure of Americans on the *Titanic*, death was met in a gentlemanly fashion. As Mark Girouard has written, 'those with the right background knew how to behave in a shipwreck, or blizzard.'[47] The Victorians modelled their own behaviour on the way they believed knights would have acted:

all Gentlemen knew that they must be brave, show no sign of panic or cowardice, be courteous and protective to women and children, be loyal to their comrades and meet death without flinching. They knew it because they had learned the code of the gentleman in a multitude of different ways, through advice, through example, through what they had been taught at school or by their parents and through endless stories of chivalry, daring Knights, gentlemen and gallantry which they had read or been told by way of history books, ballads, poems, plays, pictures and novels.[48]

Manliness makes no allowance for the coward. The true man is a hero. Popular literature emphasized the hero and how he behaved. Newspapers were full of reports of men who distinguished themselves heroically in battle. School books were filled with stories of heroes, and sports heroes abounded. A boy growing up during the period under examination here would have had the notion of heroism drummed into him from a very early age. No doubt the emphasis on heroism, and the contempt for cowardice that went along with it, had a profound effect on the way young men thought and, in turn, how they behaved.

Displaying the Military

One of the most important ways of socializing young people during this period was through group membership and identity. From the school to the sports team or youth organization to the military itself, the emphasis was on loyalty and group pride. In these contexts, the emphasis on group participation left little room for individualism. 'Boys who did not play the game or march in step were looked upon as misfits. Uniforms, whether athletic or military, underlined the growing intolerance of individuality.'[49] The importance attributed to uniforms can even be seen among volunteer firemen. In Thorold, Ontario, the firemen pleaded with the municipal council for funds to purchase new uniforms—not for any utilitarian purpose, but simply so that they would look better at the many competitions held for firemen. It became a manner of civic pride to field a sharply dressed fire company that would make the town proud.[50]

The soldier was an emblem of national pride to the late Victorian male. Parading in uniform was a glorious way to demonstrate one's passion for one's country and one's acceptance of martial values. Such displays went a long way towards glamorizing things military. Mock battles, marching troops, military bands, cadet corps, boys' brigades, church organizations: all offered the prestige of belonging to a regiment. Constantly exhorted to be a patriot, one had to be a part of these celebrations, if not as a participant then as an observer. Occasions such as Dominion Day, Queen Victoria's birthday, or the anniversary of the battle of Queenston Heights served as visible reminders of Canadians' duty to their nation.[51]

Drawing on the cult of the Loyalist and emphasizing the connection to Britain, the militia ideal was a unique construction of masculinity in Canada. The militia reflected what Mike O'Brien calls an ethnically based notion of masculinity, a British notion of manliness, that was obvious in both the small and large centres of Ontario. The militias in the larger cities, especially Toronto, were so popular that some regiments had to be split into two. For white-collar workers, the militia provided a step up not only in society but in the realm of masculinity. The idea of belonging to a socially desirable masculine unit was especially appealing to men threatened by the dislocations of industrialization and the increased 'feminization' of society. Like firefighters and sports teams, a militia unit was an all-male fraternity, an exclusively male bastion that reaffirmed one's manly status at a time when more and more women were entering the workforce, and it provided an opportunity to socialize with like-minded men. In addition militia units were celebrated as 'important assets' in bringing communities, large and small, together. Parades and spectacles featuring local militia units did much to attract recruits.[52]

Members of all classes took great pains with such displays. According to one commentator, Canadians were naturally inclined towards soldiering; they had an ingrained 'aptitude for military discipline' and were eager to assume the obligations of defence. Serious as well as festive, military manoeuvres and parades were reported in great detail.[53] The militia was often highly visible in organizing and participating in the community's social and cultural affairs, such as dances and concerts.

Not everyone, however, viewed the organized militia in the same light. The fact that militia units were sometimes used to quell strikes made them extremely unpopular in some regions. Another reason for objecting to the militia, especially among temperance supporters, was the annual military camp, which as far back as the early 1880s had become synonymous with excessive drinking and rowdy behaviour.[54] As Lynne Marks relates:

> Young men . . . received mixed messages about their involvement in the militia. Patriotism and a sense of local pride could create cross-class support for the militia in many communities. But for

respectable Christian small-town folk, the all-male hard-drinking culture of the militia camps challenged the values they held dear and, more particularly, threatened young men who were already perceived to be at risk.[55]

Even so, the majority of citizens happily joined in the communal spirit of militiary displays. As many as 50,000 spectators came out for the first celebration of Queenston Heights Day in Toronto in 1890. The parade up University Avenue towards Queen's Park to mark Queen Victoria's birthday was illustrative of the strong patriotic sentiment in this Anglo-Saxon bastion. Cadets and other members of military organizations proudly displayed their uniforms and marching skills to the thousands in attendance.[56] The *Toronto Empire* stated boldly that 'Toronto loves her citizen soldiery and always turns out to honour them.' When, in February 1899, a group of cadets travelled to Florida, the publicity they received caused a great deal of excitement in Toronto and further glamorized the image of the cadets and other martial groups among boys in Ontario.[57] An editorial in the *Toronto Globe* stressed the positive aspects of such training and attempted to dispell any concerns about potential dangers:

> Canadians are fond of soldiering; the young men like to join volunteer corps, and the rest of the population, men, women, and children, like to watch military parades and to hear military music. . . . We do not believe that the carrying of a gun inspires a youth with a desire to kill his neighbours with lead; and for most boys and young men, military discipline with its training in neatness, precision, prompt obedience and endurance of hardships is good.[58]

British forces were stationed in Canada for more than a century. Although, after they departed in 1871, the militia stepped up its role, it remained under the supervision of British officers. The Royal Military College at Kingston opened in 1876 but served primarily as a stepping-stone to the British Army. Following the 1868 Militia Act, the militia was Canada's main defence system, yet throughout the 1870s it languished as an effective military force. Military display served political and ceremonial ends. Ever since Confederation, ministers and generals had disagreed on military matters. The interests of the (British) General Officer Commanding the Canadian Militia (GOC) conflicted with those of various politicians, especially in the patronage and financial realms. A significant step towards the making of a wholly Canadian army came with the opening up of the GOC post to Canadians in 1903.[59]

The Loyalists' repulsion of the Americans in 1812 was, in the words of Cecilia Morgan, 'a crucible in which concepts of loyalty and patriotism were forged'. Loyalty and patriotism came to be linked with the heroic exploits of General Isaac Brock and the militia. Significantly, the War of 1812 firmly demonstrated Upper Canada's (Ontario's) complete loyalty to Britain. As well, the War of 1812 was a rallying point for images of loyal, patriotic militia men doing their duty for their nation. This demonstration of loyalty came to occupy a central place in the political discourse of the region for many decades. In the 1880s, the story was given new life not only by the wave of imperial sentiment sweeping across the country but by the Northwest uprising of 1885, the second 'Riel Rebellion'. Militia regiments travelled west on the new railway and after a four-day siege Riel surrendered. The success of this brief excursion blinded Canadians to the realities of war—the need for preparation of troops, professionalism, discipline, and adequate planning—and led to a general consensus that there was no longer any need for British military leadership.[60]

In the 1890s Major General Ivor Herbert, GOC, instituted several important reforms in training that helped to revitalize military morale. From infantry schools to cavalry schools, he created a solid and capable core army that would function much more like a professional army than a citizen militia. 'What volunteers needed, as much as training,' writes military historian Desmond Morton, 'was a model of professional efficiency.'[61] This did not necessarily sit well with the militia and its supporters.

Well into the new century, the idea of a citizen army was lauded and glamorized, even though training and resources were often inadequate. Militia officers were a highly visible part of the social landscape in most urban and many rural areas. With almost 40,000 men and 2,000 officers, at least on paper, numerous communities were represented throughout the province. Young boys, especially in the cities, would see volunteers on their way to the yearly drill camp and watch their parades. And, although F.J. Campbell, writing in *Queen's Quarterly* in 1902, stated that he was 'not inclined to regard [the uniform] as a serious inducement no doubt it did help to attract young boys to the militia as did the opportunity it offered to mimic fathers or older brothers.'[62]

Indeed, military paraphernalia of all kinds were incorporated into many youth organizations, and likely contributed to the success of the Boys' Brigades, the Boy Scouts, and the cadet corps. Thus the middle and upper echelons of society created a militaristic code that males of all classes would be willing both to live and to die for.[63]

3

Ideas, Myths, and the
'Modern' State

*Why did I enlist? Well, my motives are mixed. I was only just
past my twenty-first birthday. The prospect of adventure and
travel and so on had a very strong appeal for me. I would say
I had other reasons for it too. My reading was almost
entirely based on* Boy's Own Annual *and* Chums *and Henty
and so on. So I had the belief that Britain always won its
wars and that they were always right.*

(Larry Nelson, b. 1893, enlisted CEF, 1914)

*Everybody wanted to be a hero, and everybody wanted to go
to war. Hadn't had a war since the Boer War in 1899–1900
which I remember. There was nothing between that in wars
and everybody was going to be a hero, and I wanted to be a
hero too.*

(Bert Remington, enlisted CEF, 1914)[1]

The Culture of War

Many young men have gone to war for the same reasons as Larry
Nelson and Bert Remington. Yet the desire for adventure and the
chance to become a hero took on added potency in the late Edwardian
era as a result of several concurrences. Foremost, perhaps, was the
advent of modern industrialism, which made many jobs little more
than routine drudgery and subjected workers to the regime of the

clock. For most men, the traditional outdoor life had become an unattainable ideal.[2]

War offered the hope of social and personal regeneration through the sorts of experiences no longer available in everyday life—the chance, as T.J. Jackson Lears puts it, 'to escape the demands of bourgeois domesticity and reintegrate a fragmented sense of self by embracing a satisfying social role. As heroic actors in a *theatre of war* and members of a tightly-knit (though manufactured) male community, men have sometimes temporarily eluded the contradictions and confusions of modern culture.'[3] What is important here is the perception of possibility rather than the actual experience of social reality.

One could argue that the overriding importance of this perception reflects the more widely available and accessible media of communications. On one hand, increasing levels of literacy led to a proliferation of newspapers, broadsheets, chapbooks, and popular literature. On the other, newspapers and posters made the image of the military hero, bedecked in medals and standing proud, a common stereotype. It is impossible from the vantage point of today's media-saturated society to appreciate just how revolutionary these developments were. Taking the lead from Raymond Williams, Daphne Read suggests that industrial capitalism spread 'its control over the literary world, transforming cultural enterprise into business enterprise'. She continues:

> As the mass of the population became literate it was transformed from a forum of participants into a reading public and a market of consumers. The growth of widely circulated periodicals initiated an important change in the cultural relations of industrial society. As moulders of opinion, journals with wide circulation came to view their readers as relatively passive clay to be shaped by the persuasive arts of the publicist. The contexts for popular self expression shrank drastically as the circulation of the media grew.[4]

As opinion-makers and possible career-shapers, the media wielded enormous power. Educators and politicians were well aware of the role played by the press in socializing and conditioning young minds.

Some saw war as a necessary stage in the process of nation-building. Others saw it as a noble, almost holy experience, as cleansing and character-affirming. Typical sentiments were that 'war itself was a chivalrous enterprise.' Speakers preached that 'war would be a fiery furnace from which Canada would emerge purified.' At the same time, war was widely accepted as a plain fact, part and parcel of the human condition. The influential William James wrote that

'We inherit the warlike type, and, for most of the capacities of heroism that the human race is full of, we have to thank this cruel history. . . . Our ancestors have bred pugnacity into our bone and marrow, and thousands of years of peace won't breed it out of us.' Captain William Wood of the Royal Rifles reiterated the pseudo-Darwinian idea that war was 'an essential part of the universal struggle for existence' and was still an important part of *realpolitik*. Canada might be a source of world-class specimens of manhood, but it would need more than just 'our sedentary militia'. Typical of the popular literature of the time was an article in the American magazine *Harper's Weekly* that stressed the proclivity towards warfare in men and advocated training in the military arts from a young age: 'the military instinct is innate in the American boy. All that is wanted is that it should be properly fostered.' The article went on to suggest that if military drills were implemented in the schools, 'in a month the slouchy lad would have all the warp and wobble taken out of him. More, however, than the finer bearing of the boy, he would be taught obedience, respect, and thus a high sense of patriotism. . . .' Tellingly, the author concludes, 'the early lesson of the soldier would then become an integral part of the boy's life, and he would not be likely to outgrow it.'[5]

Significant in the Canadian context was the fact that by the late 1890s, war and warriors were celebrated topics. The War of 1812 was especially notable, and war heroes from James Wolfe to Isaac Brock were 'the stuff of legend', providing inspiration in the form of songs, poems, and paintings. The fact that ordinary citizens had participated in Canada's few 'conflicts' gave war a meaning for everyone; in essence, 'war was the duty of citizen soldiers—a people's crusade.'[6] By the late 1890s, the notion of citizen soldiers was receding and the idea of the professional soldier, devoted completely to the life of the country, was coming to the fore. War was seen and portrayed as the supreme test of manhood as well as the defining mark of a nation.

While their neighbours to the south were embroiled in the Spanish-American War, Canadians watched, perhaps without emotion, but surely with interest. Young boys were well aware of what was going on and many followed developments in the press.[7] They anxiously awaited their own test of manhood.

The Boer War and Imperial Unity

The Boer War was the first conflict in which Canadians had made a substantial overseas military contribution, and it found Ontario extremely excited about the prospects for imperial adventure.[8] As Arthur Lower relates in his autobiography, with the outbreak of the war in South Africa:

> A thrill went over English Canada, and impassioned verses about the young lions answering the old lion's roar began to appear. The tone of these poems was one of passionate loyalty, of heightened significance, for this provincial people was being drawn into great affairs, and an opportunity was presenting itself for all that mixture of passion, prejudice, generous impulse, duty that has marked us. The Boer War rapidly became our own Canadian war.[9]

For Canadians caught up in the 'imperial fervour', 'frenzied flag waving' and 'resolutions of sympathy' were not enough to express their loyalty and solidarity. Full participation in a war was the only acceptable path, no matter how tenuous the connection to Canada. The Boer War would serve as a tune-up for things to come. Though on a much smaller scale, the war in South Africa foreshadowed many of the sentiments, changes, and implications that would develop during the Great War. A great deal of newspaper coverage was devoted to Canada's role in the war. Although thousands of miles away, this extremely violent conflict came to occupy a pivotal place in both the public and private lives of English Canadians, especially in Ontario. The emotional response had everything to do with supporting Britain in a quest for imperial solidarity.[10]

The memory of the Boer War was consistently strong in the minds of many Edwardians. School books discussed it. Sir Robert Baden-Powell created the Boy Scouts out of his experiences in it. Veterans looked back on it with heady nostalgia. 'The major things', relates Arthur Lower, 'that young chaps like me brought out of the Boer War were familiarity with the names of glittering generals— Roberts, Kitchener, French, Baden-Powell, and many others—and a strong conviction that in the fighting what was necessary to victory was the presence of the Canadians.' Canada's—and Ontario's—Boer War participation reinforced the imperial connection in a truly significant way.[11]

As the last great international struggle prior to the Great War that English Canadians had engaged in, it provided easily remembered notions and powerful iconography. The Boer War, according to Robert Shipley, 'gave rise to a greater number of memorials than any previous wars.' While 8,300 Canadians enlisted for the Boer War, the Canadian war dead numbered 242. Monuments appeared in large cities such as Ottawa and Toronto but also in smaller communities such as

Brantford, Sarnia, Newmarket, and Southampton.[12] The emotional impact of these memorials, located in prominent downtown sites, could have been substantial. Explicitly designed to inspire notions of immortality and the glory of war among young boys, these memorials may well have succeeded in fulfilling that aim.

Participation in the Boer War marked a watershed in Canadian imperialism and Canadian nationalism. Carl Berger's seminal work, *The Sense of Power*, establishes the foundation for all discussion on this topic. According to Berger, Canadian imperialism was 'one variety of Canadian nationalism—a type of awareness of nationality which rested upon a certain understanding of history, the national character, and the national mission.' The threat of annexation by the US was a concern, but the cult of empire also reflected high hopes, especially among United Empire Loyalist descendants from Ontario, through association with Britain's commercial success, power, and 'prestige'. Foreign outposts and wars, acquisitions and 'jewels' in the British Crown, were all matters of national pride to English-speakers.[13]

The three major spokesmen for the imperial unity movement in the last decades of the nineteenth century—Colonel George Taylor Denison, George Munro Grant, and George Parkin—all held influential positions in the upper echelons of Ontario society. Prime Minister Laurier's decision to commit Canadian troops to fight in South Africa was a direct result of the growing imperial sentiment promoted by Denison, Grant, and Parkin, and it encouraged their supporters to push for a much more substantial Canadian role in the affairs of the Empire. Ontarians, as enthusiastic about Canadian statehood as they were about the British connection, were eager to take on such roles. Yet many in the imperial unity camp felt that more had to be done to strengthen connections with Britain. To ensure the support of the young, organizations and movements dealt with subjects of interest to children—Empire Day, cadets, and other ideas—permeated the classroom and the playing field. History, defence, and general cultural issues were widely discussed, with the purpose of fostering Canadian nationalism, patriotism, and closer ties with Britain.[14] In addition, as historian Norman Penlington explains:

> by demonstrating national purpose and national prowess Canadians found also that they could indulge in personal adventure. The rigidities of Victorian society had broken down sufficiently to enable the young men to relish an adventurous type of life. The careers of men like David Livingstone, Sir Harvey Johnston, and Sir Frederick Lugard provided the inspiration and appeared to

indicate high moral purpose, for their work was being done in the name of Christianity or civilization. What Victorian boy inspired by the writings of Rider Haggard, R.L. Stevenson, and Rudyard Kipling would fail to take advantage of the opportunities which the imperial movement afforded! Ambition for adventure thus became entangled with the resolution to defend Canada.[15]

Penlington's reference to 'personal adventure' as a matter of self-indulgence points to an important component in young men's motivation to embark on journeys of war. Fourteen years before the Great War, young men were being encouraged to undertake some form of adventurous exploit. As the shackles of class and religion loosened, various forms of manly adventuring became increasingly popular, and if the adventure could be framed as a quasi-religious or moral endeavour, it was seen as noble and highly praised. It was an auspicious time for any restless young man to turn his craving for adventure towards the defence of Canada and the glory of the Empire.

For those concerned about Canada's place in the Empire and military readiness, any attempt to improve in these areas would be welcome. Sensing their opportunity, certain individuals stepped up their efforts at channelling the province and the country in the desired direction. Militarists and imperialists alike harnessed the mood of discontent and capitalized on the vogue for adventure.

Denison, Grant, and Parkin all had impeccable imperial credentials, but Denison, a well-known and highly respected military writer, was the most vocal. He was involved in numerous patriotic, nationalistic, and loyalistic organizations. Much earlier, during the American Civil War, he had agitated for military preparedness in an alarmist essay entitled 'Canada: Is She Prepared For War?' This work paralleled 'invasion scare' writing and concerns about fitness in Britain; it proved to be an extremely powerful propaganda technique. George Grant, too, lauded the greatness of the Empire: the 'British Empire was the highest secular instrument the world has ever known for bringing about the universal reign of freedom, justice and of peace.'[16] Together, Denison and Grant were able to weave an extraordinary number of causes, ideals, and concepts into the Canadian imperial ideology.

Most imperialists had a direct relationship with the élite of Ontario and the Protestant Orange Order. In the 1890s they were the prime proponents of reform in the army and militia, an increased profile for the cadets, and drill in the schools. Carl Berger suggests it was the imperialists who most vociferously agitated for involvement in the Boer War. Plain and simple, they wanted increased military action and responsibilities within the Empire and on the continent. If not, as one observer put it, 'we shall live in the depressing sense that we are a dependency... and so our citizenship will be of uneasy self-consciousness.' The issue of the erosion of national character, placing the spotlight on the condition of Canada's youth, reflected the influence of British paramilitary organizations such as the Boys' Brigade.[17]

Imperialism in Canada was extremely resilient. 'Even when imperialism waned in Britain', writes George Woodcock, 'it waxed in Canada.' Canadian imperialists took hold of the idea of Empire and disseminated it with fervour to all levels of the population; indeed, some proponents of the imperial ideal in Canada were even more passionate and vocal than their British counterparts.[18]

The popularity of imperialism and women's determination to have a greater say in public matters coalesced around the formation in Canada of the Imperial Order Daughters of the Empire, in 1900. Composed largely of former teachers, the IODE focused on patriotism in education and played an influential role in the provincial school systems. Believing that 'children held the best hope for the country', the IODE aimed 'to develop in Canadians a love and respect for the British Empire and an understanding of Canada's role as a member of the Empire'. Its main avenue to this end was the public school, and its official magazine, *Echoes*, often carried articles stressing that, for students, citizenship was as important as learning to read and write.[19]

Among the imperial organizations and commemorative activities that blossomed at the time of the Boer War were the United Empire Loyalist Association and the Sons of England. The newly established Navy League picked up members and popularity with its specific militaristic theme. Empire Day was the schoolchild's opportunity to bask in the imperial sun and to celebrate the greatness of Britain. 'Ambition for adventure and the apprehension for the safety of Canada and the Empire account for a marked increase of interest in military affairs after 1895', writes Penlington. One alderman told a group of Toronto schoolchildren in no uncertain terms that 'Canadians might in time come to be called upon to defend, not their own homes, but those of the Empire at large.'[20]

War talk permeated much of the Western world around 1900. But Canadians, as Berger has noted, were blinded by myths and misperceptions about what a modern war entailed.[21] Accounts of Canadian participation in South Africa tended to be whitewashed, emphasizing personal heroics of the kind common in popular adventure stories. Beginning with the Boer War and picking up steam afterwards,

'Imperial zeal became the medium for youthful idealism.' Former military personnel were excited at the prospect of armed conflict. Imperialism provided the umbrella, the Boer War the memory, for a push towards more militant responses. As R.J.D. Page says of the situation:

> the horrors of war had long been removed from the Canadian experience and colonial campaigns of the late nineteenth century usually sustained only very light casualties. The enthusiastic attitude to war was very close to that of the athlete to sport. This military group had read with a growing sense of frustration about the glorious deeds of Kitchener's forces in the Sudan and about Teddy Roosevelt's charge up San Juan Hill; they yearned for active service. As there was virtually no opportunity for military service in Canada, they sought to involve Canada in imperial service.[22]

Only 7,000 Canadians served in the Boer War. For such a small number to have had such an impact suggests that the climate for militarism was ripe in Ontario; during the next decade and a half, it ripened even more.

Although he was exceptional, men like the newspaperman, fitness enthusiast, and former schoolteacher Sam Hughes embodied the values of Victorian warriors who had spent their whole lives training for battle. Hughes distinguished himself during the Boer War and was later to be the guiding force behind the Canadian Expeditionary Force and the Minister of Militia when the Great War broke out. Brother of Public School Inspector James Hughes—a major proponent of drill in the schools[23]—Sam Hughes exemplified the connection between manliness and militarism: a natural outdoorsman, healthy, robust—a 'man's man'. Sigmund Samuel relates how on Saturday afternoons he would watch the best lacrosse teams from Montreal play the élite Toronto teams led by Sam Hughes. Hughes believed that military training was inextricably linked to the development of moral fibre. As a youngster he had immersed himself in books about military campaigns, participated in hunting, and excelled at sports. As a teacher, he organized the first drill squad among students at the Toronto Collegiate. He was a 'strong supporter of the Cadet Corps, and Boy Scout movements, a believer in the Strathcona Trust ideal of military training in the schools', and 'he did everything possible to encourage these developments.' Hughes combined all the essential elements of a man, according to the popular opinions of his day.[24]

If the Boer War was the 'great high water mark for imperial zeal in Canada', however, it also drew attention to the 'poor quality of soldiers' and, by extension, the social conditions from which they came.

The poor performance of British soldiers not only highlighted fears of national inadequacy but pointed a finger at the poor health and difficult living conditions of the lower classes from which most of the British servicemen came. Although these concerns led to improvements in sanitary and social conditions, they also contributed (among the élite) to a view of the population in general as 'a national resource'.[25]

The Family, Feminizing Influence, and the Modern State

The idea of childhood changed drastically between the middle part of the nineteenth century and the early years of the twentieth. Increasing emphasis was now placed on children as the 'future of the country'. With various organizations moving to take control of this now important 'commodity', the role of the family became intimately linked with the ideals of the state through new legislation and social agencies. Rules were put in place to protect, aid, and teach the nation's children. There was a general assumption that the basic family unit, in particular the parents, needed professional guidance. Newly created professionals such as home economists, juvenile experts, and social workers modernized the tasks of motherhood. The guidance of these professionals was now considered essential to the proper upbringing of children. Motherhood came to be portrayed as a science —an idea that further alienated fathers. Greater emphasis was now placed on logic, routine, and reason in children's diet, habits, and hygiene.[26]

Although the family attempted to remain the model, modern urban industrial culture had an impact on its role. Formerly silent or nonexistent actors stepped in to fill the void. Everyone from the press to the churches, from civic groups to military organizations, was interested in the health, well-being, and fitness of youth. New methods of teaching, novel theories on child development, and studies of juvenile delinquency all expressed concern for the state of 'our' youth.

The family took centre stage. In the words of the Reverend J. Edward Starr, 'Take care of the children and the nation will take care of itself.' At the same time, agencies were at work breaking down the centrality of the family in bringing up the youth of the nation. Reformers and social engineers attempted to make the state and the school the primary agents of influence and sought a reduced role for the family. They believed that, in harmony with developments in science and industry, the independence of the family would give way to the dictates of the state. A rapidly changing time required drastic measures. The appropriate information became codified in manuals and books, spiced up with impressive-sounding terminology.[27]

One part of the Boer War story that was not well publicized was the fact that Britain (and, by extension, Canada) did not perform as well as expected. The search for explanations led in several directions, but two culprits in particular were singled out: immigration and industrialization. The shift to an industrial economy caused enormous growing pains. In Ontario by 1911 the urban population for the first time was greater than the rural population. Between the years 1890 and 1914 although the Canadian population had increased by 34 per cent, most of this growth was due to immigration —three million people had entered the country between 1896 and 1914. Among native-born Canadians, the birth rate was beginning its historic descent.[28]

The increase in immigration raised questions. What would be done with all the people flooding into the cities? How would immigrants be socialized to internalize the values of the ruling Anglo majority? By the last decade of the century, more than a third of Toronto's population was not native-born. Like many others, the Methodist minister James Shaver Woodsworth—the Winnipeg social gospeller who would later become the founding leader of the Co-operative Commonwealth Federation—believed that the new immigrants had to embrace Anglo-Canadian Protestant values in order to become true Canadians. Non-assimilable people were seen as obstacles to the national good. Therefore, immigration policy should be integrated with other national policies.[29]

New child-rearing philosophies, a stronger role for the schools, and an array of social experiments were implemented to combat what were perceived to be negative influences on Ontario's youth. The effects of mass immigration, rapid industrialization, and urbanization were seen as especially detrimental to young boys. At the same time, the traditional agencies of control, such as the family, the church, and the school, had 'enough holes', in the words of one commentator, to need supplementing.[30] Concern was expressed over everything from the content of stories to bad habits. Edward Bok's *Successword* (1896), a book for boys, warned of the evils of cards, wine, and tobacco. With regard to reading material, a typical opinion of the time was that

> Parents in this Canada of ours have too little concern in what their children read. It is in the training of the children that the hope of our country lies. If children's minds are kept pure in the early

stages of their growth, fewer preventative laws will be needed for adults. And yet only a small percentage of the fathers and the mothers recognize their duty in this particular.[31]

Agencies of every conceivable origin came to the fore to remedy the various problems, both perceived and real. Toronto, in particular, played a significant role in the experimental procedures in the fields of public health, social welfare, and education. The concept of 'the family' became singularly important at this time. Joy Parr writes, 'children's lives and their experience in families are entwined in the political, social, and economic relations of which family relations are a part.' Children, according to Anna Davin, 'belonged not merely to the parents but to the community as a whole; they were a "national asset"; the "capital of a country"; on them depended "the future of the country and the Empire".' The welfare of society was bound up with that of the family.[32]

As with so much of modern culture, there were formulas to follow and research to be done. 'Mothers were advised to search out methods of child-rearing that practice had shown to be successful so that their own efforts would be consistent instead of arbitrary or capricious—the result of impulse.'[33] Many family reformers believed that the nation would need a large, healthy pool of future male citizens to provide both the army and the economy with the right quality of soldiers and workers. Consequently, it was vital for the future of the state that mothers demonstrate their commitment to the national interest. In other words, it was implied that mothers must improve as well.

From a sentimental construct the family became an agency for socialization charged by the state with producing the best possible product. Mariana Valverde describes one example:

> The Methodist Church's sex educator for boys typically believed that one of Canada's untapped natural resources was its young people, and he saw his own educational work as furthering the production of 'self': 'Our young men themselves are producing a product, self, that will command in the market of the world a value—we are building this young manhood into some kind of product, that in later years we will have to offer in the markets of the world.'[34]

There was a radical shift in emphasis, from 'economic production' to 'nurturing children' as the *raison d'être* of family life. This change, in turn, placed more pressure on the mother. Motherhood was made 'to seem desirable' and was afforded 'new dignity'. In the context of declining rates of fertility, childbirth was seen as 'a great reward'.[35]

Community leaders and social improvement societies were adamant about training girls for the domestic world of motherhood and housekeeping and, at the same time, steering boys into arenas in which they would be sober, moral, and industrious. It was important for the young boy to gain an appreciation for work, commitment, and honesty, which would carry on throughout life. Carroll Smith-Rosenberg suggests that books, child-rearing manuals, and guides on etiquette dissuaded women from masculine endeavours 'such as scientific or commercial pursuits'; instead, 'they were encouraged to be coquettish, entertaining, nonthreatening, and nurturing.'[36]

The concerns focusing on the future and rearing of young boys and girls were often contradictory. As Ontario society moved into the industrial age, thousands of young males and females flocked to the major centres in search of work. Large congregations of young men had always raised concern, but even in Toronto they did not arouse the same suspicions and fears that the increasing numbers of young women did. That drink and the culture of the gang would lead to outlandish behaviour among men was expected. What was new and, to many reformers, more frightening was that now single women were not only competing with men for factory jobs but abandoning their traditional domestic role. The family and the home were threatened as women abandoned the 'hearth' for the workplace.[37]

The desirability of a clear separation between the upbringing of boys and girls was one of the most talked-about social issues of the late nineteenth and early twentieth centuries. The informal education and general rearing of girls were to be accomplished in a purely domestic setting, under the watchful control of the mother. The upbringing of boys was much more problematic. How was a boy to assume his rightful masculine place if his mother was raising him? A boy had to learn how to cope in a much more demanding setting. He had to be trained to be competitive. To qualify for a life among men certain tests and demands had to be fulfilled. Whereas a 'woman becomes a woman by following in her mother's footsteps', the boy, to become a man, 'must prove himself—his masculinity—among his peers.' The founder of the Wood Craft Indians/Boy Scouts, the well-known writer of wilderness animal adventure stories Ernest Thompson Seton, was enormously worried about the boy 'who had been coddled all his life and kept so carefully wrapped up in the "pink cotton wool" of an over indulgent home, till he is more effeminate than his sister, and his flabby muscles are less flabby than his character.'[38]

In the increasingly modern West, the ideal of masculinity would be inculcated in the home, at work, and in all-male groups. Community leaders railed against juvenile delinquency and forces that might lead to moral degeneration. The simple—and vague—solutions were development of character, a sense of responsibility, and a focus on self-improvement, which could be instilled either by the family or by an external agency such as the school.[39]

According to some commentators, the school posed a peculiar problem. John Abbott states that the increasing female domination of the teaching profession 'threatened the cult of true manhood'. Fear and parochialism reigned. As one school trustee expressed the common opinion: 'If men cannot be got to teach our boys and hence leave their training to girls I fear it will tend towards effeminacy and eventually breed a generation more fit to be apparelled in petticoats than pants.' Secondary-school teaching should be a wholly male occupation because 'the primary role of the secondary school was still seen as the education of boys.' The perceived feminization of society and, in particular, educators was a great source of worry.[40]

One of the great fears was that modernism, coupled with material luxuries, would lead to a soft society. The perceived danger of female teachers' influence on young males was compounded by the fact that, in this industrial environment, men were off at work, not at home, leaving mothers to exert a disproportionate influence on their young sons. Moreover, 'mechanization, by minimizing the importance of brawn to production, had opened up a host of new areas to the potential of female employment.'[41] These developments led one self-appointed authority, commenting on 12-year-old boys, to stress the need for male perspective and guidance:

> It is important that they begin to look at the world, into which they will soon enter, from a man's point of view, for much will depend on his training from twelve to fifteen years of age. . . . The same is true of the home. Boys should not be left to the mother alone. The wisdom of both parents, but particularly the father, is essential for a boy's development. It is men they must come in contact in the world of business, and they will be best prepared for that association with men in school and at home.[42]

Even on the shop floor, boys' masculinity was a matter of grave concern. Craft unions, as Craig Heron has written,

> urged women to stay in the household while the menfolk ventured forth in the world of paid work to earn the family's wages. Crafts-

men tended to want their women at home, and deeply resented the ways that employers were using them as unskilled help in efforts to degrade crafts such as printing, shoemaking and tailoring.

Respect for the masculine skills traditionally handed down from father to son or through apprenticeships was threatened by modernization, mechanization, and feminization. Reassertions of masculinity, through emphasis on physical strength and exclusion of women, represented attempts by men to remain the primary wage-earners and to preserve their manliness.[43]

Uncertainty in the workplace translated into unease in the home. The middle-class home came to be seen as a feminine environment, with two consequences: first, the creation within the home of a sphere of refuge for men—dens, libraries, and so on—and, second, an outward push to define new areas of masculine identity through associational life.[44]

If the home was taken over by women, then other, purely masculine environments had to be created to counter this trend. Various programs with hidden ideological motives were undertaken. The Boy Scouts, athletics, and the cadet corps reflected a systematic effort to make sure that boys became men. Many of the more formal associations organized by men for boys had a very strong military foundation. Of course, this kind of thinking also found its way into the classroom, where, increasingly, the influence of women had to be counterbalanced. The most time-proven method of making sure that boys became manly men was to expose them to the martial life. 'Indeed,' writes one commentator, 'from the late 1890s to the outbreak of the Great War', the movement to militarize Canada's public and private schoolchildren 'intensified dramatically'.[45]

Social Darwinism and Society

The connection between Darwin's theory of natural selection, racism, and militarism is of essential importance. As the historian Richard Hofstadter has pointed out, the distorted version of Darwin's view known as 'social Darwinism' was employed to vindicate both militarism and imperialism. To justify the 'subjugation of the weaker races', imperialists took Darwinism out of context, using terminology intended to explain animal behaviour and applying it to men. The concept of the elimination of weaker specimens, from Darwin's *Descent of Man*, was also used to justify the imposition of military values on society at large.[46]

Social Darwinism provided the definitive rationale for imperialist excursions; significantly, it also came to be almost synonymous with militarism and an excuse for drilling military principles into the minds of the young. As Walter Houghton has observed, 'Social Darwinism could equally justify war and militarism.' Its applicability was boundless. 'It could give philosophical sanction to the chauvinism that grew up in the second half of the century with the increasing intensity of national rivalries and the scientific development of ever deadlier weapons of destruction.'[47]

During the 1890s George Parkin, the ardent imperialist and headmaster of Toronto's exclusive Upper Canada College, often used Darwinian illustrations and 'survival of the fittest' jargon to expound his racial, moral, and political ideas. The impact on Parkin's students must have been substantial. According to Robert Page, Parkin 'viewed the world situation as a struggle between nations and races for survival and it would be survival of the fittest.' In Parkin's own mind, the fittest were the Anglo-Saxons.[48] Parkin was not the only influential educator promulgating a social Darwinist point of view.

An offshoot of social Darwinism, the eugenics movement, used the idea of national fitness to express racist views. The eugenics message was particularly appealing to Canadians worried about the decline of 'pure Canadian stock' at a time of increased immigration and the perceived social ills that accompanied it. Eugenicists cloaked their arguments in pseudo-scientific language that served to buttress long-held racist assumptions. War was a way to save the white race, according to the influential Edwardian eugenicist commentator Karl Pearson, because it worked as a direct check on the fertility of inferior stock. In 'Eugenics and Military Service', published in *The Eugenics Review* of 1910–11, Pearson wrote that the 'occasional war is of service by reason of the fact that in time of danger the nation attends to the virility of its citizens.... A military service is therefore eugenically useful because it keeps prominently before the community ideals of physical fitness and efficiency as well as courage and patriotism.'[49]

Indeed, the connection between the idea of the survival of the fittest and the aggressive instinct had been made at the turn of the century, when William James observed that 'ancestral evolution has made us all potential warriors.' James's comments were reiterated by Georg Simmel in his book *Soziologie*, in which he wrote that he assumed 'the human mind is endowed with a "fighting instinct", an "inborn need to hate and fight".' Sigmund Freud, in 'Thoughts for the Times on War and Death', wrote that regardless of the advances made in civilization, 'primitive human aggression, the desire to inflict pitiless violence upon an enemy, apparently endures obstinately in fact.'[50]

An incessant stream of theories on violence, war, and aggression flowed between 1867 and 1914. From the school to the pulpit there was always something to say on the subject. Social Darwinist, racist, or eugenicist interpretations of war were often linked to nationalism; dictums such as 'man was created to fight' or 'man is a born soldier' went hand in hand with the phrase 'for the nation'. George L. Mosse suggests that in all nationalisms the idea of historical precedent takes on extreme importance. As well, symbols such as flags and national anthems become the physical or emotional representations of the national consciousness. To salute the flag or to stand at attention during the playing of the national anthem becomes an act of patriotism.[51]

Nationalism and Myth

During the nineteenth century nationalism became a prominent force in world affairs. Nationalism could take many forms: militaristic, popular, racist. In most cases, nationalism was linked with the idea of war. As nations grappled with defining their past, what rose to the forefront was the history of their conflicts. Wars between nations occupied a place of respect and honour and served as defining moments in the life and history of a nation. As Michael Howard has observed, the idea of any nation became closely linked to the conflicts in which it had participated. The history of battles becomes the history of a nation. The Canadian journalist Richard Gwyn has made the point that unlike most Western nations, Canada did not come into being by war and, as a consequence, its history is not as exciting as that of, for example, Britain, Germany, France, or the United States. As a result, Canadians have had to grasp at virtually anything that resembled conquest, war, or militarism to express their nationalism. One of the reasons why Canada's involvement in both the Boer War and World War I was so important to the country's collective psyche is that it finally gave Canadians the chance to demonstrate their political and military maturity. On the other hand, J.L. Granatstein and David J. Bercuson point out that these were not the first wars in Canada's history: 'wars between French and Indians, between English and French and between Britain and the United States determined not only the map of Canada but also its political institutions, its trade patterns, its rate and direction of expansion, and even, to a surprising degree, its cultural and social institutions.... Military events have moulded the very shape of Canadians.'[52]

Battles could be woven into the fabric of a country's history in many ways. Textbooks, for example, could offer patriotic national histories, complete with long accounts of battles highlighting the solidarity of the nation. Certain events became rallying points in the collective memory of the nation—occasions for celebration or for mourning, for recognition of those who gave their lives for the country. These often sombre occasions had an almost religious feeling to them. Of course they could also be festive and joyous, but in most cases they remained fixed in the minds of citizens as occasions for reflection and national contemplation—in some cases to the point of becoming secular holy days.

'Mass-producing traditions' such as ceremonies, parades, and symbols was a vital part of the nationalism of most nations in the period. In an emerging modern society, with an increasingly diverse populace, 'new devices to ensure or express social cohesion and identity and to structure social relations' had to be put into place in order for the nation to function in the desired way. To ensure specific loyalties, new 'traditions' were established in a 'conscious and deliberate' manner. To gain public support, all people were to be given a stake in the well-being of the nation—or at least the perception that this was the case. Education, both formal and informal, was crucial in this process. Taking the place of churches and their rituals, public monuments and ceremonies began to play a carefully orchestrated role in the celebration of nationalism and the creation of patriotism. The effectiveness of this approach was first proved in the France of the Third Republic.[53] Boer War monuments and Empire Day celebrations went a great distance towards achieving the same effect in the Canada of the early twentieth century.

Commemoration of sacrifice and achievement became a sign of one's desire to live in and participate in the life of the nation. Monuments to those killed in war reminded citizens of their sacrifices and fused nationalist feeling with an almost religious sentiment. Memorials, monuments, tombs of unknown soldiers all gained a 'collective power' in the 'national psyche'. According to James Mayo, such constructions 'express symbolically our political and emotional response to war and peace, victory and defeat, justice and destiny, or horror and revolt.' Because monuments and memorials are symbolic expressions of war as a political act, they can have a strong emotional effect—hence the importance of the memorials to the Boer War in creating positive attitudes towards participation in the Great War.[54]

There were also tangible displays of nationalism, such as dolls, flags, mementoes, toys, and coins, all of which had special appeal for children. Robert Coles has claimed that these artifacts are 'sources of instruction and connect a young person to a country. The attachment is strong. . . . and is as parental as the words imply—homeland, motherland, fatherland. It becomes subject to the same fate as other attachments.' A child 'seizes symbols' and 'craves a general explanation for a particular set of experiences.' In turn, these give young children 'handle[s] as they shape and assert their personalities'. When the symbols and experiences provided are militaristic or martial, the child has a clear idea of what is expected of him. For example, equating athletics with war goes beyond the mere discipline and teamwork ethic.[55]

All these images blend into myths. New nations are particularly dependent on myths to establish their legitimacy. The newer the nation, the newer the myth—and, of course, 'the more ancient its claims'. Canada and America have been particularly dependent on invented myths, transported traditions, and a steady series of heroic figures representing various aspects of the national ethos. Wilbur Zelinsky asserts that 'modern states could neither exist nor operate effectively without an adequate body of symbol and myth.'[56]

The myths that a nation chooses to form itself around are often keys to its national character. The transmission, over time, of essential aspects of the past that a society values has been a way for nations not only to keep in touch with their history but to give contemporary realities a historic bent. Citizens need myths on which to build a mental construct of the nation. By substituting myth for history, the inconsistencies of the past can be ironed out into a smooth, comprehensible tableau. When translated into myth, historical anguish and experience become simplified and are less likely to give rise to questions and doubt. This is where heroes become especially valuable. The hero embodies the myth, not the history. Flawless, blemish-free, he represents the greatness of the past. The national hero is thus held as the definitive illustration of the national man, and heroic individuals usually embody the characteristics that a nation holds dear. Elevating certain individuals above the level of the average citizen gives the latter something to aspire to. When heroes and their deeds are shrouded in a veil of near-divinity, they stand as the physical embodiment and personification of the nation. These individuals become essential to the concept of nationhood. Their deeds become frozen into legend, often as a result of their being glorified in print. That is why fiction is often much more potent than 'straight' history. History attempts to tell the whole story. As Robert McDougall rightly notes, fiction, while 'still within the bounds of the plausible, can make the hero bigger and better than life'. And such representations transcend borders. Citizens of one nation can respond to the achievements of superior individuals from another. Canada, so closely attached to both its southern neighbour and its mother country, was particularly ripe for the exploits of American and British heroes. Individuals who were popular or newsworthy in their own countries—especially Britain and the US—often seemed just as newsworthy in Canada during this era.[57]

Young children respond to heroes with intense enthusiasm and almost addictive interest. The 'cult of the hero' was a virtual industry in the years leading up to the Great War. Heroes were used to provide direction and demonstrate qualities of leadership, to exemplify morality, and to serve as role models. In a time of great change and flux, heroes stood out as the embodiments of tradition, especially masculine tradition, and examples of almost otherworldly accomplishment at a time when this was especially needed. As traditional society waned and spiritual longings were left unsatisfied, the hero filled an important void. As technology and money came to matter more, as religion to matter less, heroic figures served as examples for many young men. In an age that glorified materialism and threatened traditional notions of masculinity, the dedication and courage of the hero, especially in the service of the nation, mattered a great deal.[58]

In novels of adventure and in athletics, the hero was always the type of man that young boys aspired to become. In America (and to a great extent in Canada) Teddy Roosevelt was a natural hero, but there were many others, actual and synthetic, for the young boy to worship. Military men such as Nelson, Wellington, Gordon, and Kitchener were often singled out for worship and were lauded as great men. There was a strong tendency to elevate heroes who were manly, aggressive, and militaristic in their exploits. The nineteenth century was a heroic age, with an ample supply of heroes to choose from. At the same time the military life came to be equated with patriotism and duty and to be surrounded with a 'mystic aura'.[59]

In the late nineteenth century the image of the soldier underwent a transformation that elevated the army's prestige in the eyes of the general public. This could be partially attributed to disillusionment with modernity; the professional soldier, after all, moved within a world completely different from the mundane, prosaic factory or office. The soldier became, according to Wendy Katz, one of the most potent and durable representations of 'daring and strength'—'a symbol of spiritual destiny of Empire'. With heroes so sought after during this period, the soldier's life became synonymous with the highest reaches of national spirituality.[60]

For young boys, as for the nation, heroes were flesh-and-blood examples of manliness, personifications of the 'dearest values and aspirations of the society, the perfect expression of the ideal of a group in whom all human virtues unite'. As heroes of the modern day, soldiers appealed to diverse elements within society. Boys interested in science and technology could marvel at a general's use of the new machines and inventions for war, such as balloons, aircraft, and submarines; young men interested in sports could admire the athletic qualities of military men.[61]

The importance of heroes to a nation was talked, written, and taught about at length. Carlyle equated history with heroic enterprise: 'Universal History, the history of what man has accomplished in this world, is at bottom the History of the Great men who have worked here.... all things that we see standing accomplished in the world are properly the outer material result, the practical realization and embodiment, of thoughts that dwelt in the Great men sent into the world: the soul of the whole world's history, it may justly be considered, were the history of these.' By the 1880s, many had come to believe what Carlyle had suggested: 'The national hero was now a warrior and a patriotic death in battle was the finest masculine moral virtue.'[62]

For a country as young as Canada, the hero—Canadian, British, or American—became the model of the supreme citizen. Military heroes, in particular, became linked to the glory of the nation. The narratives they inspired—in novels, histories, newspapers, and textbooks—took on the stature of myths—myths that became coherent and tangible ideals around which the nation, and particularly young boys, could rally. They could be used not only to solidify aspects of nationalism—to define the qualities of the nation—but also as examples to be followed.[63]

Also relevant here are the commentaries and discourses on nationalism by the nineteenth-century French philosopher Ernest Renan. Renan felt that ties of the past, 'a rich legacy of remembrances', were a major constituent of the soul of the nation. Renan's ideas about nationalism are particularly pertinent to Canada's situation. Specifically, Renan highlights the 'heroic past, of great men, of glory... that is the social principle on which the national idea rests'. Codifying the past and great men, he writes, 'The worship of ancestors is understandably justifiable, since our ancestors have made us what we are.' In a young country like Canada, the most potent heroes were often military men. War meant 'suffering together', a concept that Renan believed was more important than happiness: 'national sorrows are more significant than triumphs because they impose obligations and demand a common effort.' Rallying young men to become soldiers and imposing a patriotic frame of mind led them to accept the idea of sacrificing themselves for the country. 'A nation is a grand solidarity constituted by the sentiment of sacrifices which one has made and those that one is disposed to make again.' This willingness to die for one's country was vital, fostering a sense of pride among those making the sacrifice.[64]

The initial stages of hero worship in the realm of spectator sports paralleled the glorification of military heroes. This development coincided with the rise of the modern Olympic Games, first held in 1896, as a test of national or racial strength, possibly in place of actual combat. In his classic studies *Imperialism* and *Jingoism*, published early in this century, John Hobson suggested that such vicarious experiences of action fed a neurotic national imagination. The athletic hero was the imaginary reflection of a society fascinated by manliness and sheer physical power.[65]

Sports came to be seen as a model for war. By the late nineteenth century the connections between sporting and military manliness were already well established. 'Sports as war games had many promoters', writes Michael Adams. 'Men and boys felt that they were in training, keeping themselves steely-eyed for some great violent test.... War became a Victorian game and like other sports it provided some men with a missing sense of vitality and community. This helped to make the enthusiasms of August 1914 possible.' Sport and related endeavours taught strength of personality, manliness, and the importance of winning—ideals that were easily transferable to the arena of warfare.[66]

To be a man meant to engage in action and competition and to strive for physical prowess. It also meant being able 'to cope with pain without showing distress' as a demonstration of courage. This ability predisposed one not only for success as a man, but also for service in war. To offset the changes that accompanied industrialization and modernization, a heavy emphasis was placed on the physical. As Anthony Rotundo puts it, 'toughness was now admired, while tenderness was a cause for scorn.... Indeed, the body itself became a vital component of manhood: strength, appearance and athletic skill mattered more than in previous centuries.' As men became less their own masters and more the employees of others, the most significant aspects of their masculinity disappeared in the sphere of work. 'Men believed they faced diminishing opportunities for masculine validation and that adolescents faced barriers to the development of masculinity', writes Jeffrey Hantover; 'the enthronement of "muscularity" is evident in leisure activities, literary tastes, and cultural heroes.'[67]

In Victorian culture, no topic preoccupied the public mind more than health. Naturally, then, the public in the late Victorian era marvelled at the endeavours of the athlete. Those athletes who reached the apex of achievement in their chosen sport were worshipped as heroes. As in ancient Greece, the ideal athletic form was singled out for special praise. According to one study of turn-of-the-century magazine articles, 'heroes were most often described in physical terms with an emphasis on their impressive size and strength.' Body-building in particular exemplified the North American and British public's fascination with the perfect physique. But gymnastics, cycling, and rowing also took hold in the public mind. Perfect specimens in sporting and physical culture had an impact on the national image. World-champion rower Ned Hanlan of Toronto was acclaimed as both a local and a national hero in the late nineteenth century. By the turn of the century the revival of the Olympic Games confirmed the equation between physical culture and the national hero.[68]

Demographic, economic, and ideological conditions came together to aid in the soaring popularity of most sports that required equipment. By the 1870s, young men from all classes were either participating in or watching every sport available to them. Whereas in an agricultural society physical strength was valued for its importance to work-related activities, in an increasingly industrialized society the athletic body was admired for its value in war and as a tangible demonstration of manliness. In Victorian culture, an interest in sport, in physicality, was considered exclusively masculine—in diametric opposition to femininity. This idea was central to the development of manliness as a contributor to war.[69]

A powerful physique was a metaphor for a potent and virile man, one capable of leading in war, government, or industry.[70] Lads who were considered manly were up to any challenge, constantly testing their manhood against other men and nature. Physical size, strength, and agility were admired as definitive aspects of the masculine ideal essential to the manly character that was projected as heroic and patriotic. At the same time the 'muscular Christianity' or 'Christian militarism' diffused through the 'public school ethos' was closely tied to sports and athletics. Keith A.P. Sandiford discusses the linkage between Victorian sport and religion:

the influence of the churches was doubly profound since a number of clergymen also served as headmasters in the public schools. It was at these institutions that they implemented their ideas of 'muscular Christianity' and tried to train outstanding civic leaders by exposing them to organized sports. In their view, all the requisite civic virtues could best be inculcated in a physical education program that made cricket, soccer, rugby and rowing almost essential features of the public school curriculum.[71]

Sandiford is talking here about Britain, but he could just as easily be describing Canada and its schoolboy culture. 'Muscular Christianity' was also embraced in the Dominion, 'where eager disseminators of British culture reproduced its best traditions'. David Brown notes that as early as 1859 the Ontario educator Egerton Ryerson was aware of the novel *Tom Brown's Schooldays*, which fostered 'muscular Christianity', although 'a time lag occurred before the term appeared on a national basis in the periodicals which burst into circulation in the 1870s and 1880s.'[72]

The English-speaking settlers who came to Canada from Britain brought with them the basic elements of British 'public' school education. Throughout the nineteenth and early twentieth centuries, private schools such as Upper Canada College and Trinity College School 'promoted with conviction an education based on Christian morality and character formation in turning out future citizens of true "Christian manhood".'[73]

Games and physical exercise became the prime means through which this moral character was to be instilled. Games, it was generally felt, inspired virtue, developed manliness, and formed character. All the attributes of manliness could be learned on the playing field— initiative, loyalty, self-reliance, obedience. In short, in addition to creating confidence in young men, games created young men with a disposition to follow rules—an important quality for future soldiers. As the Ontario education expert James L. Hughes put it, sports developed 'an erect, graceful figure, and easy carriage, benefitted the health and aided in securing effective discipline'.[74]

The British public school ethos was disseminated through the Canadian general education system in a number of ways. First, the headmasters of many Canadian schools had been educated in Britain. Headmasters generally, writes David Brown, 'were the most ardent proselytes of the "techniques of persuasion and instruction" utilized by their British counterparts. Organized sport, sustained by the ideological rationalization of athleticism, was used intentionally as a means by which to nurture character.' As well, the public school ethos filtered down through school stories in books such as *Tom Brown's Schooldays* and magazines such as the *Boy's Own Paper*. *Tom Brown* was extremely effective in transmitting the ideals of the public schools as exemplified by Tom's school, Rugby, to the general public. As more magazines entered the field, such stories reached a wider audience, as did the public school code. The ideals of the closed public school system were now permeating the public at large. By the time of the First World War, the results of this kind of propaganda were becoming evident. 'Each school', writes Peter Parker, 'had its proud boast' of enlistments and deaths; 'few English schools could claim, as did St. Andrews, Aurora, Ontario, that 98 per cent of its Old Boys fought in the war.' It is no exaggeration to say, as David Brown does, that 'Christian, nationalistic and imperialistic ideals were prominent features in the pedagogical rhetoric at Canada's élite schools.'[75]

Filtered through the English public school model, sport, games, and drill—all things athletic—functioned as convenient media for the delivery of specific messages. Headmasters, church and civic leaders, and others in positions of power assisted in this process. 'Athleticism . . . was the esteemed consort of militarism. Games maximized the physical development of the individual and ultimately, the nation and Empire for the struggle of war.' In an environment where war, sports, and athletics were so closely related, it was not much of a leap to perceive athletics and war as training grounds for manliness.[76] As later chapters will show, the inclusion of drill in all levels of school, the rise of the Boy Scouts, and the popularity of hunting all contributed as well to strengthen the relationship between manliness and militarism.

World War I was, in the words of Peter Filene, 'the ultimate test of manliness'. Men 'envisioned the battlefield as a proving ground where they could enact and repossess the manliness that modern . . . society' had lost. Why turn to the model of soldiering in particular at this time? Perhaps surrogate warfare had run its course and all the substitute formats no longer held sufficient appeal. From a very young age, boys were raised to be soldiers. They were prepared from early on to view war as both a thrilling adventure and an honourable endeavour. Military heroes abounded. Patriotism, pride in a young boy's future manhood, the romanticization of war in toys and books, and the extreme emphasis on competitiveness, winning, and sacrifice in sports combined to train young man for eventual sacrifice in war. This social conditioning had been highly effective.[77]

It has been argued that, since the end of the nineteenth century, sport has been the premier source of masculine representation. The athlete/warrior has come to stand as the ideal in masculine achievement. With advances in technology, more and more products—from tin cans to cigarette cases—featured pictures of the popular heroes of the day. Advertisers turned their attention to manliness and the promotion of the ideal man, seeking to create a connection between youth and health, between the athletic body and sporting success. This connection was strengthened by the new preoccupation with personal hygiene and the perception of poor health as a reflection of failure.[78]

The hundreds of enlistment posters that appeared at the beginning of the war graphically depicted the essential elements of manliness and militarism so pervasive at the time. Models of manliness, in the form of everything from the characters of popular fiction to sporting heroes, constituted a well-established and well-known cultural symbolism. Sport as a metaphor for war was widely used at numerous levels of society. From games to language, militarism permeated discourse on all levels, and sporting metaphors influenced public perceptions. Paul Fussell relates how the early battles of the Great War were often framed in terms familiar to readers of various heroic exploits, such as Peary's 'Race to the North Pole'. Fussell writes that the words 'race to' 'had the advantage of a familiar sportsmanlike, Explorer Club overtone, suggesting that what was happening was not too far distant from playing games, running races and competing in a thoroughly decent way.' With the desire to fight inculcated in them from all sides, 'In August 1914 they . . . responded to the call of patriotism and adventure.'[79]

4

The Culture of Reading

How often have I been vituperated by rose-water critics because I have written of fighting and tried to inculcate elementary lessons, such as that it is a man's duty to defend his country and that only those who are prepared for war can protect themselves and such as are dear to them.

H. Rider Haggard, *The Private Diaries of Sir H. Rider Haggard, 1914–1925*, ed. D.S. Higgins[1]

In late nineteenth- and early twentieth-century Ontario, numerous facets of society were anxious to rear youngsters with the values and attitudes that opinion-makers and educators thought were proper and upstanding. Patriotism and nationalism were pervasive ideologies ingrained into the minds of the young. There was also a specific concern to create militarists willing to defend the country should the need arise. A survey of boys' literature of the time reveals that it was saturated with examples of heroic endeavour and military conquest. Encouraged from above in the hegemonic sense, this body of literature was designed to provoke specific responses. If much of what a man becomes reflects the influences of his youth, then the impressions made by his reading as a boy can determine his particular path and contribute to the destiny of his nation as well. To dismiss adventure stories, boys' magazines, and popular histories and their impact on attitudes and behaviour would be to dismiss a substantial proportion of pre-World War I boys' culture.[2]

During World War I many important authors were enlisted in the cause. This was a significant development, for it highlights the influence that writers had in moulding public opinion. For many writers this was not a difficult transition, since much of the work they had done for their entire careers fitted easily into a more official package. As they built a following through their novels and short stories, and as their names and works reached larger audiences, some branched out into other areas, such as journalism and drama, further cementing their hold on audiences.[3] This chapter highlights the themes and subjects that were part of a young man's reading material in the period prior to World War I.

Canadian Publishing

Situated in a remote, barren colony with a sparse and widely dispersed population, two languages, and the rapidly developing United States next door, the Canadian book industry did not have a very auspicious beginning. Many of the first settlers—if they knew how to read at all—lacked the time, the money, or the desire for reading. Those who did want to read depended on a very small number of booksellers. Government officials, officers of the military, clergymen, teachers, merchants, and well-to-do women attached to these persons were the main consumers of printed material.[4]

Before a printing press arrived on what is now Canadian soil, books were few, often brought from England by settlers:

> From the outset, the book trade was organized to import books and periodicals, just as other mercantile activities brought in manufactured goods: this was the corollary of being a colony, which existed to absorb excess populations and to serve as a market for home products as well as to ship out raw materials.[5]

When, in 1751, the first printing press did arrive, its sole purpose was to serve the government. The printing of proclamations and official notices allowed the authorities to disseminate their views on law and order and codify their rule. The press was not intended to publish native literature or even to reproduce British books. As technology improved and more presses were made available (often from the US), a publishing industry did emerge. Still, in order for it to survive and to ensure sufficient profits, government patronage was essential.[6]

Although printing official documents ensured an income, entrepreneurial spirits sought to expand their business by printing other material. The almanac was the most popular and durable feature of early publishing. Various religious pamphlets and prayer books were also produced, especially after the arrival of the Loyalists. One of the main hindrances to the creation of a unique industry was the tendency of Canadian settlements to look to more established American centres, both economically and culturally. Canadian booksellers got their books from American cities like Boston, not Montreal or Toronto.[7]

As technological innovations increased and restrictions on printing relaxed, those who possessed presses had to combine activities such as newspaper printing and bookselling. This made practical economic sense. Vital to survival of a nascent Canadian publishing industry were reprints of American popular stories and British 'classics'. Works already guaranteed to sell (if not presold by subscription) were far less risky then indigenous Canadian works. By the early nineteenth century, the Canadian reading public preferred lighter American works and the familiar British standards. Canadian publishers did not go out of their way to nurture homegrown work, which was generally considered immature and unappealing. Even by 1850, the desire for both American and British writing was still strong. 'Thus was established a tradition: a parasitical dependence upon the dreams, the romances, the adventures, the tragedies, the plays, the epics, all the stuff of fantasy, manufactured outside.'[8]

When reasons for the paucity of indigenous Canadian writing are sought, a pervasive feeling of homesickness cannot be dismissed. As a relatively new colony still inextricably linked to Britain, the settlers preferred stories from home. Folktales, fables, and old stories in general had a natural appeal for those seeking escape from everyday hardships. People who spent time and money on reading material did not want to read about the monotonous and difficult existence they knew in Canada. Books from the US, a country with full independence, and an expanding sense of nationhood and a vibrant cultural life, were also readily accessible.

As the colony moved into mid-century, however, the English-speaking population was beginning to evolve into a more independent citizenry. A growing desire for more control of the national culture among those living in Canada West was reflected in a trickle of works 'detailing the routine of the real world, works which however derivative, were stamped as uniquely *Canadian*'. Yet few Canadian works were profitable, and thus Canadian publishers relied on reprints and agency contracts. Together, the aggressive tactics of American publishers, the caution of native publishers, and the short-sightedness of British publishers who benefited from the lingering colonial mentality ensured that an indigenous Canadian literature would be slow to develop.[9]

Technological advances and cultural changes led to the establishment of more Canadian publishers, but most depended on their agency/reprint function to survive. Between 1896 and 1913 over a dozen new publishing houses were established in Toronto alone. They published the odd Canadian title, but most continued to be branch houses selling British and American titles. Widespread compulsory education meant that more Canadians were now readers, and technological changes made inexpensive books available in great quantities,[10] but with a few notable exceptions—Ernest Thompson Seton, Charles G.D. Roberts, L.M. Montgomery—the majority of books read in Canada came from 'foreign' sources.

The Impact of Modern Publishing

In his study of nationalisms, Benedict Anderson asserts that what has held many nations together in space and time was the development of printed literature or, as he terms it, 'print-capitalism', which 'made it possible for rapidly growing numbers of people to think about themselves, and to relate themselves to others in profoundly new ways.' In his view, the West was increasingly defined by capitalist culture and book publishing was one of the earliest forms of capitalist enterprise. As profit concerns became inextricably linked to economic survival, booksellers 'sought out first and foremost those works which were of interest to the largest possible number of their contemporaries.' Anderson argues that the introduction of printing was, in this respect, a stage on the road to our present society of mass consumption and standardization. In turn, a national literature established a basis for national consciousness.[11]

Marshall McLuhan was also intensely aware of the power of print and the eventual commodification of books. Reading a printed book changed the relationship of the reader to his or her environment and decreased the importance of oral culture. Reading, according to McLuhan, removed the reader from 'the collectivity' and encouraged a focus on personal identity. At the same time memory became less important. The ability to follow the thought process in a linear fashion became so essential as to make literacy no mere skill but the 'dominant cultural frame of mind'. In effect, the printed word gained a monopoly: if one could not read, then one was excluded from certain sectors of society and aspects of life. The distinction between oral and book culture, as Neil Postman makes clear, proved to be the dividing line between illiteracy and childhood. Those who could read were beyond the stage of childhood.[12]

The invention of printing, then, is seen as crucial to the invention of modern childhood, and literacy became the primary focus of schooling. At first the emphasis was on the 'good book' that depicted proper moral attributes and contributed to the building of character. By the 1870s, books emphasizing manliness and feminine virtues, character training, and the prevention of vice dominated the titles presented as gifts; the book prizes presented to students by the Toronto Board of Education tended to be beautifully bound English classics and character-building studies.[13]

The prescriptive literature market gave way to different kinds of works that began to challenge the authority of church and family. In turn, enjoyment and entertainment became increasingly linked to literacy. The rhymes and games so typical of children's oral culture were transformed in the nineteenth century into published formats. Middle-class and upper-class parents, who were very concerned about their children's education, were the primary purchasers of these books. By the middle of the nineteenth century, traditional oral culture was 'being overshadowed rapidly by the medium of print'.[14]

Didactic and morally rich stories serve to buttress various 'attitudes, ideas and preconceptions', especially in the realm of the popular.[15] Their power as agents of social control is evident in the fact that they played 'a large role in the socialization of infants, in the expression of official norms such as law and religion', and 'in the conduct of politics'. There is a full 'psychological sense of participation' involved in reading certain kinds of fiction—adventure, for example—one that asks the reader to merge his or her personality with that of the protagonist. The reader is proud to inhabit the fictional world and takes great pleasure in it. Joan Rockwell writes that 'If literary characters personify social norms and values, they also set patterns for imitation which are very much wanted in times when society is being unmade and reassembled in new and strange ways.'[16]

Popular literature of the period was expected to provide role models. Perhaps this outcome is not as relevant where serious literature is concerned, but lighter fare has a tendency to rely on formula, archetype, and stereotype. The same 'plot' or tale type is retold again and again, reinforcing and confirming a particular kind of gratification. Easily digested messages are prominent in popular literature, measured out with equal doses of suspense, adventure, violence, and romance.[17]

Between 1820 and 1860, most children's books in effect were a 'record of what adults wanted of and for the next generation'. Not only were they infused with moralism; they were specifically intended to provide and sustain moral education. The patterns of the evolution of children's literature are similar on both sides of the Atlantic. With regard to American children's periodical literature, R. Gordon Kelly maintains that there were three stages. The first stage, from 1789 to the 1840s (coinciding with the founding of the first children's periodical), saw a full-fledged religious instruction flavoured with moral lessons. A transitional period from the late 1840s to the outbreak of the Civil War brought experimentation, with alternatives reflecting 'a more relaxed attitude toward the duties and characteristics of childhood and a lessened emphasis on religious conversion'. The final stage in the development of periodicals for children was marked by a general move towards 'wholesome entertainment', except among those still concerned primarily with religion. Kelly suggests that the proportions of wholesomeness and entertainment varied considerably, and that even if the intent was to entertain, a didactic quality was never too far removed. Nonetheless, the essential feature of late nineteenth-century children's publishing was the move 'from instruction to entertainment'.[18]

In England, the *raison d'être* of children's publishing was instruction. While entertainment came to the forefront after the 1850s, there was still a strong didactic component in children's literature. According to one authority on the 'moral' period, this type of literature was meant to provide children with instruction on how to live a moral and virtuous life. Among the principal lessons learned by the main characters in these books were perseverance and resistance of temptation. Characters of questionable morals, of course, always came to a bad end. But those who worked diligently at the business of life would triumph.[19]

Until the 1840s there was no specific lighter fare for children. The tales of Daniel Defoe, Walter Scott, and James Fenimore Cooper were exciting, but they were not directed specifically towards young readers. By the mid-1840s, however, the adventure tale for boys was well on its way to establishing itself. Captain Frederick Marryat, in particular, is credited with establishing the boys' adventure story.[20]

By the late 1860s the content of the books had begun to change. Work, for example, was portrayed as an 'act of heroism', no longer an obligation. This shift represented a 'quiet, almost unnoticed revolution'.[21] By the end of the nineteenth century fiction for boys was radically different from that of 40 or 50 years earlier. As the concept of masculinity became more concrete, boys' works followed suit.[22] Boys' literature was supposed to 'help build up men'—in essence, to distance boys from the world of their mothers. Escaping the female-dominated domestic world was a common theme in the new boys' fiction, in part because women had now become 'the chief agents of socialization' in the home. Action and adventure did not leave room for introspection. The boy characters in the books of this time 'endeavoured to do: to explore, challenge and master.' Girls, by contrast, 'aspired to ethereal benignity'. Boys were being drawn ever deeper into the 'dramatic fantasies of heroism' and 'daydreams of conquest'. The authors of many of these books were themselves examples of manly action.[23]

Typically, the boy escapes domestic socialization by running away from home and undergoing a different kind of socialization through his experience in the world. Whereas the young female protagonists of this time are 'rewarded' by submission and service in the home, male protagonists are 'rewarded' by becoming men in the world of external accomplishment. The hero in boys' books of this period is often an adolescent 'bad boy' who goes through a series of trials before becoming a man. From Stevenson's Jim Hawkins to Twain's Tom Sawyer, the emphasis is on becoming a man in the outside world and on learning and preparing to meet the challenges of business, nation-building, and war. The heroes of these books cultivate the virtues that were supposed to constitute true manhood. The young hero of a boys' book has an adventure that removes him from the domestic realm and allows him a taste of manly resolve through 'violent action' that, according to Sally Allen McNall, 'validate[s] his courage and determination'. In the opinion of Claudia Nelson, towards the end of the nineteenth century children's novels imparted not practical knowledge but 'something more precious still: manliness or womanliness'.[24]

Publishers began to realize they could increase sales by focusing on the current interest in manliness. The flood of books on adventure and war that followed also created a sentimental yearning for boyhood and the fraternity of an all-male world. Over time, a literature emerged designed to be shared by men and boys. Promoted as manuals of manliness, such books were meant to show boys how to behave like real men. Their authors did away with any attributes in their protagonists that could be interpreted as feminine. At the same time, they enlarged all the quintessential manly ideals. This magnification of masculine elements led to the construction of hyper-masculine fictional boys who were 'manlier than manly'. Boys and their heroes were constructed as 'more loyal, more patriotic, more cunning, more masterful and more reticent than ever before'.[25]

In this context of magnified manliness, violence and other active emotions were shown to be useful as long as one never lost full control. Heroes channelled their anger by attacking bullies, or boxing to settle a dispute. In part, being courageous meant having control over one's emotions; it was even permissible to display fear—provided it was a one-time occurrence. Experiencing fear was part of the testing, the coming of age; mastering it meant that one was brave. American novels for boys after the Civil War were saturated with this message: 'An injured lad was urged to "keep up a good heart" '; ' "A little pluck does more for a wound than a good many bandages." '[26]

The emphasis on being able to 'take it' removed emotion from such stories and possibly from the reader's stock of expressions—a highly desirable consequence when the intention was to create soldiers. Significantly, this emotional neutralization produced an 'anti-intellectual strain' that is evident in much of this fiction. As Kimberley Reynolds writes, 'muscle and morality are celebrated over intelligence and inspiration.' The sporting events, boys' play, races, rescues, and fights that made up a substantial portion of these novels encouraged boys 'to see themselves, their trials, opportunities and triumphs, as belonging to a public sphere of action rather than taking place internally.'[27] In other words, boys' fiction of the period was oriented towards performance.

For a number of male writers of boys' stories, there was a close connection between masculinity and economic success. The insecurities that many men felt during this turbulent period took numerous forms, but the male's role as breadwinner seems to have been particularly challenged in the last years of the nineteenth century and the first decade of the twentieth. Being an economic provider was an essential attribute of a man. Industriousness was thus equated with manhood. In an urban industrial society, one way to tell a manly man was by his success as a provider.[28]

The popular Horatio Alger stories, for example, suggest that, in order to be taken seriously as a man, one must not give into temptations that would bring about economic and moral downfall. Alger's books were a fictional complement to the manuals of instruction and advice, interspersing examples of courage, self-reliance, and manliness with warnings about the evils of alcohol, tobacco, and loose living. Life was portrayed as a struggle that, when successfully won, would lead the young boy to wealth.[29]

Interestingly, it was male writers who focused on industriousness and stressed the value of work. By contrast, female writers of books and manuals directed to young men had a tendency to stress the spiritual—a 'higher state' often attained through reading, especially fine literature and poetry. Male writers, though, seemed reluctant to go too far in this direction. Not only were certain kinds of poetry and literature seen as 'effeminate', but men concerned about their sons feared that too much time with this kind of 'amusement' would take boys away from learning how to earn a decent wage. Boys should read, but their reading material should be inspiring, uplifting, and encouraging in a manly fashion. Reading should groom a boy in masculine ways.[30]

In their manual *Moral Training in the School and Home*, E. Hershey Sneath and George Hodges suggested that moral training had been most successful when the instruction was indirect. Schools and parents played a role in this process, but reading material of the right kind was the most persuasive:

> We should introduce the children to the virtues and vices, with corresponding rewards and punishments, through fairy tale, myth, fable, allegory, parable, legend, stories of heroes and heroines, biography and history. The child is easily brought into sympathy with the story, and grasps in this concrete and interesting way its moral import; and the lesson, because of the child's intense sympathies soon sinks into his sensitive mind and receptive heart.[31]

The development of a child's identity as a male or female was seen a pressing need between the ages of seven and 11. It is not surprising, therefore, that during this stage 'there is sometimes a split between books concerned with conventional masculine characters and attitudes' and other, more traditional fare. Here there is a full-fledged emphasis on heroic adventure and clearly delineated masculine models.[32] Who to be was of prime importance. In many cases, words were buttressed by illustrations, just to make sure the portrait of heroic masculinity was not missed. In many cases, even if the books were not read, the dynamic pictures on the covers and the daring suggestiveness of the titles effectively conveyed the content; Captain Marryat insisted that the covers of his books contain illustrations of such eye-catching appeal as to hook the child's eye immediately. This technique marks the beginning of marketing for young adults. In an increasingly visual world, pictures, drawings, and photographs helped to inculcate manly ideology in young readers in a provocative and accessible way.[33]

Older books with adventure themes and masculine elements that had not been specifically designed for juvenile readers were now reissued to take advantage of the popularity of the new genre. Works by Defoe, Swift, and Cooper were reissued in the last quarter of the nineteenth century with illustrations, maps, and bolder print. Many such works were also often re-edited to weed out the more difficult passages that might discourage a younger reader. Abridgements of well-known adult works and classics, with shorter sentences and simpler prose, became common.[34] This reorientation was particularly pronounced with the so-called adventure series, which favoured recurring themes and familiar archetypes.

Investigations have shown that the tactics of repetition and emphasis produced a set of patriotic images that came to define manhood, action, and Empire for a generation of young boys. The actual deeds of real explorers and true men of action further tightened the bond between the 'world of boys and the world of men'.[35] Joseph Conrad wrote of Marryat, who had legions of devoted followers from all walks of life:

> He is the enslaver of youth, not by the literary artifices of presentation, but by the natural glamour of his own temperament. To his young heroes, the beginning of life is a splendid and warlike lark, ending at last in inheritance and marriage. . . . To the artist his work is interesting as a completely successful expression of an unartistic nature. . . . There is an air of fable about it.[36]

Whether it was Conrad with his sophisticated prose style or more popular writers such as Marryat and Henty, the young reader was immediately captured by the fabulous, even supernatural elements within the story and embodied by the protagonist. The key was the rendering of horrific situations such as war and violence in exciting and meaningful terms. The use of illustrations only added glamour and reduced the complexities of moral problems to a level of access that served to reinforce what Robert MacDonald has called 'the social reproduction of aggressive virility'.[37]

From 1870 onward, advances in newspapers, technology, reporting, and education all aided in the creation of a massive reading public. Books reached a much wider audience as new production methods made them more affordable.[38]

Late nineteenth-century purveyors of fiction had an enormous influence; as J.S. Bratton has observed, 'Anyone educated to the level of basic literacy was accessible through a story.' Books became an excellent vehicle for propaganda, for eliciting specific reactions. Popular fiction legitimized, glamorized, and romanticized new ideas. The rise of particular genres for boys reflects the fact that the demand for great quantities of literature required publishers to play it safe and make the most of what was already selling. A certain formulaic element was inevitable.[39]

Books became more than just instruments of pedagogy in the late nineteenth century. Excitement often took over from 'pious ascetics', resulting in tales both magical and marvellous. Stephen Kline has written that 'The stories took on the ability to enthral and delight the child, an ability that emerged as the prime attraction of reading.'[40] This was the era that brought us a substantial number of 'enchanting' works, even if not every one was a *Peter Pan* or a *Secret Garden*.

Noting that the Victorians believed 'self-improvement, respectability and even entertainment could be obtained at home through the written word', Steven Mintz remarks that at a time when family traditions and local customs were losing their authority, children's literature filled the gap by providing models for speech, taste, etiquette, and fashion. Fiction served to shape and mould moral standards by furnishing people of varied backgrounds with 'a common frame of reference and a shared set of norms and aspirations'.[41]

Even so, the so-called 'democratization of the word' was not without its critics. Many feared that the new mass culture—the dime novels, serialized stories, and 'trashy' fiction—threatened social morality. This concern was not new: from the beginning of mechanized print, the guardians of culture had worried about what the masses were reading. However, new technology, coupled with growing literacy, exacerbated the situation. Consequently, according to Dee Garrison, numerous articles, books, and pamphlets were written by the 'better educated' on how to 'give direction to the less educated'. Titles such as 'Books, Culture and Character', 'The Abuse of Reading', 'Books and Ideals', and 'Good Habits in Reading' suggest how intent certain members of society were on guiding the new reading public.[42]

A paradox is evident here. On the one hand, the systems of public and private education that evolved in nineteenth-century Ontario clearly succeeded in the basic task of creating a functionally literate population. Reading was increasingly popular and consistently on the rise—a development that pleased most educational and some moral reformers. On the other hand, there was a strong suspicion that the content was in questionable taste and might lead young readers astray. Those concerned about the quality of the literature available to young boys were often vigilant in their censorship, and in many cases lobbied to make 'quality' literature—Bible stories and morally uplifting works—accessible to youngsters. Many books were advertised as suitable 'for the family circle' or 'for the fireside'. Yet as Jane Pettigrew has pointed out, 'children also read alone in the privacy of their own bedrooms or in the schoolroom.'[43] According to one commentator in the first decade of the twentieth century:

> Some of the boys in the schools found pleasure in trespassing into forbidden fields. Teachers have complained that these boys were reading Henty and Ballantyne and neglecting the text-book. Yet these boys sometimes surprised us with information that we did not suspect, and when questioned about where they had found out these things, blushingly admitted that they had obtained the knowledge from books that were hidden from parent and teacher.[44]

Many people were determined to ensure that the contents of all books were morally suitable for young minds.

As early as the 1840s, attempts were being made to control the impact of rising literacy rates. Books, schools, and libraries were all subject to various political and social pressures. Reading at home, ideally within the family circle, was supposed to prevent idle and undesirable activities. 'Regulated reading was seen by many middle-class and upper-class reformers as the best means to limit the apparently unbridled independence of the mass of the population that had resulted from the breakdown of earlier relations of domination and subordination.' One typical manual suggested that once a boy had experienced the pleasures of reading, it was up to his parents to make sure that what he was reading would have a 'helpful moral effect'. The author of *Training the Boy* wrote, 'It is not enough that the literature merely entertain, it must instruct, it must tend to inculcate wholesome juvenile ideals.' Recognized as a 'potent force' capable of both good and bad, reading should provide the populace with the desired attributes of character and manners; social order would depend on it.[45]

The library became an environment in which issues of class, leisure, and access to information were contested. The efforts to create and regulate the Ontario library system drew on British and American models and regulatory structures. The properly regulated library would improve society as a whole. 'Social stability' and the prevention of 'class antagonism' were the goals of library bylaws. Official and quasi-official actors stepped in to voice their opinions or exert their moral weight. People, given the chance, were reading—newspapers, journals, magazines, and books of every kind. It was what they were reading and how they were reading it that was of greatest concern. In this context, the reading habits of young boys were especially problematic.[46]

People were not reading what teachers and moralists had hoped they would read. Fiction, particularly fiction of questionable taste, was the preferred choice for patrons of the libraries and bookstores. In 1878–9, 80 per cent of the 33,000 volumes borrowed by members of the Toronto Mechanics Institute were works of fiction. Murray G. Ross, who has listed the YWCA's holdings at 1,556 volumes in 1873, states that in 1874, Toronto reported 400 visitors daily to its reading room. In his autobiography, Sigmund Samuel praises the Toronto Mechanics Institute library as a kind of oasis, providing him with reading material during his childhood: 'I would look through the *Illustrated London News* of the day and borrow exciting adventure books such as *Robinson Crusoe*.' When the Institute closed in 1882, its assets and books were incorporated into the Toronto Public Library system. In Toronto in 1907 and 1908, fiction accounted for almost 40 per cent of the books borrowed from the Toronto Public Library. Mary Vipond speculates that popular novels at this time may have reflected 'heightened nationalistic or imperialistic feelings, or [served] as a counter to the uncertainty of rapidly changing times'.[47]

The *Catalogue of Books* published by the Education Department of Ontario in 1895 reveals what was popular and also, perhaps, what was considered valuable by libraries and readers. In fact, it offers a tailor-made course in manliness and militarism. Fiction, for example, is divided into such subcategories as Adventure, Historical Tales, General Fiction, Religious Literature and Moral Tales, and Juvenile Literature. Under Juvenile Literature, one finds Horatio Alger, and General Fiction includes numerous works by Dickens, Rider Haggard, and Scott. Other categories are also illuminating. The lists headed History of Great Britain and Great Battles and Sieges are both lengthy, the latter including works by Henry Morton Stanley and Teddy Roosevelt. Yet the largest list of all is Historical Tales. The author with the most titles (45) is G.A. Henty; among them are *With Wolfe in Canada*, *By Sheer Pluck*, and *Held Fast For England*. The biography section runs eight pages and is peppered with lives of 'great men', as well as numerous military heroes. The extensive Travel and General Adventure list contains a veritable who's who of boys' authors. Present and accounted for are Ballantyne, Fenn, W.H.G. Kingston, Mayne Reid, Marryatt, Oliver Optic, and Gordon Stables.[48]

The almost insatiable demand for novels by a mass audience affected the way people read. This trend became even more pronounced when mass-market magazines entered the field. It has been suggested that because cheap and ephemeral books and magazines were abundant, 'they were purchased for their novelty and quickly discarded', which, in turn, changed the nature of reading.[49]

Prior to the innovations in technology, publishing, and mass education, reading and book ownership were the privilege of a small, wealthy élite. Books were treasured possessions. A private library was a mark of wealth, prestige, and education. Circulation of journals, often expensive to produce, was limited to institutions, a few private individuals, and possibly the odd coffee house. Michael Denning has accurately observed that the 'ideals of the gentle reader' and of 'reading as a leisurely, contemplative process gave way to a reading based on brevity, information and manipulation of the reader.' The mechanization of printing and the democratization of the book led to the emergence of readers from all classes and walks of life. General fiction magazines designed to appeal to the whole family offered light and entertaining fare. The popularity of these illustrated magazines led to circulations in the millions. In an article on the 'demise' of the 'gentle' reader, Christopher Wilson cites Burton Bledstein: 'Detached from any face-to-face confrontation, apart from any mass audience, oblivious to any restriction of time, the individual alone could read and reread the written work in the privacy of any room. . . . Isolated, the reader required no intermediary as interpreter, no set stage, no responsive listener.' Fredric Jameson argues that the commodification of book culture and the 'reification of reading' at the turn of the century led people to 'read for the ending'. Among the reasons for this shift, he suggests, were the rise of genre and the 'best-seller', and the general desire for satisfaction.[50]

The rise of mass-market book and magazine publishing reflected the fact that people had more money to spend on reading. In 1874 fewer than 500 periodicals, including newspapers, were published in Canada; by 1900 there were more than 1,200, and by the 1890s more than 400 newspapers were being published, many of which included the added attraction of illustrations.[51]

Many young boys were avid newspaper readers, especially during times of war. Arthur R.M. Lower recalled reading everything he could about the Boer War, surveying all the news and memorizing the maps: 'A wide-awake youngster could hardly fail to be well informed on the day-to-day aspects of war. The geography of South Africa became more familiar than our own.'[52]

Thanks to Egerton Ryerson and the Carnegie Foundation, Ontario had numerous libraries. By the end of the century most adult Canadians could read, and most had access to 'some kind of organized collection of library material'. As well, the cities and larger towns had bookshops offering everything from the classics to books on religion. Joseph Schull writes that 'It was said of the province that there was a good bookshop in every town of over a thousand, and Toronto had at least twenty.' Eaton's offered cloth-bound, illustrated editions of Henty's works for $1.15; Horatio Alger's books, described as 'good healthy reading for boys', were available for as little as 19 cents. A significant number of books and magazines came from the United States or Britain. Although there were some indigenous publications and Canadian editions aimed at the youth market, for the most part young people depended on periodicals imported from Britain and the United States. In popular literature, adventure stories by Cooper, Kipling, Scott, Stevenson, Alger, and Henty reigned supreme, and the Tarzan stories gained a broad readership. Although figures from one authoritative source show that Canadians read primarily American fiction in the early part of the twentieth century, boys living in Ontario probably devoured more British adventure stories than anything else,[53] internalizing the values that they conveyed.

The Adventure

As with hunting and athletics, there is a long history of association between literature (including poetry) and war. During and after the American Civil War the linkage became stronger still. First a boom in production of paperback books, especially adventures, helped to drum up interest in the conflict and had a 'significant' impact on 'Northern wartime psychology'. After the war, a flood of books glorifying 'heroic and manly behaviour' was unleashed on the North American continent. The equation of manly heroism and the Civil War would affect many generations of boys.[54]

Perhaps the most famous novel about the Civil War is Stephen Crane's *The Red Badge of Courage*. Its publication in 1895, some 30 years after the conflict, coincided with a renewed sense of manliness and militarism. The hero, Henry Fleming, eventually demonstrates true heroism and courage after mastering his fear, panic, and shame. The message contained in the *The Red Badge of Courage* is unmistakable: 'war was the ultimate catharsis in life that tests true manhood.'[55]

The soldier hero was a particularly durable expression of the definitive masculine role. Since ancient Greece, stories presenting the soldier as the 'quintessential figure of masculinity' have served as the foundations of national myths and provided solid role models for young boys. English literature and culture always held the soldier in high regard and the colonial translation elevated the soldier to new heights and the epitome both of patriotism and of manhood. Again and again, across all boundaries of class and age, a real man was defined by his willingness to sacrifice his life for his country. War was both the ultimate test and the ultimate opportunity and though not all could participate, readers, especially the very young, could still dream.[56]

Whether books with their suggestive titles or magazines with their cover pictures 'of big game in furious conflict with white hunters', charts of naval ships, and illustrations of army life, the common theme was a blatant and consistent 'reiteration of racial pride, militaristic values and . . . enthusiasm for conquest'. The incorporation of real places and actual events in fictional stories provided imaginative involvement for readers and a means of tangibly embodying moral and political ideas.[57] The nautical adventure tales of Captain Marryat, the novels of Henty and Kingsley, *Tom Brown's Schooldays*: all served as propaganda vehicles for militarism and recruitment promotions for the army, instilling nationalistic and patriotic ideals while constantly reinforcing the theme of manliness.[58] According to the education secretary of the IODE, Constance Laing, reading was essential:

> Let the boy roam with Hiawatha, sail the seas with Sinbad, build stockades with Crusoe, fight dragons with Jason, let him play at quoits with Odysseus and at football with Tom Brown. These playmates will never quarrel with him or bully him, but from them he will learn to be brave, self-reliant, manly, thoughtful of others, straightforward, with his face toward the light.[59]

One of the oldest and most widespread literary forms, the pure adventure story is what Martin Green has termed a 'masculinist' form that has always been written for boys and men. Such works often have a deeply ingrained subtext focusing on conquest, attrition, and heroic endeavour. 'Vigorous individuality' and 'action' are two of the defining characteristics of the genre. Today all this seems commonplace, but before World War I the basic adventure story was finding myriad new manifestations, including the spy novel, the invasion scare, and the pulp serial, all of them featuring a gentlemanly young hero. From the 1870s on the adventure evolved, in the words of Graham Dawson, 'as a gendered form contributing to that general splitting in cultural imaginaries'. This polarization of gender was extremely obvious in the adventure genre in two particular ways. First, there was the emphasis on ultra-masculine heroes with ultra-masculine names, such as Frank Fearless and Dick Dare; second, female characters were almost totally absent, and women writers were very scarce.[60]

This kind of work could straddle both ends of the culture spectrum, appealing to admirers of Kipling and Conrad as well as those of Henty and many lesser writers. C.D. Eby, commenting on Henty's plots, states that common to all of them was 'a fledgling protagonist [who] graduates from boy to man through adjustment to and enjoyment of honest combat and conflict.' The line of descent from Ballantyne to Stevenson to Henty was often direct. As editor of a number of successful magazines, many of which reached the juvenile and young adult market in Ontario, W.H.G. Kingston could use these podiums as places from which to preach the importance of the colonies and the British traditions. Henty's historical adventures were 'infused with elements of British commercial enterprise, physical courage and national strength and portrayed to his youthful readers what many late Victorians regarded as the essence of the country's greatness and uniqueness.'[61] Acting as recruiters for the army, 'juvenile journals' and adventure novels reached out forcefully to young readers either by having the protagonist act as saviour or by placing the young hero in the presence of some great mythic figure.[62] Henty's development of the boy-hero was unparalleled. Appealing to young boys all over the Empire, he served as a wonderful protagonist, to whom any young boy could relate:

> Having such an accessible and predictable hero is plainly to encourage the reader to project himself into the character and thereby to take a personal interest not only in the details of battles and campaigns but in the hero's ultimate success. Ideally, some sort of imprinting process will take place, and the manliness of the hero will become the manliness of the reader.[63]

Such writing was praised by teachers and influential social reformers as having all the attributes required to inspire young boys.

Tom Brown's Schooldays, which went through six printings within a year of its publication in 1857 and 70 printings in author Thomas Hughes's lifetime, had an enormous influence in Ontario. Full of references to battle, war, and the glory of Britain, it describes a wholly male world, 'one of violent challenge and male comradery', and its overriding theme, according to C.D. Eby, is that 'life equals combat. From first to last the narrative is crammed with scenes of internecine warfare.'[64]

Yet Tom Brown is tame compared to some of the more popular fare that followed. The specifics of manliness and adventure are summed up in Rider Haggard's *Allan Quatermain*, published 30 years later. 'Adventurer', writes Haggard, 'is defined as he who goes out to meet whatever may come. Englishmen are adventurers to the backbone.'[65] This idea of adventure became the sustaining notion of the Empire and, in the case of the United States, the 'energizing myth' of imperialism. Martin Green, who coined that term, writes that 'as everyone knows, adventure was and is the "rite de passage" from white boyhood to white manhood, and ritual of that religion of manliness which in mainstream books of the nineteenth century quite displaces Christian values.'[66] Green goes so far as to say that the unofficial religion of the nineteenth century, if not the twentieth, was manliness. The adventure experience, at least as depicted by certain authors, was 'the sacramental ceremony of the cult of manhood'.[67] The use of adventure stories as surrogates for actual deeds provides a vicarious sense of transitory drama. The ethics and cultural values embedded in the narrative convey to the reader a strong sense of what manly action and masculine drama are all about.

The sum of a particular society at any given time is often mirrored in its books.[68] George Orwell has written that 'the worst books are often the most important because they are usually the ones that are read earliest in life.'[69] If penny dreadfuls, adventure stories, and the like are deemed trash, then according to Orwell the influence of trash is vast. Praising the willingness to fight, to take initiative, and to run risks, the adventure story served as a central vehicle for both manly and nationalistic/patriotic ideals.[70]

While the future historian Arthur Lower was convalescing from a bout of the measles, his mother read him Kingston's *True Blue* and Henty's *Under Drake's Flag*. Both had a lasting impact. Subsequently, Lower devoured dozens of similar adventure stories. In his autobiography, he notes that these books

> took many small boys into worlds utterly different from the simple Canadian society that surrounded them. Lake Simcoe would do very well for a life on the ocean wave, but where were pirates, admirals, and all the panoply of war? A good many of us were to find out in due course, and I rather suspect that all that Victorian literature helped to prepare us for what we were to encounter. Good churchgoing Methodists that we were, I can recall nothing from church or community about the wickedness of war. War, as I remember the atmosphere of the day, was part of life. And it was always somewhere else and since the British were fighting it, necessarily just![71]

Lower's response was undoubtedly typical. The adventure story provided boys with a magic carpet to exciting places and action-packed dreams, laying the foundations for future activity and sentiment. And as Lower makes quite clear, no critical references were made to the actualities of war. War was not only the ultimate adventure, but a noble one—as long as the British were involved. If the popularity of adventure stories is any indication, many in the generation before 1914 held the same idealized view of war.

The period when adventure novels and stories were most popular, from 1867 to 1914, was also the period when Western imperialism reached its height. Writers were thus able to include in their work references to contemporary events such as the Crimean War, the Indian Mutiny, the Fenian Raids, the Franco-Prussian War, and the Spanish-American War, helping to create an appetite for any writing related to war. Many critics came to see this genre as 'wholesome and patriotic'.[72] 'Literature on the theme of war', writes Cate Haste, 'had enjoyed immense popularity since the publication in 1871 of Lt. Col. Sir Tomkyns Chesney's serial, "The Battle of Dorking".' The stories of William Le Quex, Erskine Childers, and Saki greatly intensified the interest. According to C.D. Eby, popular literature during this period was 'so steeped in militant nationalism that the Great War when it finally arrived came like an ancient prophecy at last fulfilled.' Stories suggesting over and over again that 'war is fun' were 'fed into young minds during the years in which the soldiers of the Great War grew up'. Popular poetry and school anthologies also began to emphasize military and patriotic themes. The martial spirit was evident in the works of Kipling, Conan Doyle, Sir Henry Newbolt, and Sir Francis Doyle. Boys' magazines such as *Chums*, *Boy's Own Paper*, and *Gem* 'consistently prepared their readers for wars in the future and unflaggingly pumped up their morale by depicting English victories'. Noting that these boys' periodicals 'were a powerful force in educating and indoctrinating children', Robert Macdonald adds: 'what is written and published for children may later influence adult behaviour—even if, or especially if, children can choose what it is they read.'[73]

By 1890, literature about war was beginning to 'glorify it as a good in itself'. War was increasingly lauded not only as character-forming but as a way to purge the nation of many of its negative qualities, especially the trend towards effeminacy.[74] As 1914 grew nearer, 'the monthlies and quarterlies turned ever more attention to the topic [of war],' says John Gooch, 'a common approach being the glorification of war as a theatrical event of sombre magnificence.' In fact, it can be argued that the press, led by Lord Northcliffe in England, was agitating for war. Some writers and opinion-makers, it seemed, were 'spoiling for a fight'. As Peter Parker writes, 'they did their best to encourage belligerence under the guise of chauvinistic adventurousness.'[75]

Works in the adventure genre were available to readers from all levels of society. According to C.D. Eby, 'in this epidemic of martial feeling nearly all young Englishmen were exposed to the contagion, and there was little reason to believe that other western powers were quarantined from the disease.'[76] Although the largest audience for adventure and war stories was composed of boys and young men, men, women, and girls were also reading them.[77] In effect, by 1914 all levels of society had been inculcated with martial values, tantalized with the possibilities of military glory and heroic adventure, and bombarded with patriotic jingoism.

These works contributed in no small way to a young boy's perception of who he was and what his destiny should be. 'We were brought up on the *Boy's Own Annual* and *Chums* and on novels like those of Henty and Ballantyne', said Edgar Harold, a Canadian World War I veteran.[78] 'My reading was almost entirely based on *Boy's Own Annual* and *Chums* and Henty and so on. So I had the belief that Britain always won its wars and that they were always right', stated Larry Nelson, who was born in 1893 and enlisted in the Canadian Expeditionary Force (CEF) in 1914.[79] It is clear that these works reflected both the opinions already in the public mind and the ideas circulated by the authors.[80]

In some cases, adventure stories served as an introduction to history for boys who had not been stimulated by school lessons. The authors of such stories took the opportunity to present historical 'facts' that not only gave their tales verisimilitude but suggested how citizens could serve their country.[81] G.A. Henty had an enormous influence on boys' perceptions of history and was recommended as an excellent source. Accuracy of history took precedence over moralizing in most of Henty's works. Henty was especially concerned with facts because he realized that many boys took his stories for the authentic picture. While his works served as propaganda for Britain's might and the glory of its Empire, his boy heroes from the past demonstrated to contemporary boys how they could help to keep England great. As Claudia Nelson has observed regarding Henty, 'A knowledge of the glorious past is essential to a glorious present.' Henty was considered a 'publicist for the British empire, and a recruiting officer for a generation of schoolboys'.[82]

Of course, writers determined to support the Empire inevitably portrayed other peoples and other places as not only alien but inferior. As Gail Clark puts it, Henty's descriptions of race 'seem merely to encapsulate crudely a widely-held vision of Anglo-Saxon superiority previously elaborated by Victorian intellects such as Thomas Carlyle.'

If other European nations were substandard, however, they still stood several ranks above those outside the industrial Western world.[83]

Wendy R. Katz writes that the imperial hero, 'whether soldier, an adventurer, or simply an embodiment of "manliness" ', has 'no ideological dispute with society. His mission is to prevent his country from getting soft, losing its integrity or straying from its righteous course.' What a wonderful formula for future soldiers to follow: never having doubts, always knowing what is right.[84] What David Stafford has written about the appeal of the spy-adventure story is relevant in this regard:

> In an age when the values which had reflected and reinforced the social order of nineteenth-century England were under siege from the onslaught of new political philosophies and social forces, the spy as gentleman patriot emerged as hero who defeated not only the threatening foreigner, but also exorcised the demons of social disorder and political unrest which troubled the imaginations of so many in Edwardian England.[85]

Broadening this new category wide enough, one might also include the super detective, from Sherlock Holmes to Bulldog Drummond. Whether fighting the Empire's enemies abroad or at home, the 'spy as gentleman patriot' was now a common character, used to great effect.

Of course, one of the many new social forces that 'threatened society' was the crisis of masculinity, and the literature of the time provided a wide selection of both genres and heroes to remedy the situation. Robert Ballantyne created supremely manly heroes who were consistent and easy to understand. In works such as *Young Fur Traders*, Ballantyne made masculinity a simple matter for young readers to grasp. Like many of the more popular adventure novelists, he scoffed at boys who could not rise to the occasion, who were fearful or prone to contemplation. To prove one's worth as a man, in Ballantyne's books, calls for action: saving, guarding, fighting, being bold.[86]

The heroes created by the prolific novelist G.A. Henty were always fearless and resourceful in their duty. In a posthumously published article in the *Boy's Own Paper*, Henty boasted: 'I know that very many boys have joined the army through reading my stories and at many of the meetings which I have spoken, officers of the army and Volunteers have assured me that my books have been effectual in bringing young fellows into the army.'[87] Jeffrey Richards has observed that Henty wrote with a singular purpose, 'to teach boys how to behave'. And the right way to behave was to be manly.[88]

Some less-celebrated authors wrote about Canada itself, as a place where a young man could test his manliness in a struggle with the elements. Most of these writers are quite unknown today, but their popularity in the years before the Great War was considerable. After Argyll Saxby, a contributor to the *Boy's Own Paper*, visited Canada he wrote a number of adventure tales with such subtitles as 'A Tale of Adventure on the Canadian Prairie'. The ex-Mountie John Mackie, author of *The Rising of the Red Man* (1904) and *Hidden in the Canadian Wilds* (1911), was reputed to have based his work on his own experiences. Such writing created a picture that Canadian boys could relate to, no matter how far-fetched that picture was. Like other authors of the time, these writers were, 'quite unashamedly, guardians of imperialism, protectors of and propagandists for the British way of life which espoused a firm belief in wholesome adventure'.[89]

Rudyard Kipling, the quasi-official spokesman for the British Empire, also contributed his fair share of advice on how to behave. Concerned about both the moral fibre of British citizens and imperial decline, in a number of stories he sought to instil the proper characteristics in his young male readers. Among those characteristics, according to Carole Scott, were 'stalwart indifference to pain' and 'suppression of softer "feminine" feelings that . . . made men vulnerable'. Kipling's *Stalky & Co.* became a kind of manual for 'training administrators of the British Empire' in the manly virtues of courage, self-sacrifice, and heroism. Joseph Bristow makes the interesting observation that even when Kipling's stories are not about boys and men, 'they depict a "Jungle Book" of predatory creatures—foxes, bears, tigers—[that are] both fierce and friendly, exciting and sentimental at once, in a domain based on emotional extremes of protecting and fighting.'[90]

In the early years of the twentieth century, a Canadian clergyman named Charles Gordon, writing under the pen name Ralph Connor, published a series of novels that were extremely popular in Canada and even sold well in the United States and Britain. Stressing the importance of physical activity and clean living, books like *The Man from Glengarry* fitted neatly into the 'muscular Christian' framework.[91]

Mounted policemen, specifically the members of the North-West Mounted Police, stood for all that was good and manly. Mounties were quickly co-opted by dime novelists and serious writers alike to represent the virtues of clean living, obedience, and deference to British justice. The heroic mythology surrounding these noble tamers of the Canadian West quickly became central to the young nation, especially its boys. As Daniel Francis puts it: 'With the explosion of the dime novel phenomenon near the end of the nineteenth century, the Mountie became a stock figure in fiction. Writers of stories for children picked up the scent—"The scarlet tunic! What a story!" gushed an author in *Chums*, a British adventure magazine for boys—as did best-selling authors like Ralph Connor and James Curwood.' Blessed with quantities of determination, patience, skill, discipline, and good judgement (a list not too different from the ideals of manliness), a single Mountie was capable of standing down an unsavoury group of American whiskey traders or a scruffy bunch of cattle rustlers —as Ralph Connor describes in *Corporal Cameron of the North-West Mounted Police*. One reason the Mounties were successful despite their small numbers had to do with the 'moral force' behind them, a moral force that, according to Francis, combined British justice with the 'weight of the Empire'. Ne'er-do-wells were quick to back down once they remembered the Empire connection. Another source of the Mountie's strength, in the view of the popular historian Pierre Berton, was the fact that he was a member of a group rather than a brash, showy individual. This, of course, is in complete harmony with the British games tradition. Interestingly, Berton also suggests that the anonymous individual, as part of a group, is a typical example of Canadian sacrifice and heroism. Vimy Ridge and Passchendaele would prove the truth of this observation.[92]

The Magazine

The market for all types of juvenile literature expanded rapidly beginning in the late 1870s. At first, magazines for boys tended to be a bit crude. In 1879, in response to the perceived threat from these 'penny dreadfuls' or 'bloods', the Religious Tract Society in Britain launched the *Boy's Own Paper*. This was to be a more wholesome, more patriotic magazine promoting proper Christian values. Aiming to 'combat evil by treating goodness as ordinary unemphasized decency and honesty' and to combine manliness with 'naturalness', it played down the vanity of success in favour of quiet good deeds. Jack Cox, in his history of the *Boy's Own*, writes that all of the over 200 Gordon Stables stories that appeared in it stressed the virtues of manliness, courage in the face of danger, and cheerfulness in adversity.[93]

By the end of the century, changes in taste had created a market for literature with a more militaristic and nationalistic tone. New publications appealing to different classes of readers had entered the market. Magazines such as *Gem*, *Magnet*, *The Captain*, *Chums*, *Young England*, and even *Young Canada* and *The Young Canadian* offered variations on the themes of manliness and militarism.[94] Although they circulated at all social levels, these publications were much more class-specific, and each had its own editorial objectives. In the end, though, their ideological goals were essentially the same—a masculine world with manly actors doing their part for the country and eventually for the army. These magazines achieved high circulation levels, and one reason was that their tone was not 'morally rectitudinous', which proved increasingly unpopular. The juvenile magazine of this type, by the turn of the century, had moved away from 'religious didacticism or secular rationalism toward moral entertainment where an extrovert, imperial manliness mattered more than introspective piety or dry memorizing'. Characters like Jack Harkaway, 'fighting for the flag', or the 'Captain of the Hussars' demonstrated manly deeds in exotic settings. Over and over again, young readers were told to emulate these fictional heroes, to 'bear yourselves like British boys'—in short, like men.[95]

Sigmund Samuel, whose favourite adventure author was W.H.G. Kingston, subscribed to the *Boy's Own Paper*. He and his friends eagerly awaited 'its thrilling stories of courage and loyalty abroad and at school, lavishly illustrated with engravings of sailing ships and fierce savages'. The fiction was not the only thing that appealed to Samuel. In his autobiography, he relates how he learned about heraldry, gymnastics, British history, and current events from articles in the *Boy's Own*. The paper was so important to him that at the end of each year he had the issues bound, and he kept his collection into old age.[96]

Ramsey Morris of Pembroke, Ontario, a member of the first Canadian contingent, and his sister Grace were also avid readers of adventure tales. She writes, 'We had always regretted that in our peaceful world nothing exciting was ever likely to happen; certainly there would be no wars.'[97] The magazines and adventure stories that the Morrises devoured made war seem exciting, especially in contrast to their parochial existence.

War was a supreme preoccupation in the magazines that youngsters read. According to Samuel Hynes, '*Chums* in fact anticipated the war by some nine months; it ran a serial about a war between England and Germany beginning with the December 1913 number.'[98] Lord Northcliffe, a pioneer of mass-circulation journalism, and the other publishers involved in politics ensured that their periodicals and magazines supported their own favourite nationalistic and patriotic causes.

Supplementing the action-packed fiction in these magazines were non-fiction articles that provided more practical instruction: for example, how to build a fire in the wilderness, how to construct a telescope, how to swim, and how to enlist in the navy. As well, most issues contained information about collecting stamps and coins. The Victorian mania for classifying and collecting made these two pastimes extremely popular among armchair imperialists. Advertisements for chest expanders, rifles, medals, and other war paraphernalia added spice to the stew of manliness and militarism.[99]

Numerous articles in these magazines served as surrogate recruiting stations for the navy and army. *The Canadian Boy*, published in Guelph, Ontario, for a while featured a monthly column on the Boys' Brigade. In a typical description, it sang the praises of the Brigade and lauded the honour and camaraderie of being part of a battalion. In the October 1901 issue, the Premier of Ontario, G.W. Ross, commented that the Boys' Brigade was 'one of the very best organizations to train young men for public usefulness', and suggested that Canadians should learn from Great Britain how to train boys properly: 'There is no room in Canada for idle men or idle boys.'[100]

Another example of this approach is found in the *Boy's Own Paper*. 'How British Sailors are Trained' begins with the following: 'Probably every British lad, at some period of his youth, desires to become a sailor—to "follow the sea". . . . The love of adventure, and the alluring call of the open sea, still exercise a powerful influence. . . . The sea life is admittedly a hard one; it is a vocation in which the "slack" youngster will either go to the wall, or, which is equally possible, become a manly, vigorous sailor.' Although the article romanticizes the sailor's life, it also offers technical data on training methods and information on duty and discipline.[101]

The popular *Chums*, like other such magazines of the period, used illustrations as a means of projecting its militaristic and manly message. Images of power, in many guises, grace the covers and pages of *Chums*. The glory of the British uniform and the superiority of British technology in the form of a new battleship—to cite just two examples —emphasize the link between 'virile manhood' and the unshakeable foundations of the Empire. These illustrations 'carried their own rhetoric: fighting was reduced to a code in which reflection was absent, bravery instinctive, suffering rendered as endurance, and death presented only as dignified sacrifice.'[102] In essence, the characteristics of manliness and militarism were presented as natural.

The men featured as heroes in the boys' periodicals were typically described as 'powerfully built'—'a man of commanding presence', 'a fine specimen of the ideal English gentleman, manly, straightforward, brave, and true'. The titles in the *Young Canada Illustrated Annual* of 1902 suggest similar qualities: 'Hard as Nails' (fiction);

'A Great Arctic Explorer', and 'A Mighty Hunter' (both non-fiction). The emphasis was usually on heroic endeavour of some sort, whether fictionalized or apparently true, with the hero triumphing over extremely long odds. Usually combining narrative and interview, the articles are filled with advice: 'Be utterly unselfish'; 'work hard'; 'obedience to superiors is imperative'.[103]

Popular historians were often commissioned to write about manly and military themes that would appeal to young boys. In 1897, for instance, the *Young Canada Illustrated Annual* published a series entitled 'Our Great Living Generals'. In his profile of Commander-in-Chief Field Marshal Viscount Wolseley, Arthur Temple, the author of the popular *The Making of the Empire*, quickly sets the tone: 'We have generally had to fight against overwhelming numbers, in terribly trying climates, and often in unknown bits of country where the utmost skill of our generals and the most desperate courage of our soldiers have been needed in order to win.' Temple makes it clear that the skill of the generals, coupled with the courage (or willingness to die) of their soldiers, has been the reason for success. 'Scarcely a year has passed without our being engaged in some sort of warfare in one part or another of our vast empire.' And this is a good thing, for without these yearly exercises, which are always 'troublesome', 'our swords might have grown rusty, and we could not be sure that we had a single great general or a single regiment which would face a cavalry charge.' Fortunately, these minor actions ensure that, if a European struggle should break out, we 'should have full confidence in those who would lead our armies.' At this point Temple introduces Wolseley, who has 'steadily fought his way to fame and fortune'. Noting that the general has been 'wounded dozens of times', lost 'an eye in the Crimea', and possesses scars all over his body, Temple declares that if the general had not lived a clean life and refrained from the temptations of the typical soldier he would 'have been dead long ago'. There follows a list of the Field Marshal's qualities: courage, nerve, high spirits, self-reliance, a strong will. In short, he is a man 'able to make himself at home in any sort of country and with any kind of foe.' Our hero's life reads like a Henty novel. From the Ashanti campaigns to the Red River District of Manitoba, from Cyprus to Burma, he has been involved. The motto on his coat of arms —'Man is as a wolf to his fellow man'—prompts Temple to write that 'to those who are England's enemies he is as a wolf—swift, strong, patient, and untiring.'[104]

A second profile, of General Sir Henry Wood, begins with ominous warnings of war. 'No one knows', Temple writes, if the 'storm-clouds of war' will pass or not, but General Wood certainly will be ready because 'he has been a fighting man from his boyhood', 'valiant in the field of battle'. The descriptions of this 'fearless warrior' continue, complete with a description of his wounded body. Wood has always been where the fighting has been fiercest. As a young lad, Wood was 'eager, daring, and altogether careless of danger... one of those boys who have made Britain what she is.' Having 'played the man' in the Indian Mutiny, becoming a Lancer, with his 'astonishing courage' he won the Victoria Cross. Thereafter he participated in conflicts small and large, from the Fenian troubles in Canada to the Ashanti War in Africa. Both profiles follow a pattern that suggests to young readers how they too can make themselves into brave and courageous men. The army was one very popular route.[105]

Whether the featured hero was a scholar, a military man, or an athlete, he was made to look regal, successful, and contented. In the *Boy's Own Paper* of 29 June 1907, a piece entitled 'Extraordinary Athletic Feats of Schoolboys', by George A. Wade, listed the heroic accomplishments of boys attending schools from Rugby to Charterhouse. Whether the sport was riding, throwing, or jumping, the intention was to demonstrate how certain boys surpass the norm and achieve things no one thought possible. In another issue of the *Boy's Own Paper*, the short story 'A Brave Man', about a North American 'native's' bravery, serves as a reminder to English-speaking readers that examples of courage could be found in many places.[106] One prominent theme is nostalgia and historical tradition. An informal 'chat about armour' starts with a direct appeal to the historical tenacity of the myth of chivalry as embodied by knights:

> Probably no subject excites a greater degree of interest in the minds of all of us than the stories of the old knights. The legends of King Arthur's Round Table, the records of the Crusades, the histories of Crecy and Poitiers, all possess a charm for the imaginative or romantic mind. We often try to picture ourselves as warriors, and we seem to see them before us clad in all their splendour.[107]

A veritable mania for collecting seems to have struck the middle classes beginning in the 1870s. This had its counterpart in museums and other institutions, which began to accumulate objects of every kind, from zoological specimens to the ancestral treasures of colonized peoples. The prevalence of coin and stamp columns in the pages of the boys' magazines reflected this desire to code, possess, organize, and display items from all over the Empire. As one article on 'The Colonial Coins of the British Empire' puts it, the coins 'not only mark the spread and progress of the English nation in various parts of the globe, but from the story which they tell, something is to be gleaned of the struggles and difficulties of the . . . colonists and of the social and economic condition under which they lived.'[108] This was especially important to colonial boys, as an affirmation both of Canada's place within the British Empire and of the Empire's place in the world. Coins were tangible displays of nationalism, embodying the importance of a country's leaders and sense of place. They were, and still are, ideal for conveying the majesty of Empire.

In the pages of boys' magazines, direct expressions of militarism, such as an article on the content of military music, were to be found next to references on the 'strenuous life', the outdoors, and physical exercise. Stories and essays on everything from camping to fishing, in conjunction with advertisements that appealed to boys, can be seen as conscious efforts to create boys who would be ideal soldiers.[109] The Canadian versions of these magazines were no different, although the picture they painted of Canada was certainly unique.

When *Chums* and the *Boy's Own Paper* featured adventure stories set in Canada, most often they focused on the 'Wild North' and painted Canada as a vast untamed wilderness to which one went to test one's manliness, to flex one's muscles in a natural environment, and to live the strenuous life. This was no place for effete sissy-boys—only for young adventurers with imperial zeal, those 'healthy well-knit Saxons' who proved they could be heroes anywhere in the Empire. Readers were reminded that they could contribute to the success and grandeur of the Empire in many different ways. Any time Canadians distinguished themselves in war, invention, industry, or sports, a mention was made of the colony's contributions. *The Young Canadian*'s intent was clearly to 'foster patriotic sentiment' among the adolescent inhabitants of the 'Brightest Jewel in the Crown of the British Empire'. The editor of *The Canadian Boy* subtitled his publication 'A Journal of Incident, Story and Self Help' and said it was designed to be 'literary, patriotic and entertaining. We have before us always the attainment for boys of manliness in mind, morals and muscles.' One issue from 1901 featured an address by the Right Honourable Joseph Chamberlain entitled 'The Unity of the Empire', a poem by Kipling, a story of the war in South Africa, a profile of King Edward VII illustrating his 'manly qualities and regal characteristics', a piece on how Andrew Carnegie made his fortune ('thrift and hard work bring success'), a column on boys' drill exercises, and another on collecting stamps and coins. This format was much the same in the periodicals that came from Britain—the classic recipe for grooming young boys in a specific manner.[110]

Written just after World War II, E.S. Turner's lament—'If only the present generation had been reared on the heroic exploits of fictional character Jack Harkaway, how much manlier they would be for it'— suggests just how important this kind of literature had been for the generation of 1914. Robert MacDonald writes simply that a boy 'who learns from a boy's magazine that war is exciting, a grand adventure', will eventually march off to fight. According to Jeffrey Richards, 'it is now widely recognized that it was the saturation in the literature and imagery [that] prepared the youth of England for enthusiastic participation in World War I, an enthusiasm that produced two and a half million volunteers in the first sixteen months of the war.' In his essay 'Boys' Weeklies', George Orwell suggested that these publications had a great deal in common with the Boy Scout movement, which had begun at the time that these works were most popular. The Scouts' motto, 'Be Prepared', had a particular resonance at this juncture in history and, like the stories, the movement served to instil in boys the political and social mindset that would soon lead them to enlist.[111] Both inside and outside the classroom, reading material was focused more and more upon heroic adventure, and the organization of the school took on a strong political and patriotic flavour.

5

The Politicization of Schooling

'To die will be an awfully big adventure.'

J.M. Barrie, *Peter Pan* (1904)

In most Western countries the introduction of formal schooling[1] served a number of purposes. Getting children off the streets was one. Another was to ensure that citizens had the basic skills of reading, writing, and arithmetic—skills that became increasingly important in the age of industrialism. Perhaps the most important purpose of formal, institutionalized schooling, however, was to create functional citizens.[2] A barometer of Ontario's success in this project was the enormous number of former students who answered the call of their country in 1914. Formal schooling for citizenship emphasized two interrelated goals. The first was to stimulate patriotic loyalty by focusing much of the curriculum on Canada's ties to Britain. The second goal was to inculcate the character-forming qualities associated with sport, which was intimately linked to the condition of the state. The emergence of military drill as a form of exercise served to instil a love of country in a concrete manner. Formal education was often equated with national well-being; socialization was geared to reinforcing the equation.

In his book *National Dreams*, Daniel Francis notes that the children who attended Canadian schools from 1890 until shortly after World War II 'were taught to venerate Great Britain and its empire'. The imperial connection informed virtually every aspect of the school program: the flying of the Union Jack, the pledge of allegiance to the monarch, the singing of 'Rule Britannia', the naming of schools and teams after members of the royal family. Students were taught that anything worthwhile in Canada was derived from Britain. 'Every subject in the curriculum was expected to reinforce the British connection, but none more so than history.' In addition to providing civics and moral lessons, history courses were geared above all to teach students about Britain and the Empire. Pupils 'were educated to become citizens of an empire as much as to become citizens of Canada.'[3]

Patriotism

In developing the Ontario school system, Egerton Ryerson drew on a variety of educational philosophies that reflected nationalistic, patriotic, and militaristic ideals. Many of these philosophies were European; for example, Friedrich Froebel (the originator of the kindergarten) and Father Jahn (who saw gymnastics as central to both manliness and patriotism).[4]

In the course of the nineteenth century, as the pace of social change accelerated, schools were increasingly charged with the responsibility of 'ensuring political stability'.[5] By the end of the century education had become directly linked to national economic well-being. Besides cultivating 'citizenship, loyalty, respect for property and deference to authority', those responsible for schools in Ontario hoped to emulate the US educational reforms that appeared to be reflected in the booming American economy: in effect, 'schooling itself became a fundamental feature of the state.' At all levels—municipal, regional, and federal—those in power worked to ensure that their opinions were represented in the schools. Thus 'school knowledge [became] increasingly synonymous with state knowledge'. Beginning in the early years of the nineteenth century, children were trained, guided, and taught to conform—in a word, socialized.[6]

Citizenship, patriotism, and sacrifice were consistently invoked as the building blocks of the new nation. If, as educator A.A. Jordan put it, 'One of the main purposes of education is to make a man a good citizen', then 'training should be given to fit a man to perform the duties of a citizen in such a manner as to advance the best interests of the state.' 'We want men ready to die for their country', stated teacher A.C. Todd; 'patriotism consisted in dying for one's country', wrote educational observer E.W. Bruce. Loyalty and sacrifice in this period were not just idle words.[7]

At a time when both the church and the family were losing influence, the schools were seen as 'the only nation-building force over which the state [had] absolute control', and they were expected to use the powers bestowed on them by the state for the purpose of making citizens. Classroom teachers staked their reputations, not only as educators but as patriots, 'on the observable outcome of the process of schooling'.[8] Patriotism was a constant theme of conferences and journals. 'Patriotism', wrote a school principal in 1886, 'is an essential factor in national greatness, and the greater the degree to which this love-of-country spirit is developed the greater will be the height to which such country will ultimately and inevitably rise among the nations of the world.'[9]

In 1892, a teacher, Miss E.J. Preston, wrote that 'It is time our youth were taught to love the land we live in, and admire the constitution that protects us.' 'Britain is the mother who nursed our young colony, and gave us protection, even at the peril of her existence.... Like human children, we have often been ungrateful and discontented.... And shall we let our children grow up in comparative ignorance of all we owe to her?' Preston answered her own question with a resounding 'No!' Patriotic songs, geography lessons, and literature would instil the desired sentiments.[10] Such instruction was especially vital, of course, for students from non-British backgrounds.

If education and citizenship were synonymous, then, according to Principal W. Irwin, 'it follows that the teacher who fails to instil into the hearts and minds of his pupils a feeling of loyalty to their fatherland fails to perform one of the highest functions of the true teacher.' If teachers were principled individuals of integrity and 'uprightness of moral character', then the children around them would develop into 'men and women of the same stamp'. 'Let us have true patriotic teachers, and we'll soon have a patriotic people that will defy the very worst forms of despotism.'[11]

In an article that appeared in 1896, Irwin commented that teachers wielded more power than members of the clergy. The teacher has the potential to shape the future, the 'opportunity of wielding a mighty power in influencing the life and character of all future generations'. The teacher's personality, his (or her) likes and dislikes, are important, for they surface in the classroom. Those with noble ideals of patriotism, the 'mind-moulders' and 'character-builders of a nation', are charged with an enormous responsibility in constructing patriotism and stoking the passions of love for one's country. Pride in being Canadian should be taught in such a way as to ignite the 'spirit of enthusiastic loyalty' and to be so 'infectious as to be caught' by all. Canada had a unique place in the British Empire, and its greatness should be lauded. Students should be urged to exalt in the 'great actions of great men', and should know, too, that the British Empire would be there for the protection of all, 'ready and willing and able to protect us from any insult that would bring dishonour upon our national escutcheon'. Principal Irwin then writes that patriotism is usually seen to be waning during periods when peace and order reign. The threat of war, however, is enough to jolt citizens out of their complacency. With this threat, 'we soon find a people who are willing to sacrifice time and property, yea, even life itself, in defence of their country.' This is the kind of patriotism that Irwin wanted to emanate from the schools. This was, in Irwin's words, a fully 'rational' approach. Schools, boards, and teachers needed to work on the 'emotional' aspect of patriotism. As he wrote, 'We can hardly hope to make true patriots through intellectual training alone.' Irwin encouraged the reading of poetry to instil the emotional aspect of patriotism, because poetry is the most powerful way to reach the emotional element of 'a man's nature'.[12]

Virtually every issue of the *Canadian Educational Monthly* devoted considerable space to issues of patriotism and character formation. The school system in Ontario increasingly came to be seen as an agency of socialization, expected 'to improve the moral tone of society; to solve the problems associated with urbanization; [and] to assimilate the immigrant [by] foster[ing] sentiments of national unity and national identity'.[13] Often, traditional pedagogical concerns were overshadowed by concern for loyalty and moral character.

The formation of character, specifically moral character, was a vital part of the schools' role—in part because the church and family could no longer 'meet the needs of youth' in this regard. 'No other agency', wrote one superintendent, 'can be relied upon for the proper training of all citizens.'[14] Character became an even more explicit part of the Ontario school philosophy following the appointment of John Millar as deputy minister for education in 1890, a position he would hold until 1905. Fond of maxims such as 'the highest aim of education is the formation of character' and 'morality is essential to the welfare of the state',[15] Millar fused moral character with citizenship and physical culture in his book *School Management* (1897):

The fully educated person has stored his mind with knowledge in such a way that his intellectual faculties give him skill and power. His moral nature is so developed that he has a delicate appreciation of duty, and a will that readily responds to the dictates of an enlightened conscience. His body has been trained to perform its functions in obedience to the intelligent demands of his moral impulses.[16]

Millar believed that a 'complete education' would prepare individuals both physically and mentally, to the benefit of the whole community. An avid supporter of physical exercise—'bodily exertion' promoted 'moral restraint' and helped to secure 'better discipline in school'— he believed that moral training and physical exercise were ideal for inculcating the manly qualities of 'courage, fortitude, determination and obedience'; as he put it, 'the object was to tame the individual child and mould an upright citizen who respected authority and controlled his baser passions.'[17] With due attention to 'personal character', the desired 'national character' could be assured. Given the essential qualities of manliness, obedience, and a sense of duty, students would grow into proper citizens of the British Empire.

Empire Day

For most English-speaking Canadians before 1914, Britain was, to all intents and purposes, the centre of the universe. Although attempts were made to add more purely Canadian elements to the curriculum, more often than not these were secondary. As Neil McDonald has observed:

> An emphasis on using material published in Canada and adapted to its uses was not the same thing as promulgation of a strident or even standard Canadian chauvinism in the schools. In the short run, English Canadian educators tended to Canadianize by emphasizing 'the rich heritage of British history ... reflected in our national escutcheon.'[18]

Before Confederation, both textbooks and teachers were commonly imported from Great Britain, and the practice continued after 1867. It was never easy, therefore, to distinguish where Britain ended and Canada began and in general Canadian nationalism tended to pale in comparison to the 'greater emotional appeal' of British imperialism. Robert Stamp suggests that certain politicians and educators, such as Ontario Minister of Education George Ross, who attempted to promote a form of Canadian nationalism in the schools, 'actually spent more time strengthening the imperial sentiment'. Ross was a tireless promoter of patriotism among Ontario youth, and the concept of Empire Day, to be celebrated on the school day before the 24 May holiday that commemorated Queen Victoria's birthday, reflected his political views. In 1897, a housewife from Hamilton, Mrs Clementine Fessenden, wrote to Ontario Education Minister George Ross, suggesting that one day of the school year be set aside for patriotic festivities, in particular, the celebration of Canada's place within the British Empire. Ross was enthusiastic about the idea, and immediately put the concept into play. It was first observed in 1899, and Ross publicized the event across Canada. The appointment of Richard Harcourt as Minister of Education at the end of the nineteenth century was significant in that Harcourt, too, was extremely sympathetic to strong connections with Britain. A lover of cricket and an ardent Anglophile, Harcourt lauded the glorious achievements of the British.[19] Empire Day gave Harcourt 'added opportunities to expound his imperialist nationalist views'. Harcourt hoped that, in addition to instilling a love of British institutions, Empire Day would encourage students to reflect on 'the relationship of the various units to the "central authority", and the "admirable heritage" of which they were an integral part'.[20]

Harcourt's successor as Education Minister, Robert Allen Pyne, also believed that 'Canadians delighted in their unique privilege of holding "double citizenship".' During the Great War, Pyne 'was pleased to point out the practical results of [the] emphasis on imperial sentiment. The large number of young men who volunteered "to fight the battles of the Empire" was, indeed, attributable to the lessons in "love of home, loyalty and patriotism" so effectively learned "in our educational institutions." '[21]

'Physical action or embodiment', writes Anne Bloomfield, 'is a powerful means of expressing ideological belief. This method was used effectively in the creation of an imperial mentality through the symbolic and ritualistic use of dances and drills performed as public spectacle by children.'[22] In the new age of visual display and imagery inaugurated by Victoria's Diamond Jubilee, commemorating 50 years on the throne, there was a desire to surround all such occasions with tangible embodiments of nationalism. The Union Jack, the visual symbol of the Empire, was held high and waved often.

Empire Day was an invented tradition intended to strengthen the ties of far-flung colonial outposts to the imperial centre. No country more enthusiastically celebrated this ritual than Canada, and no place in Canada was more enthusiastic than Ontario.[23] Empire Day came into being:

> at precisely the same time when enthusiasm for the imperial connection was at a fever-pitch in English-speaking Canada. This enthusiasm was aroused by the Imperial Federation League in the 1880s and the Diamond Jubilee celebration of 1897, sustained by the South African War and the Imperial Conferences during the first decade of the new century, and reached its crescendo with the outbreak of the First World War in 1914.[24]

Patriotic groups were quick to involve themselves in Empire Day celebrations. The IODE offered prizes to students who wrote essays that demonstrated their solidarity with Britain. It also sent members to schools to talk about Canada's place in the Empire and distribute materials buttressing their position.[25]

Specially commissioned pamphlets were authorized for use in the Ontario school system. They were specifically intended to help the pupil grasp the full significance of his 'duty as a single member of that grand membership of nations, the British Empire'. In one such pamphlet, *The Empire Day by Day*, a listing of famous dates in British history—'a journal of triumphs'—is mixed with quotations from poets like Tennyson. As well, a reassurance states that 'Imparting this knowledge' to the student 'should not in any way make him bellicose or foster in him an undue military spirit.'[26] This is an interesting statement, and one can speculate that perhaps the author believed that with all the 'love' and loyalty, an overt martial quality would not be required if war broke out. Suggested topics for teachers on this day included British loyalty, patriotism, the majesty of Empire, Canada-Great Britain relations, and the work of the Empire.[27] While it was important to recognize Canada's own accomplishments, its place in the British Empire was something to cherish. One of the goals of the school was to reaffirm this link and to 'encourage those students to internalize, for future use, a set of values which supposedly represented the ideals of imperial citizenship.'[28]

The ties between Canada and Britain were further strengthened by the Cadet movement. In a speech to the members of the Empire Club in 1905, Inspector of Schools James L. Hughes remarked:

> In our own City we have had for thirty years one institution which I think is of vital interest and of great consequence in the development of the Empire, in the establishment of the true relation between the young men of the Empire and the Empire as a whole. I refer to our cadet work in the schools. If you saw us on Empire day you would see we had forty-nine companies of well-drilled boys in line.[29]

Physical Conditioning, Drill, and the Cadets

Growing concern with the physical condition of Canadian adults led to the introduction of physical conditioning in the schools. In 1909 Dr J.E. Hett wrote, 'Many of our Canadian people boast of our physical race, but I cannot see anything to boast about. We are neglecting physical culture and cadet drill.' He goes on to quote statistics from the British army showing that between 1893 and 1902, 34.6 per cent of potential soldiers were rejected. This high rate of rejection led to the formation of the National League for Physical Education in the UK. As an expression of the militarism pervasive in the era, 'some Canadians called for general fitness, military drill, and cadet corps to be included in the school program.' Sir Frederick Borden desired that 'boys acquire "an elementary knowledge of military drill and rifle practice" so that they could, if necessary, "take part in the defense of their homes and country".' Addressing the Faculty of Education at the University of Toronto in 1909, a Lieutenant Colonel Merritt 'told the students that though war and bloodshed were horrible, they were, like death and disease, nevertheless inevitable.'[30]

Those who favoured military training drew their inspiration from the British Navy League, the Lads Drill Association, and the National Service League. The creation in 1909 by Lord Strathcona of a trust to provide funds for cadet training gave official sanction to this idea. In two of its aims, the constitution of the Strathcona Trust reflected the goals of British youth organizations and emphasized qualities that would be useful in the event of war: first, 'to improve the physical and intellectual capabilities of the children, by inculcating habits of alertness, orderliness and prompt obedience'; and, second, 'to bring up boys to patriotism'.[31]

By 1900 there were cadet corps in 33 Ontario schools, and with the establishment of the Strathcona Trust in 1909 interest increased. The funding, administration, and organization represented the first direct involvement of the federal government in the promotion of physical culture. The Strathcona Trust encouraged elementary teachers 'to qualify themselves, under the guidance of military instructors, to teach physical education'.[32]

As a result of security concerns stemming from the American Civil War, military drill had been considered for adoption in Ontario schools since 1864. As early as 1862, Ryerson had insisted that nothing else was so well adapted to secure the habits of obedience and discipline in the schools as military drill. In 1863, Major R.B. Denison took charge of a group of senior common-school boys from Toronto, who were drilled for an hour a week. Many, not just Ryerson, thought that 'military drill provided an indispensable lesson in citizenship and patriotic duty.' Gradually, drill was blended into physical education and calisthenics, though it did retain its own distinct group of supporters. Physical education as a significant part of the philosophy of education was introduced in 1866. Interest in both drill and physical education reflected the chauvinistic belief in Anglo-Saxon superiority, as well as the related ideals of nationalism, patriotism, character-building, and respect for authority. Patriotism in military drill and physical education served to Canadianize new immigrants; character-building led to manliness; and drill in general served to instil obedience, punctuality, and loyalty.[33]

The most powerful tool for Canadianizing new immigrants was, of course, the system of national schools. Given that, as J.R. Lumby said, it was 'out of the question to prevent the influx of the various nationalities into Canada, each bringing its own racial traditions and peculiarities', the singing of patriotic songs, observing of patriotic holidays, and flying of the flags of Canada and Britain were essential to guide newcomers along the right path. In addition, a tough physical regime would not only strengthen schoolboys physically but help to counter both the influence of female teachers and the moral decline brought about by urban materialism.[34]

By the early 1880s, physical culture was a common subject of patriotism and physical abuse discussion in professional educators' journals. The *Canada Educational Monthly* presented the argument that the physical health of the pupils should be of primary concern to the teacher who 'desires to see them succeed in their studies'. Although some believed that the emphasis on sport was out of line with the realities of modern schooling—the requirements of time conflicted with other subjects already filling up the day—one commentator suggested that physical education was 'an absolute necessity of humanity'. Physical exercise was essential for students who had been sitting all day long, neglecting their muscles, straining their eyesight, and in general developing bad habits of demeanour and deportment. 'Individual exertion' through sports—cricket, baseball, football, lacrosse—would foster 'a self-reliant manliness'.[35]

Advocates hoped that physical culture and, later, the teaching of physical education in the school system would help to offset the so-called modern 'luxuries' that were said to be making boys soft. The new emphasis on mental exertion, as opposed to the physical exertion demanded by an agrarian society, left much to be desired in the physical arena. In his *Manual of Drill and Calisthenics*, published in Toronto in 1879, James L. Hughes emphasized the importance of balance between the two natures, mental and physical. Hughes believed that too much study drew blood from the brain and left the limbs weak and powerless. In his opinion, drill was the ideal remedy, for it allowed the blood to flow evenly around the body.[36]

Hughes, of course, was not alone in advocating drill. Archibald Cuthbertson felt that marching and drill were not only excellent physical exercises but were ideal for maintaining discipline. In an address to the Dominion Educational Association, one speaker even suggested that drill was the panacea for all the ills of the age. By fostering habits of obedience and bringing out the manly spirit in boys, drill would help to mould good citizens.[37]

Scientists and pseudo-scientists alike maintained that it was vital for students to engage in some kind of physical activity. Using the agricultural model as an example, another authority observed that 'the physical, being less immediately essential, and not being kept up to its previous standard by the necessity to wrest the means of subsistence from the forest and the furrow, has been suffered to decline.' All the maladies affecting the populace, from insomnia and dyspepsia to insanity, were, according to this authority, 'tokens of outraged nature's righteous wrath'.[38]

In the second half of the nineteenth century, women increasingly took responsibility for raising and teaching boys. The challenge to manliness was obvious. As the population increased, more schools were built and more teachers were needed. Male teachers began to look for jobs that were better paying and women, as a consequence of growing educational opportunities, swelled the teaching ranks. The possibility that women teachers would have a detrimental effect on young boys' masculinity led to preventative measures. A good dose of drill and some vigorous exercise would certainly ameliorate the situation![39] The growing numbers of female teachers alarmed those concerned about 'the feminizing influence'. By 1900, out of 8,569 teachers in Ontario, only 2,612—31 per cent—were men; the remaining 5,957 were women.[40] In the next decade the number of women teachers in the Toronto secondary schools would double.[41] The patriarchal alarm went off, and men began asking questions:

Can women prepare our boys for the social, political or moral duties which devolve upon them in the world? How can they, when they themselves form no part of it, know practically nothing of it, and in the nature of things never will know much about it? Boys must be taught by men who have a wide experience in public matters. . . . Who can estimate the influence of the male teacher who takes part in the boy's sports? Or who can estimate the loss to those boys who have never had a male teacher to direct their sports? The teacher who will not take part in the boyish sports with his pupils is not worthy of the position. This is a realm entirely beyond the female teacher. . . . A strong moral man will have twice the influence on the average boy.[42]

Whether engendered by prejudice and fear or by sincere concern for the manliness of young boys, such sentiments were common among Victorian and Edwardian men in positions of authority. Early in the twentieth century, one commentator worried about the influence of female teachers on boys concluded that their pupils were less aggressive than others and overly sensitive, with a tendency to be more receptive and less deductive—a sure sign that their masculinity had been arrested. Perhaps the 'sterner discipline of male teachers would do more to develop the masculine qualities, than the sensitive and nervous restraint exercised by a woman.'[43]

Concerns about masculinity made it easy to advocate the inculcation of military virtues in young men. Drill, it was felt, appealed 'to the natural instinctive interest of a boy in soldiering'.[44] The enthusiasm for drill in the schools was so great that one commentator feared that the claims for its effectiveness were out of all proportion: in addition, male teachers must become exemplars of military virtues. Thus male teachers were instructed never to let down their guard, never to lose their self-possession, always to be in control. In 1878, male candidates for a first-class Ontario Teaching Certificate were required to be able to conduct military drills. It was the teacher's job to protect and develop the male student's body for the benefit of the nation.[45]

Other military influences also found their way into school culture. Schools were organized on a hierarchical model, with a military-style chain of command; group activities such as recitation in unison were favoured; and the idea of the mind as a 'machine or muscle' that could be 'sharpened, honed and polished' was widespread, as was the view of students as 'raw material to be processed'. Following the industrial model, the day was strictly divided into periods: 'Knowledge was broken into pieces, reduced to its elements and compartmentalized.'[46]

Many believed that increasing urbanization was creating pockets of 'rot' in various neighbourhoods—prime locations for vice and crime. Just six years into the new century, in an address to the Ontario Educational Association, W.E. Groves lamented the physical condition of the pupils committed to 'our' care. He blamed the changing nature of the country on the fact that 'we' were not doing 'nearly enough' about the unnatural conditions of urban life and modern society. If students 'roamed the woods, drank in the life-giving ozone of God's free atmosphere', there would be no need for physical education to 'correct the resultant evils of our artificial life and society'. Groves nostalgically lamented the fact that the urban community had removed the responsibilities formerly entrusted to young boys. No longer was it necessary for young males to contribute to the family in any significant way. 'The conveniences of the fuel companies and the municipal furnishing of the water supply free the boy from his duties in those directions, so that it seems difficult to find suitable employment for the energies of an ordinarily healthy boy.'[47]

In 1875, a member of Parliament made a passionate speech in the House of Commons pleading for the introduction of military drill into the school systems. Military education was an absolute necessity in this day and age of war, said the member from Grenville South. This speech led to a long series of debates on the merits of drill for school-age children, following which the MP's request was rejected. Yet by the end of the decade, Ontario was encouraging drill both in its schools and in its teacher-training programs. Throughout the 1880s, participation in and support for school drill companies increased. By the end of the decade these school companies 'had become a proud show piece for educators, civic officials and citizenry'.[48]

Ontario finally allowed military instruction to become a practical program in 1898. This idea had been considered for almost a quarter of a century. According to Desmond Morton, 'Since the militia instructors promised by the 1879 regulations had long since failed to appear, the province would grant $50.00 to any school board which could boast of a cadet corps of more than 25 boys, provided its efficiency was certified by an inspecting officer.' Education Minister George Ross suggested that the main purpose of drill was not to instil habits of aggression, but rather to develop 'a manliness of form and bearing, as well as physical force and independence'. Jarvis Collegiate in Toronto is credited with having the first 'active cadet corps', which was initiated in 1899 at the request of the federal government.[49]

Lord Strathcona, born in Scotland and named Donald Smith, worked his way up the hierarchy of the Hudson's Bay Company and become CEO in 1889. A successful railroad financier, he was a major contributor to the Canadian Pacific Railroad. During the Boer War he financed his own regiment, known as Lord Strathcona's Horse.[50]

The Boer War had much to do with the increasing interest in military preparedness. A circular sent to parents of Trinity College schoolboys in 1900 stated that 'the War has taught the value of straight shooting.... It is sad that such an education should be necessary, but as long as War lasts, we must be prepared for War.' In the fall of 1900, the *Canada Educational Monthly* printed an article by J.J. Findlay on the links between the British army and the school system. Noting that 'it is a truism to observe that the soldier is a boy at school before he takes service under the Queen', Findlay advocated military exercises for adolescents, in the hope of guiding them along the desired patriotic path.[51]

Looking back on his long service as a teacher, principal, and school inspector, James L. Hughes was aware that for many years the cadet idea had been subject to ridicule. Nonetheless, he was convinced of its 'ethical value in the development of character'. He also believed that cadet corps in the schools were more important than either the church-oriented Boys' Brigade or the more secular Boy Scouts—groups that, for all their admirable qualities, 'cannot take the place of the cadet system as a means of physical and moral training, or in revealing the duties of citizenship to boys.'[52]

From 1898 until just before the Great War, the cadet movement in Ontario experienced explosive growth. Interest in all facets of the corps increased as the public became more aware of their activities. Most members of society, with only isolated pockets of opposition— such as church groups—completely accepted the idea of military training. After 1911, the 'military orientation of the cadet movement intensified' with the appointment of Sam Hughes as federal Minister of Militia. In a speech before the Ontario Educational Authority, Hughes said that if every school had a cadet corps, perpetual peace would surely result. By the outbreak of World War I, '44,680 youngsters had drilled with various cadet corps.' Carl Berger succinctly highlights the point: 'nearly all appeals for cadet training were phrased in terms of loyalty to the Empire and assumed that the martial spirit was a desirable ingredient of national character.'[53]

Sports and Games

Three kinds of physical education dominated the Ontario school system: drill, gymnastics, and calisthenics. Games and team sports were secondary. Although athletics became more important as the century closed, drill remained the most common form of physical education in Ontario in the years before the Great War. The number of children taking drill and calisthenics increased threefold between 1880 and 1900, and in 1889 physical education was made compulsory in the schools. The introduction of drill had more to do with finding a cheap means of defending the colony than with anything else. Military drill in the schools was justified by Ryerson as both a patriotic enterprise and a vehicle for fostering obedience.[54]

Inspector Hughes's 1879 *Manual of Drill and Calisthenics* stressed the teaching of proper form in saluting, marking time, and marching, squad formations, and so forth. He also noted the wider applicability of drill to school life, suggesting that it would promote habits of order, neatness, and obedience. The Ontario Teachers' Association adoption of the manual gave it a broader public profile.[55]

Some concern was expressed over teaching young children the fundamentals of soldiering, but the overwhelming support this facet of the curriculum generated was enough to silence critics. 'Little soldiers' would hone their skills from secondary school on through university. John Millar was born in 1842 and received a BA from the University of Toronto in 1872. He taught school, became a principal, and was appointed by Oliver Mowat's government to the position of deputy minister of education in 1890. He was a frequent contributor to the *Canada Educational Monthly* and held positions in the Dominion Educational Association. As a Methodist, he believed in the strength of Christianity as a necessary precondition for both moral individuals and a civilized nation, two notions close to his heart. In his book, *Canadian Citizenship* (1899), he stresses the relationship between the character of citizenship taught in schools and the impact it has on the country at large.[56] John Millar, as always, claimed drill was not only 'an excellent method of forming habits of attention, order, subordination and prompt obedience', but a remedy for an 'ungainly walk, stooped shoulders or sluggish movements'. The incidence of 'round shoulders, weak chests, and defective vision', to name just a few, seemed to be reaching near-epidemic proportions. Gymnastics, outdoor exercises, and drill were most often suggested as remedies that would result in 'a healthy, vigorous frame with an active, graceful deportment'.[57]

Increasingly, the body seemed to belong to the state. E.B. Houghton's *Physical Culture* (1886) retained a focus on uniformity as well as hygiene.[58] Concern over the physical and mental effects of schooling, the fact that boys were often sitting at desks all day, as well as the quality of citizens helped to revive interest in the physical culture of youth. One of the core objectives of physical education was to instil the desired manly characteristics in young boys before they became too soft.

A debate over this issue raged in the years before World War I. Helen Lenskyj mentions that the theories on adolescence, aggression, and child-rearing of the time tended to stream boys into more active pastimes, whereas girls were led towards more passive activities: 'Clearly, teachers were expected to channel the "instinctive" play drives of girls and boys into appropriate directions.'[59] With the 'crisis of masculinity' in full force, added emphasis was placed on those elements of physical culture that reaffirmed the manly values associated with militarism.

Much stress was also put on the benefits of physical exercise to the mind. As Ryerson wrote, 'A training which gives superiority in one department of active life must be beneficial to another.' Physical culture would not only aid in the development of mental capacity but would contribute in the realms of nationhood and manhood. Although this emphasis could be taken too far—in the opinion of one observer, 'a strong physical boy is more needed than a strong mental mind'[60]— there was little doubt that physical culture was an effective means of promoting both good citizenship and strong moral character. Athletics 'will develop perseverance, courage, and power to adapt one's self to emergencies. Gymnastics will develop endurance and faith in one's powers . . . and calisthenics will promote grace of movement.'[61] Indeed, 'proper care of the body was itself a moral attribute.'[62]

British immigrants brought with them a wide variety of games, and in the general desire to emulate all that was British, specific British games and physical exercise programs were adopted by Ontario private schools as well as the regular school system.[63] Ryerson was a huge supporter of the British sport tradition and through his *Journal of Education* sought to influence public education in this direction. These definitive 'British sports' aided in maintaining 'old world values and traditions' and reproduced the ideologies of Rugby and Eton in the heart of Ontario.[64]

Typical of this mindset was the view that sports were the main reason for British achievement. According to the advocate, the team player had 'a determination strongly characteristic of the Briton, which has led him in all quarters of the world to victory, conquest, and fame'.[65] While cricket—synonymous with 'Anglo-Saxon greatness' all over the world—was ideally suited to foster discipline and self-control, by the mid-1880s the indigenous game of lacrosse had become '*the* major popular team sport in Canada'.[66] Thought to be ideally suited for 'cultivating Canadian nationalism, manliness, and respectability in male youth, and [for keeping] the leisure activities of males in check', and played enthusiastically both under and outside school supervision, lacrosse was inextricably linked to the creation of a nationalist vision. Owing much to a game played by various Native peoples, the sport was developed by the Montreal dentist Dr George Beers and, like cricket, was to become closely associated with its country of origin.[67]

Within the British public school system, soccer (British football) was closely allied with military rules and regulations and became the central link between sport and war. Harrow boys were compelled to play football so that they would make good warriors. Football, it was claimed, brought out all the qualities necessary for bravery in combat.[68] Like British football, rugby, and baseball, cricket had also caught on among the Ontario élite, although it never permeated the mass public in Canada the way it did in other colonies.

While American team sports were also played in Ontario, its élite schools preferred British forms. At Toronto's Upper Canada College, for instance, 'the Association game of football was played until 1876. In that year one of the masters introduced some features of English rugby, and by 1877 the school had completely adopted the English rules.'[69]

At first, rugby, cricket, and football were confined to the élite private schools. But towards the turn of the century they began to move out into the broader society. As a result, specific messages embedded within the games began to filter down. As Peter Bailey so elegantly puts it, 'Sport could be effective in indoctrinating hoi polloi as well as public schoolmen.' Advocates believed that any team sport was capable of fostering the patriotism and teamwork deemed so important, especially in the event of war.[70]

Textbooks and Curriculum

In her study of the history of the use of textbooks in the schools of Ontario, Viola Parvin states that the textbook is an important tool for the teacher and one of the chief sources of indirect experience available to the pupil. Yet the construction, writing, and publishing of a text or (more to the point) 'a reader' is not an apolitical matter. Recent work by Michael Apple and Linda Christian-Smith, drawing on ideas proposed by Raymond Williams, highlights the fact that texts are written by 'real people with real interests', making them 'particular constructions of reality' and embodiments of the characteristics of 'selective tradition'. According to Robert Lanning, in Canada this 'selective tradition' was that of the 'superior' British culture, and he notes that 'much discussion centred on how its representation in Canada could be further entrenched in, and by, state power.'[71]

Canadian boys, it was thought, should know the British version of their history, according to which Canada owed its existence to the mother country and the Empire. Among the central themes of this history were a romantic view of war, a preoccupation with heroic death, and the glorification of the British Empire and English-speaking peoples. These themes appear again and again in the content of the readers used in the Ontario school system in the years prior to World War I. From Shakespeare to 'The Charge of the Light Brigade', school texts fed Canadian students a steady diet of Anglo-Saxon heroes and neo-chivalric values. As Alan R. Young suggests, this diet was to make 1914 an opportunity for many young men to 'live out the cherished fantasies of their barely completed adolescence'.[72]

If the purpose of education was to ensure the future of the state, it is no surprise that state schooling had a particularly masculine thrust. Not only was it intended to turn boys into the kind of men the state desired, but by taking the 'great men' approach to history and civics, the school curriculum confirmed 'the importance and durability of masculine forms of power and participation'.[73] The idea that 'the men who make history become models whom the learners consciously imitate' served the objectives of trustees and government officials. Problems arose, however, when women attempted to present the glorious story of male dominance. Among the concerns was that female teachers would introduce emotions and forms of expression that 'were not traditionally seen as masculine'. Opinion at the time was quite specific as to the difference in the 'kind of mental training that a boy gets under a male teacher compared with that received under a female teacher'.[74]

The administrators of the Ministry of Education also placed great weight on values, a category that could cover everything from general moral standards to class differences. The readers that were authorized for use in the province would, in some cases, contain as much as 50 per cent 'value' content. Social differences were portrayed as natural, and the school readers often encouraged children to accept the existence of such differences as a *fait accompli*. When 'the poor' were depicted, they were presented as trying to make do with their situation and striving to improve it. One value that was particularly stressed was social harmony, which depended on acceptance of the idea that different levels of wealth and abilities were natural. Students were told that they must never upset the social structure and never let unrealistic or false hopes cloud their judgement. Perhaps the most important themes of all the readers used in the Ontario school system were the Protestant work ethic and Methodist maxims promoting humility and a 'modest way of life'.[75]

The content of the Canadian, Royal, and Ontario readers was designed to inculcate the proper appreciation of the British Empire and Canada's place in it. This patriotic intent became even more prominent just after the Boer War. Students were told that 'second only to the expansion and consolidation of the dominion, the "most important fact of recent Canadian history has been the strengthening of ties binding Canada to the British Empire".'[76] Among the great events outlined in various histories and readers from this period, such as *The Ontario Public School History of Canada*, was Canada's role in the Boer War: 'In marching, scouting, and fighting, the Canadian troops proved themselves worthy sons of the Empire.'[77]

Authorized history and geography books were similarly geared towards impressing young readers with the Empire's enlightened and benevolent achievements in places like Africa and India. The *Ontario High School History of England* (1911) begins with what would now strike us as extremely offensive comments about various minority groups and finished with a list of Britain's triumphs at the expense of everyone else in conflicts from the Indian Mutiny to the Boer War. Like an Empire Day pamphlet, it suggests how fortunate Canada is to be part of the greatest empire since Rome.[78]

National historical narratives were designed to foster nationalist sentiments in harmony with Britain-centred patriotism. In addition to national heroes and nation-building events, appeals to national prejudices ('us' versus 'them') found their way into history readers. In this way schoolbooks helped to teach patriotic nationalism and reaffirm the desired values.[79]

As we saw in Chapter 4, increasing levels of literacy were cause for concern. 'School officials feared these books—popular novels, adventure stories—like the plague.'[80] 'The moral consequences of literacy were so great', wrote Susan Houston and Alison Prentice, that one 'could not take for granted the outcome of exposing children . . . to just any kind of printed material.'[81] Despite relatively tight controls on access, inferior products inevitably found their market. It worried some observers that library books were 'selected for all classes of readers, and too often without sufficient care and judgement. Children and youth are not competent to choose what is best for them; they read too much fiction, and that not of the best quality.'[82] Reading habits had to be carefully cultivated and monitored in order 'to develop the literary taste of pupils, and where necessary to create such a taste, so that they may themselves have some way of distinguishing good books, great books, and those that are worthless.'[83] Great books, of course, were mainly those written by members of the familiar British pantheon: Defoe, Scott, Henty, Kipling, Stevenson.[84]

Next to the family, the school was the single most important source of attitudes and beliefs for a child. 'The home is the state in miniature,' according to one authority, 'and as the school is considered a means of extending the training received at home for the wider duties of life, it would seem that the school should also be a field for the training of citizenship.'[85] In short, the school was an important agent of socialization.

Socialization is initiated and enforced by the dominant political group. An important part of that group's power is its ability to define relationships and determine who or what is important. In Ontario, the socialization process was well served by textbooks and readers that the world presented to students from the perspective of élite British culture. The dominance of what Robert Morgan called 'Englishness' in the Ontario school environment was a clear message to people from other backgrounds that there was only one 'motherland', only one legitimate set of identities: English. Morgan goes on to argue that this constructed sameness had enormous ramifications regarding state power, especially where the 'ideological production of a national neutral language' is concerned.[86]

The Empire Élites

Some of the most potent conveyors of both the imperialist ethos and the British ruling class tradition were to be found in Ontario's private schools, specifically Upper Canada College ('the Canadian Eton') and Trinity College School. Modelled on the famous British public schools, these institutions were intended to serve as training grounds for the country's future leaders. According to Paul Bennett, they forged 'powerful and enduring class and gender identities', inculcating the personality traits that were essential for the perpetuation of the ruling class and training boys for 'male rulership'.[87]

Drill was introduced at private schools as early as 1865, and was a significant feature of everyday school life. The dual message of 'love of country' and 'a disposition to defend it'[88] was conveyed with much more force in private than in public schools. Whatever the subject— history, classics, physical education—the emphasis was on the higher sacrifice expected of those endowed with the capacities required to rule. An editorial in Upper Canada College's *The College Times* leaves no doubt as to why such a high proportion of 'old boys' enlisted:

The school is the nursery of the state, and its duty is to train and send out boys strong and vigorous physically, as well as mentally, who will be able to perform manfully and with good heart their appointed task among life's workers. We have no need of a school that turns out weak-backed, spectacled wonders, but we . . . need a school that promotes a stamp of boy whose very appearance is a guarantee that his education has been, primarily speaking, complete. . . . Nowhere can the great qualities of life be better learned than on the playground. The boy that has learned to 'play the game', be it football, cricket or hockey, in the best sense of the word, has learned a great lesson, and one that will be of life-long benefit to him. He has learned to take hard knocks like a man, to accept a superior's decision with good grace, to be unselfish and consider the glory of his club rather than his own, to struggle against heavy odds, and if need be, to acknowledge himself beaten; in short, he has learned to be a manly boy.[89]

This passage could have come directly from an English public school sermon. With its emphasis on manliness, its equation of life with a game, and its many references to the good of the country/team, it is an artful piece of propaganda and a clear recipe for manliness and militarism.

Even proud Canadians had no problem reinforcing the link between Canada and Britain. In many cases, they never even bothered to differentiate between the two. Imperialism was assumed to be a moral enterprise, and all Canadian citizens were also British subjects. Nurtured on pictures of the king and sonnets to fallen soldiers, passionate young citizens viewed England in a near-holy light, with 'feelings of reverence'. Perhaps Kipling was correct when, after a trip to Canada, he said of Canadians that 'their redeeming point is a certain crude material faith in the Empire.'[90] This faith was acquired in the schools, which hammered home the idea that Canada's place was unequivocally with Britain. By extension, the Dominion's own accomplishments and survival depended on its association with the motherland.

It is not surprising, then, that Prime Minister Borden's comment— 'when England is at war, Canada is at war'—had such resonance for young men who had grown up in this atmosphere. Nor is it any wonder that, as the historian Arthur Lower observed, 'those boys [would rush] off across the seas to fight for a country they had never seen— to fight as perhaps men had never fought before.'[91]

6

Making Boys into Men

*A SCOUT'S DUTY IS TO BE USEFUL AND TO HELP
OTHERS. And he is to do his duty before anything else, even
though he gives up his own pleasure, or comfort, or safety to
do it.*

*A SCOUT OBEYS ORDERS of his parents, patrol leader, or
Scout master without question.*

*A SCOUT SMILES AND WHISTLES under all
circumstances. When he gets an order he should obey it
cheerily and readily, not in a slow, hang-dog sort of way.*

Robert Baden-Powell, *Scouting for Boys* (1908)

The Crisis of Masculinity

Between 1867 and 1914, modernization, urbanization, and an
increasingly visible and vociferous women's movement accentuated
masculine self-doubt. With the separation of the public and the private spheres, as a result of industrialization, men no longer spent
much time with their sons. With women in both the home and the
school taking control of the socializing process, many men worried
that women were instructing boys on how to become men.[1]

Concern over how children were to be raised was common among
parents, educators, and the loose coalition of individuals who might be
called 'progressives'. In many cases, the worry was as much a national
issue as a family one.[2] At virtually every level of the socio-cultural

realm, discussion centred on how best to raise 'feminine' girls and 'masculine' boys. Before 1870, male infants often wore dresses; after 1870, boys were increasingly dressed in loose, functional, durable, and—above all—masculine clothes. Younger and younger boys were moved out of their breeches into pants, while kilts and skirts for young boys virtually disappeared. Any garment with a feminine connotation was banished from the wardrobe. The new emphasis on clearly masculine clothes, beginning in the late 1870s, reflected the values of a changing society. Boys who were supposed to be tough, aggressive, and competitive needed suitable clothes.[3]

Much thought was given in the years after 1870 on how to deal with the rambunctious and wild tendencies of adolescent boys. The child expert and physician Pye Henry Chavasse offered one view of this situation, claiming that boys who did not indulge in innocent mischief and play were 'unnatural'.[4] Yet there was a significant difference between little boys of six or eight and adolescents. By 1870, the term 'youth' was focused on the years 14 to 19. The modern definition of adolescence would have to wait until psychologist G. Stanley Hall popularized the term in 1900.[5]

Adolescence was often portrayed as 'a time of danger'. As scientific evidence to this effect accumulated, the association of adolescence with trouble became firmly established. Ernest Thompson Seton, an influential authority on how to deal with boys, wrote that 'not one boy in a thousand is born bad. Boys have their badness thrust upon them. They are made bad by evil surroundings during the formative period between school and manhood; between twelve and twenty years of age.' Experts advised parents to keep an eye on their children at this stage; but of course a climate of surveillance simply encouraged adolescents to be more secretive. As Michelle Perrot has observed, young people were very adept at inventing strategies to protect their privacy: 'They read novels during study time or after curfew; they wrote poetry; they kept diaries; and they dreamed.'[6]

As members of the social and political élite became more aware of the importance of younger members to the country's well-being, a 'broad spectrum of private and state-administered agencies accepted an increased responsibility for the advancement of the young.'[7] Some combination of moral training, character-forming activities, and nationalistic or patriotic themes was seen as necessary in order to create manly men. By the late nineteenth century, a transition had occurred. 'Youthful rebellion' was now increasingly co-opted in the service of the state. As various agencies increased their hold on the young, the idea of independent young people 'at war with society' was giving way to the concept of youth 'at war for their society'. The numerous recruiting posters that glorified the young, masculine male in the service of the state are the supreme examples of this shift.[8]

The typical advice manual suggested that controlled groups and monitored gatherings would have the desired effect. As with the juvenile delinquency 'problem' of the 1950s, concern about the 'boy problem' came to focus on the 'gangs' of youths roaming around aimlessly. Part of the appeal of gangs was the fact that they served as arenas for validating masculinity. Participating in initiation rituals showed courage and honour, and a gang provided one of the few environments in which a boy could demonstrate his ability to 'take it like a man'.[9] The gang was a closed clique of boys, acting and performing for each other. All-male fraternal organizations and athletic clubs were especially strong at this time, and boys saw men in numerous groups celebrating manliness in various ways, formal and informal.[10]

In 1901 the number of Canadian bachelors was extremely high, and those who did not gravitate towards the YMCA found a very appealing culture in the pool halls and taverns and on the street corners. Reformers hoped to play on the natural tendency of young boys and men to gather in groups by promoting wholesome group activities that would counteract the poor habits and unmanly qualities that gangs fostered—that would prevent what Joe L. Dubbert calls the further deterioration of the quality of young boys and offer 'an attractive alternative to street life'.[11]

In large and small towns alike,[12] young men had a tendency to hang out on the streets, where they would make lewd remarks, intimidate passersby, spit tobacco, and generally behave in a manner directly against the 'values of the evangelical Protestant moral code'. In Lynne Marks's opinion, these 'loafers' were 'visible symbols of rough culture'.[13] In his lectures for boys, aptly titled *A Manly Boy*, the Reverend Louis Albert Banks lashed out at this idleness. 'A boy,' he wrote, 'is in a dangerous position when he is lounging around *doing nothing*. Nothing can be worse for a boy than the habit of loafing around the street corners, or indeed, of loafing anywhere.'[14] The fact that most loafers came from the working classes caused indignation among 'respectable' middle-class citizens.

From indignation it was a small step to outright hostility as a general fear of public disorder took hold. Many thought that the loafers were just 'too lazy to work', or that they should be in school.[15] The best antidote, it was thought, would be to get them into some form of rational recreation.

Authorities would have preferred to see young men reading or pursuing self-improvement at the Mechanics Institute, participating in church-sponsored activities, or spending time at home. For many working-class youth, however, church-sponsored activities reeked of effeminacy. Moreover, especially in small towns, there was little available in the way of leisure-time activities for those who could not afford to pay. Even drinking or playing billiards required money that many did not have. For the poor, home environments were at best barely adequate, and certainly they did not have middle-class amenities. Thus, for many lower-class youths, the street corner was the only place to meet with their friends.[16]

Although fighting was another concern, it was often encouraged as a way of proving one's manliness. Even the most revered authority on youth and adolescence, G. Stanley Hall, did not condemn fighting: 'better even an occasional nose dented by a fist ... than stagnation, general cynicism and censoriousness, bodily and psychic cowardice.' The need to prove one's manhood to oneself was a particularly frequent justification: 'There are times when every boy must defend his own rights if he is not to become a coward, and lose the road to independence and true manhood.'[17]

Even worse, perhaps, was the fear of being labelled a 'sissy'.[18] One factor contributing to this fear was the so-called absent-father syndrome.[19] New research at the beginning of the twentieth century suggested that it was vital for fathers to be present in order to ensure the proper shaping of children's character as well as to balance the feminine influence of mothers. Yet fathers were spending increasing amounts of time away from the home—whether at work or at the 'club', the pub, or sporting events. The result, some feared, was an excessive feminine influence in the household that made it difficult to raise manly boys.[20] Nor was it enough for the father to be physically in the home if he simply isolated himself in his study. In that case, his role would be even further diminished; he would be perceived as a 'weakling', incapable of making decisions and exercising his authority.[21]

Varda Burstyn sees the need to replace the busy or absent father with an 'extrafamilial social fatherhood' as one reason for the rise of sports: 'ritual institutions with exceptionally strong and dominant masculine models', capable of providing 'both surrogate fatherhood and male socialization'.[22]

If boys were not participating in manly sports, then they 'were not developing normally'.[23] The emphasis on physical activity coincided with efforts to combat 'neurasthenic' tendencies and prevent homosexuality—now seen, in Gail Bederman's words, less as 'a punishable act' than as a symptom of 'an aberrant and deficient male identity, a case of the male body gone wrong through disease or congenital deformity'.[24] Another object of concern was masturbation. The 'solitary vice' was regarded not only as evidence of inadequate self-control—a 'mind over matter' issue—but as a senseless waste of a young man's vital energies. Many people believed that 'self-abuse' would lead to insanity if not 'race suicide', and G. Stanley Hall maintained that preserving semen for procreation was the only way men could ensure they would have happy, highly developed, and moral children.[25]

Although guidebooks of various kinds had long been popular in the family household, by the last quarter of the nineteenth century increasing numbers of them were geared to young men who were not getting the proper direction at home from their fathers.[26] Nineteenth-century advice for young men consistently associated masculinity with action. Doing something physical—preferably outdoors, away from the 'constricted life' of the city—was the best way to become a manly man. Such works also tended to refer frequently to war: being a manly soldier meant taking charge, being a doer, and, most important, showing courage—an attribute defined in one instance as 'contempt for safety and ease'.[27] In an environment that some felt suffocated the individual with modern luxuries, this last point was particularly resonant. Modern civilization was making both men and boys 'soft'. They needed tests and challenges to demonstrate their courage and define their manliness.

As challenges to traditional definitions of manliness increased, men from all classes attempted to 'remake' their ideas about what a man was. A general process of celebrating and embracing all things male was part of this orientation, but there were also deliberate attempts to make boys into men.[28] As, in most occupations, the need for sheer physical strength declined and women entered the public domain, men looked for other ways to assert their manliness. Formal and informal social organizations took on additional importance. Among working-class men, for instance, volunteer fire brigades became very popular. Volunteers would spend much of their leisure time in the pump house 'playing cards, drinking and maintaining equipment'. When the alarm sounded, they would take part in an adventure far removed from their daily routine, one that also gave them a chance to be heroes, to prove their worth to each other, and to perform an essential (often dangerous) service for their community.[29]

The fear of becoming soft or being seen as effeminate provoked men to pursue manly lifestyles both for themselves and for their boys.

Membership in organizations like the Boy Scouts and participation in rugged, manly activities served as antidotes to the fear that masculinity attitudes might be lacking.[30]

Scouting

Britain's lacklustre showing in the Boer War sparked comparisons with the decline of Rome. It also led to serious investigations into the condition of her soldiers.[31]

Robert Baden-Powell, the hero of Mafeking, major general, cavalry officer, and an individual concerned about the education of boys,[32] believed that he could help reverse this 'imperial decline'.[33] Launching the Boy Scout movement in 1908,[34] he laid down the 'Scout's Law', which included not only vows of honour and loyalty (to King, country, and parents), but a pledge to be useful and to obey orders without question. From the start, scouting had a militaristic thrust that was arguably part of its appeal, both in Britain and in North America.[35]

Powerful social and historical circumstances help to account for the rapid spread of scouting. Jeffrey Hantover suggests that its acceptance in the US 'reflected turn-of-the-century concern over the perpetuation and validation of American masculinity.'[36] Baden-Powell himself worried that 'young Englishmen would prove themselves weaklings . . . that they would fail "the supreme test of manhood" in battle.' He wanted Scouts to become 'real men'. Patriotism and duty to one's country were central elements of his philosophy, as was the essential personal attribute, character.[37] 'To combat enfeeblement and bolster boyish pride,' writes David Macleod, 'the Boy Scouts [of America] cultivated an air of determined masculinity, symbolized by awards for heroism, service alongside police at parades, and a uniform like the U.S. Army's.'[38] It was no secret that a nation with 40 million people controlling a significant portion of the earth would need a constant supply of individuals to manage, control, and fight in defence of its Empire. On the political side, then, scouting had the not-so-hidden agenda of making boys and young men into both good citizens and good soldiers.[39]

In his study of British youth movements from 1887 to 1940, John Springhall notes that they tended to be 'instruments for the reinforcement of social conformity'. They were formed during a period in which they found themselves increasingly becoming socialized into national moulds by a committed middle class that took its *Weltanschauung* from various permutations of militant evangelical Christianity, a public-school 'manliness', militarism, and imperialism.[40]

In appealing to the middle-class element, scouting was successful on both sides of the ocean. Yet its overall impact was restricted because it did not incorporate boys of visible minority or immigrant background. Baden-Powell's movement was designed specifically for the middle class and it expressed such firmly rooted middle-class values as the Protestant work ethic and the public school ethos. 'Its ideology', writes Robert MacDonald, 'was conservative and defensive, seeking to find in patriotism and imperialism the cure for an apparently disintegrating society.' Baden-Powell looked upon the movement as a way to save the Empire as well as to defend it in case of war.[41]

Scouting evolved from Baden-Powell's own experiences as a colonist and soldier. He wanted young boys to become men of high character—rugged souls who could be counted on to defend the values of the Western world. In a speech to the Empire Club of Canada, four years before the Great War, Baden-Powell stated: 'Your boys have plenty of self-reliance, resourcefulness, and independence—the only danger is that they may get too much of it. You also want discipline and self-sacrifice, then courtesy and chivalry.'[42] These characteristics are synonymous with the concept of manliness. In his writings and speeches, Baden-Powell always linked the goals of the Scouts with those of the Empire. From its opening pages, *Scouting For Boys* holds up as models 'the "real men" who do their duty to the King and their countrymen and who form part of a heroic national tradition stretching back to the knights of King Arthur.'[43]

'To make men out of them' was the goal both of the Boy Scout movement and of the army. To Scout supporters, the movement provided a character-building 'moral equivalent to war'. The 'rhetoric and content of Scouting spoke to masculine fears of passivity and dependence. Action was the warp and woof of Scouting, as it was the foundation of traditional American masculinity.'[44] One of the central themes of maleness is a stoic toughness that harks back to the days of the frontier.[45] The same sort of toughness was promoted and valued in both subliminal and overt ways with the Boy Scouts.

Scouting was viewed as a positive counterweight to industrialization in that it focused on outdoor life and traditional male activity, and, in America, as a means to prevent the 'feminization' of society. Jeffrey Hantover states that the supporters of scouting

> believed that changes in work, the family and adolescent life threatened the development of manliness among boys and its expression among men. . . . The Boy Scouts provided an environment in which boys could become 'red-blooded' virile men. Less

explicitly, scouting provided men an opportunity to counteract the perceived feminising forces of their lives and to act according to the traditional masculine script.[46]

This 'masculine script' was codified in the Scout law, which 'derived much of its mystique from an alleged connection to the knightly code of King Arthur and his Round Table.'[47] Drawing on noble and time-honoured traditions, scouting codified the concepts of honour, loyalty, and brotherhood in the form of simple rules that anyone could follow.[48] Among middle-class boys on both sides of the Atlantic, scouting channelled young boys' interests and energies with just the right doses of 'sponsored fantasy'.[49] It allowed them to act on their desire to be adventurous 'soldiers', to learn how to survive, to learn how to serve.

One of scouting's greatest attractions was its emphasis on outdoor life at a time when city living was increasingly seen as deleterious, especially for young men. In Canada, it was promoted as a way to harness the legacy of 'backwoodsmen, explorers and frontiersmen'. Baden-Powell argued that this approach would strengthen Canadian boys in 'mind and body' in preparation for the defence of the Empire.[50]

Hunting

Perhaps one of the strongest indicators of manliness and, by extension, virility was the mania for hunting—or, at the very least, shooting—that affected Ontario in the last decades of the nineteenth century and the first decade of the twentieth century. By the late 1880s, hunting for deer and moose was well established. Men and boys travelled great distances to kill them. Coupled with outdoor life, this became the acid test of one's grit.[51] One did not have to go far to indulge in the pleasure and purpose of hunting. Just outside of Toronto in the 1870s, one could hunt and fish in ample park and forest areas. Sigmund Samuel would spend hours with his friends hunting, fishing, and trapping in this urban wilderness. In his autobiography, Samuel relates that he and his friends constructed a natural history museum in one mate's house. Samuel writes that it was 'well stocked with bird's eggs, rocks, fish, and botanical samples. Its centrepiece was a large crow which I had shot and stuffed, following instructions in the *Boy's Own Paper*.'[52]

Closely related to the general principles of scouting, hunting was the next logical step in a boy's evolution. Hunting offered boys the chance to become 'real men' and was encouraged in their manly training. 'Every boy ought to learn to shoot and to obey orders, else he is no more good when war breaks out than an old woman.' This quote is from the first edition of Baden-Powell's *Scouting For Boys*. According to John Mackenzie, 'it perfectly encapsulates concepts of manliness which were conveyed through youth organisations, popular images, juvenile literature, and many other texts in the late Victorian and Edwardian periods.' In this manly world, and in 'Scouting's cult of masculinity' in particular, 'indifference to the pleasures of shooting, or the outdoors, or danger puts one's manhood in doubt.' Baden-Powell promoted hunting with enthusiasm, for it 'constituted the essence of the pioneering spirit, the source of all attributes that prepared the peace scout for war.'[53]

Hunting has been defined as 'an armed confrontation between humanness and wildness'. Because it 'involves confrontational, premeditated, and violent killing, it represents something like a war waged by humanity against the wilderness.' The war analogy is apt. The paraphernalia and strategy involved in an organized hunt closely 'resembles a military campaign.' The long tradition of comparison seems endless. 'Hunting', according to one authority, 'has been widely regarded as a sort of war game, the first step in a young man's combat training.'[54] In certain cultures it has also served as a formal initiation rite, a testing ground for youth prior to joining the ranks of the warriors. Strategy, planning, tactics, capture, weaponry, aim, and the kill are all terms that apply to both hunting and war.[55]

Hunting in archaic and classical Greece was already defined as a 'masculine, and in a sense, a manly activity'.[56] It could already be equated with the ideas of noble, heroic manhood. The ancient Greek historian Xenophon wrote a training manual called *On Hunting*, which laid out the rules and techniques of hunting. This work was more than a 'how-to manual'; hunting was a complete education in masculine mores. For Xenophon and many others since, hunting was the way boys were shaped into responsible, virile men. For the Greeks, 'hunting promoted a specific image of manliness.'[57] Xenophon likened hunters to warriors and 'thought hunting the best training for war because it cultivates manly virtues and teaches military skills such as maneuvering and attacking.'[58] For medieval lords, hunting served as an important peacetime surrogate to war, as it allowed them to demonstrate their prowess and manliness to their subjects. Hunting as the ideal model and preparation for war is an activity that permeates much of Western culture from classic times until the present day.[59] Between 1870 and 1914, this cultural inheritance was fully utilized.

Hunting in the nineteenth and early twentieth centuries held great appeal for both men and boys. For men, hunting with a rifle was a reminder of the not-too-distant past when hunting was necessary to feed one's family. In the new age of industrialization and urbanization, the nostalgic importance of this cannot be underestimated. For boys, there was simple adventure as well as the status gained from emulating an adult.[60] Contemporaries thought that there was a natural tendency for boys to want to kill animals, which combined with an instinct to be adventurous in nature. According to one opinion, 'Boys of this age are especially fond of fighting and bloodletting and will expend a surprising amount of time and energy in an effort to see something killed outright or chopped to pieces alive.'[61] There was also an issue of power and control. Man's domination over animals, the land—all living things—was of unstated but pervasive appeal. In an age of racial theories and classifications in which the Anglo male was invariably placed at the top, regard for anything below did not make sense.[62]

The most traditional hunters in the West, the élites, had justified their privileged position as necessary to the maintenance of their skills for future battles. Beginning in the eighteenth century, imperial representatives in far-flung parts of the empire could enjoy these same privileges and many recorded their exploits and experiences, making them accessible to new and larger audiences, especially young boys.[63] Hunting, practised as a manly endeavour by white settlers in various parts of Africa and India, and glorified through fiction and memoir, came to be considered the natural hand-maiden of imperialism.

The exploits and writings of Theodore Roosevelt with regard to hunting in virtually every corner of the earth served to popularize the myth of hunting and to make it synonymous with powerful masculinity.[64] Roosevelt allowed that hunting brought one closer to the land and thus gave him every chance to demonstrate his manliness in untamed nature. In *Hunting Trips of a Ranchman* and *The Wilderness Hunter*, he mixed this understanding of nature within the influence of the adventure story. His advocacy of 'the strenuous life' was closely related to military admonishments about being prepared and being tested.[65]

Dominance over others, the thrill of the chase, the trophy, in essence the power of life and death at the heart of it all, came to define the imperial, masculine ideal. The hunt came to stand for real power. 'For the imperial and Darwinian hunter, the Man in the Pith Helmet, it [the hunt] is an assertion of his competitive superiority over the natives and other local fauna.'[66] Whether it was Roosevelt hunting big game, Baden-Powell 'pig-sticking', or excursions into the new rural wilderness for soon-to-be extinct species, a masculine camaraderie in killing came into being. It came to be thought that hunting was the definitive way to harness all the supreme masculine attributes. Hunting involved and encouraged all that the imperial male valued: courage, individualism, staying power, resourcefulness, knowledge, and mastery over the environment and nature. Hunting was thus closely bound up with the symbolism of imperialism and extolled as a ritualistic, manly affair.[67] R.G. Moyles and Doug Owram explain some of this pervasive appeal:

> As they explored, and conquered, and extended the Empire, the British hunted. They rode, in a state of imperialistic fervour, all over Victoria's vast dominion, sticking pigs in India, stalking zebra along the African Veldt, and charging after buffalo across the Canadian Prairie. For many of them, unrestricted hunting was the expected rest and recreation of empire-builders—'we have done our duty, now we must play.' But for many more, hunting was part and parcel of the empire-building process; the play habits of the British, especially the aristo-military caste, were closely linked to their professional pursuits.[68]

Ritualism was involved, as was a code of conduct. One had to show 'courage in the face of danger, demonstrate fair play, give the native a "sporting chance"', and one never was to 'gloat in victory'. This kind of mentality was ideal for training in the 'manly game of war'.[69] Like war, hunting offered a clear adversary, had certain rules, offered trophies, and stressed coolness and precision.[70]

Leaving the city to hunt provided men and boys a chance to act like 'real men' in the wilderness. The mythology surrounding the hunter was a social creation designed to give those who hunted or those who read about hunting a new-found sense of masculinity. Hunting could also provide a valuable series of lessons for men and boys, and came to be seen as a way for the city-bred male to reassert his manliness and to prevent others from labelling him as 'effete'. In some instances, the hunter may have been hunting for his own masculinity.[71] As Charles Bergman so astutely remarks:

> Unlike anytime before, hunting was explicitly adduced as the agency of self-generation for men. It was a program and an ideology for the recreation of manliness. Hunting would redeem men from the very world they were busy creating at home in the cities.[72]

Stories about hunters, especiallly the great white hunter, presented important models of manliness. In either a 'natural account' or else a fictional version, the glorification of hunting reached a wide audience, especially through the stories of G.A. Henty and Rider Haggard, who were popular on both sides of the Atlantic. 'For Henty, hunting lay at the centre of the imperial experience and he had a horror of lads who shrank from shedding blood.'[73] Killing was part and parcel of settling, touring, or surveying the various outposts of the British and American empires. It went hand in hand with environmental and topographical knowledge.

Boys who had read Henty, Captain Mayne Reid, W.H.G. Kingston, or R.M. Ballantyne were intimately acquainted with all the 'gory details'. Works such as Kingston's *Peter the Whaler* or *Hendricks the Hunter* and Ballantyne's *The Gorilla Hunters* or *The Walrus Hunters* were quite explicit. Hunting, in fact, is a seminal feature of children's literature of this period—a metaphor for action and taking command. As the narrator of Ballantyne's *The Gorilla Hunters* warns, there is no place for the timid, unenthusiastic boy.[74]

The influences of social Darwinism also comes into play here, for hunting, in conjunction with scouting, required a fit and competitive society. 'If only the fittest survived, then young people had to be fit; if nature was competitive, then young people had to compete.'[75] When versions of this kind of thinking are cloaked in some agency of respectability they take on added importance. The work of G. Stanley Hall was often invoked to justify such preparation for the struggle for survival. Commenting on this, Peter Gay writes that Hall felt that 'Boys must train their capacities in "wrestling, fighting, boxing, and dueling, and in some sense, hunting," thus emulating in their lives the animal world, which "is full of struggles for survival." ' Hall, according to Gay, 'welcomed schooling in "man-making" as a defence against moral degeneration, the essential feature of which is weakening of will and loss of honor. Real virtue requires enemies, and women and effeminate and old men want placid, comfortable peace, while a real man rejoices in noble strife which sanctifies all great causes, casts out fear, and is the chief school of courage.'[76] Scouting and hunting provided opportunities to act out this 'defence against degeneration'. In essence, then, one could suggest that aggression and competition were condoned, provided they were oriented towards acceptable objectives.

But for some, the best place to organize these instincts and passions was in the realm of sport. Participation in sport, in any manifestation, could provide the barometer of manhood. The range was wide and could include the simple or the intense sporting activities to be enjoyed by active individuals or enthusiastic spectators.

7

At Play in the Fields of the Empire

God knows that for myself I have scanty care;
Past scrimmages have proved as much to all;
In Eastern lands and South I have had my share
    Both of the blade and ball.

Thomas Hardy, 'The Colonel's Soliloquy' (1889)

One of the more interesting and objective observers of late nine-teenth-century culture, the social scientist and economist Thorstein Veblen, had much to say about the combative qualities that the Boy Scouts, sports, and other agencies of masculine socialization sought to instil in young boys. For example, 'These manifestations of the predatory temperament are all to be classified under the head of exploit.... A strong proclivity to adventuresome exploit and to the infliction of damage is especially pronounced in those employments which are in colloquial usage specifically called sportsmanship.'[1] Similarly, John Hobson, an influential early twentieth-century critic of imperialism, recognized that the objective of sports and clubs was to mould young boys into men with the instincts of warriors.[2]

Ambition, competitiveness, aggression, and toughness—virtues greatly admired in the years before World War I—came to define manliness. A short temper could be a good thing, according to one authority, for it made a boy quick, alert, and courageous. Fighting, as we have seen, could help to develop the character and abilities required for battle.[3] Others believed that the best way to develop the necessary instincts and skills was through sport.

Exercise and the Outdoors

The change from a traditional rural-agrarian society to a modern urban-industrial one 'wrenched society from the moorings of familiar values'.[4] Numerous changes had already taken place and many more were to come.

The Canadian response to urbanization was 'generally unfavourable'.[5] Contemporary journals, according to George Altmeyer, 'portrayed city life as artificial: the city was seen as a place of "stone and mortar", of "rattlin' and roarin' streets".'[6] In 'Worry: the Disease of the Age', a series of articles that appeared in *Canadian Magazine* in 1906–7, C.W. Saleeby suggested that the pressures of city life were probably the most important factors leading to worry and anxiety.[7] Many city dwellers, perhaps spurred by memories of their country roots, began to look to nature as an escape. Urbanization had created a distinct change in perceptions of the rural landscape. As people moved away from the countryside and settled in cities, as cities grew and office or industrial work took over more and more of people's lives, the idea of nature acquired a new value. The wilderness became a symbolic place, a 'national symbol', a repository of all that had been lost and might be recaptured.[8] As Allan Smith writes:

the simple and uncomplicated notion that the forest possessed the capacity to uplift and regenerate those exposed to it had great appeal in a society whose population was increasingly urban, since city dwellers, functioning within the framework of a highly structured system, seemed in particular need of escape from the constraints of routine and organization.[9]

By the closing years of the nineteenth century, educators, physical culture enthusiasts, and medical experts recognized that the outdoors had benefits beyond the symbolic. As cities grew in size and as more of the population laboured inside factories, the health of the province and nation became a matter of increasing concern. By the 1870s, physical fitness was being recommended as the remedy for a whole series of discontents. Combining the outdoors with physical culture was thought to be of particular benefit to young people. Physical activity in the outdoors, close to nature, would help to arrest the deterioration of Canadian manhood. Nature was the antidote required to reinvigorate a 'rapidly deteriorating race'.[10]

For those not interested in the rigours of scouting or the visceral pleasures of the hunt, a general back-to-nature movement promoted outdoor activity for thousands of urban dwellers. Altmeyer writes:

at its mildest, *back to nature* meant leisurely rides into the countryside astride a bicycle on Sunday afternoons, tramping through a marsh or hillside thicket to get the perfect 'kodak' snapshot of some animal or bird, or taking up the popular sport of bird watching. Somewhat more strenuously, it meant hiking, camping, canoeing and alpine climbing.[11]

The back-to-nature experience was presented as transformative. Adults would lose their urban stuffiness, release the pent-up frustrations of their working lives, and be rejuvenated. For children, boys in particular, early exposure to the wonders of nature would prevent the development of any overtaxing sense of 'urban confinement' and instead encourage all the manly qualities.[12] Success in the great outdoors would lead to success in virtually any other endeavour.

For the children there were camps. These ranged from the *Toronto Star*'s Fresh Air Fund Camp for underprivileged children, which began in 1891,[13] to Ernest Thompson Seton's Indian-style woodcraft camps, which began at roughly the same time. Unlike the Boy Scouts, with their military emphasis, Seton emphasized the pure appreciation of nature. Offering such traditional outdoor activities as tracking, camping, and canoeing, Seton's camps were thought to be ideal for training citizens and forming character.[14] Perhaps following Seton's lead, a physical training instructor at Upper Canada College established a camp in northern Ontario at Temagami in 1903, which was dedicated to 'character building through vigorous outdoor living and wilderness appreciation'.[15] Camp Temagami was particularly well suited for canoe trips, in the course of which boys were expected to acquire various skills—pitching a tent, cooking outdoors, and of course, portaging —and learn to share in the tasks required for the good of all. Lessons in manliness and self-reliance were learned from interaction with other boys or from their fathers.[16] In addition, the YMCA conducted numerous camps around the Toronto area in the summer—a time when boys were at particular risk of 'moral deterioration'.[17]

Camping for pleasure in Ontario dated back to the mid-nineteenth century, but improvements in rail access—by the 1880s, the train from Toronto north to Gravenhurst took about three hours—enabled more and more people to enjoy it. By the turn of the century, increasing numbers of middle-class people were travelling to cottages and resorts. The Muskoka district north of Toronto billed itself as offering relief from the pressures of the city, a place to rest and exercise among the pristine forests.[18] Similarly, the Temagami region, farther north, advertised itself as a cure-all for the 'brain-fagged, nerve-racked denizens of our great cities', promising respite from the 'treadmill of business life'.[19]

Sports

One authoritative book on child-rearing advised that the young boy 'should spend the greater part of every day in the open air; let him exert himself as much as he please, his feelings will tell him when to rest and when to begin again.'[20] The two most popular boys' magazines of the time, *Chums* and the *Boy's Own Paper*, regularly published articles on physical fitness, profiles of athletes, and advertisements for barbells and other exercise equipment. In 1893, Captain Lord Charles Beresford made the case for sports to *Chums* readers by playing on the insecurities of adolescence, specifically the desire to be popular:

> always devote a portion of every day to physical exercise. It makes you feel nice and tired at the end of the day, and that puts you in a good temper and makes you kind. It also makes you healthy and health is invaluable in life. A healthy boy can always bear pain and worries better than a seedy one. Then exercise—sports, that is —makes you chivalrous, which leads to respect and popularity. No one who seeks after popularity ever gets it, but the chivalrous boy is almost always popular, and his popularity will last.[21]

Even the churches supported games that built character and made men out of boys. As young people spent less time in the pews and more on the playgrounds, representatives of most Protestant denominations began looking to sports and physical recreation as tools to reverse the moral and physical decay of young people. According to Bruce Kidd, middle-class people concerned about disease, street children, and even class conflict urged church elders to demand better public areas and playgrounds.[22] Speaking to a Methodist rally in 1901, the Reverend T.E. Egerton Shore complained that the few men he had seen attending a recent conference were 'delicate looking specimens', and he wondered aloud: 'Where were the young men of vigor and strength? Where were the young men of athletics and sport?... Wherever they were, they were not in the church.'[23]

Recreation of all sorts had to have a rational purpose and be directed towards a specific goal. In the past, there had been a strong suspicion that sports attracted the wrong crowd, and connotations of unsavoury actions lingered within most sports associations. As long as 'healthy activity' and 'moral training' were involved, however, sports and games could be seen as useful vehicles for teaching obedience, discipline, and self-improvement.[24] As increased leisure time became available to more people, and a structured school day framed a child's time, organized sport came to be increasingly controlled by rules and regulations.[25]

The rise of modern sport and leisure would not have been possible without urbanization. Many games may have originated in rural environments, but until they were contained and 'remade' in urban settings they were just pastimes. In cities and larger towns, games were codified, refined, and transformed into sports. Urbanization meant formal rules and control by governing bodies and businessmen, but it also meant regular competition, ease of access, more efficient equipment, newer facilities, and 'designated hours of leisure for recreational pursuits'. The bustling cities also provided the sheer numbers of bodies necessary to make team sports viable.[26] Immigrants who came to Ontario adopted the dominant sports, Canadianized their own, and pressed those in charge for more facilities and opportunities to participate.[27]

Such expansion was closely watched and heavily regulated. Local, municipal, and provincial governments, various child-centred societies and youth and social organizations, business groups, and churches determined much of what was allowed. Activities they disapproved of were prevented, while those deemed suitable received encouragement. Land for playing fields and time off in the form of holidays were two forms of official generosity; the financing of a trophy by a notable figure, such as the Governor-General, was another. It is telling that the federal government was instrumental in establishing the Dominion Rifle Association in 1888, with rules and regulations, competitions, and funds that exceeded $1.5 million by 1908. Such encouragement was an excellent way of developing expert marksmen, and at a relatively low cost compared to outfitting an army.[28]

As with virtually every other facet of their society, Ontarians selected from both British traditions and American ideas in constructing rules and standards for participation and play. In Britain, 'blood' and 'combat sports' served to train men not only for war but for leadership in military and administrative functions in the service of the Empire.

Boxing provides a particularly interesting case study. In the mid-nineteenth century, boxing belonged to lower-class urban culture and offered an outlet for those victimized by the emerging machine economy. In the midst of bourgeois urban society, boxing represented an eruption of macho power and a violent test of manliness. Usually clandestine,[29] boxing matches also represented an attempt by those on the margins of society to exert some form of independence. The 'art' of boxing put physical prowess on display in an age in which appreciation for the skills of the body was eroding.[30]

For the lower classes, the late Victorian association of manliness with economic success did not apply, for if wealth was the measure of manliness, the lower classes were surely doomed to failure. In an age of diminishing traditions, a father was unlikely to pass on a skill, or a trade, to his offspring. At a time when monotonous factory jobs made strength and skill almost redundant, boxing focused on a simpler, more primal idea of manhood—one beyond the control of the factory bosses and bureaucratic pencil-pushers. A boxer could demonstrate his manly attributes: his 'sensitivity to insult, his coolness in the face of danger, and his ability to give and take punishment'.[31]

As the nineteenth century drew to a close, boxing began to attract men from the middle and upper classes. Part of its appeal had to do with the fact that middle-class men were looking for ways to assert their masculinity; another part had to do with boxing's emphasis on physicality and action, its glorification of the body. Many young boys were keen to learn how to defend themselves, and many were encouraged by their fathers. In *Youth* (1911), Stanley Hall advocated boxing lessons for boys as a way to channel their natural aggressiveness and instil such manly qualities as stamina and endurance. Boxing filled a need for the middle and upper classes by giving them a taste of a more active and dangerous life. Boxing represented an alternative to the safety of everyday middle-class life. As an activity for men only, it also offered an escape from the smothering tendencies of mothers and wives.[32]

By excluding women, violent and aggressive sport reasserted masculine dominance and created an all-male fraternity that sanctioned the 'use of aggression, force and violence'[33] and legitimized male domination.[34] If there was a subconscious force of anger working within the psyche, sports could be used to channel it. Sport was an ideal way to transform emotional volatility into strength of character. By harnessing anger and directing it, sports allowed men and boys to blow off steam, to corral dangerous, disturbing emotions and direct them towards positive outcomes.[35]

For men and boys alike, sports represented a response to the inroads made by women and the separation of work and home. Equated with muscularity and courage, manliness and strength, sports in every manifestation—at the school or in the playground, in the clubhouse or tavern, on the sports page or in the bleachers—served as a primary stronghold against the perception of feminization. If boys were being reared by women, both at home and at school, then fathers and civic leaders felt it imperative to get their sons involved with sports 'lest they become sissified'.[36]

By the 1880s formal conditions and rules had been established by athletic unions and sport associations,[37] and informal guidelines were dictated by fashion and personality. These conditions and guidelines combined to form a powerful agent of social control that worked in conjunction with the fostering of a spirit of cohesion. Sport could be classified as having both a hidden and not-so-hidden agenda. The obvious relationship to training future soldiers has been mentioned, but other related ideas found their way into the recipe. James Walvin notes that 'football was converted from its pre-industrial turbulence into a quieter, more restrained (though nonetheless tough) team sport, ideally suited to the task of exhausting, controlling and training healthy young men and boys.'[38] Similarly, American football was lauded for fostering 'physical and moral courage, vigorous manhood, self-control, discipline, and "power of the will"'. A popular text at the time stated, not surprisingly, that these were qualities very useful to the soldier.[39] Organized sports were preparation for war, while war would become a 'sporting endeavour'.[40]

Ice hockey was another game promoted as having important educational benefits for Canadian boys. Schools, churches, towns, and organizations of all kinds formed amateur teams and leagues. 'Soon after its invention, ice hockey was recognized as an ideal vehicle for the demonstration of manly qualities. In fact, this quality provided the justification for its acceptance in society.'[41]

From the struggle to win a game to the hidden political messages of certain contests, virtually all aspects of sport could have a significant, controlled result.[42] Whether it was oriented around the repression of certain unsavoury entertainments or the regulation of improper behaviours, most sports went through a period of controlled transformation that in a way gentrified and professionalized them. Upper-class amateur codes made sure that those not of the right race and class would be prevented from polluting the pure sporting environment that in many cases had been designed to perpetuate gentlemanly traditions throughout the Empire and to keep the manly ideal unsullied.[43] By the end of the nineteenth century, 'amateur sport became more widely understood as something that promoted the *civilizing* values of hygiene, fairness, emotional control, and respectability.'[44] As more working-class participants excelled and were accepted in mainstream (professional) sports pure amateurism was left to the school or to heavily regulated associations and unions.

The professionalization of sport was tied to the rise of sports entrepreneurs. Increasingly, remuneration for participation on a team or appearance at an event became a key factor. As sports matured, they became subject to the same forces that affected the rest of society. The rationalization of sporting activity—through bureaucratic regulation and a focus on record-setting performance—merged with society's fascination with statistics and record-keeping. Sport was said to differ from physical training primarily in that gymnastic and calisthenic programs were considered more scientific, whereas athletics, specifically games and sports, seemed to fall into a category that made them more social and more dependent on courage, co-operation, and self-reliance. This important distinction was carried over into two separate realms. Educators appreciated the structured discipline of physical training, whereas young boys preferred the looser forms of play typical of games and sports.[45]

In this age of bellicose adventurism and assumptions of racial and national superiority, the concept of winning took on added significance. As Johan Huizinga explained of winning in the context of play, the evidence of superiority gained by winning a game 'tends to confer upon the winner a semblance of superiority in general. In this respect, he wins something more than the game as such. He has won esteem, obtained honour; and this honour and esteem at once accrue to the benefit of the group to which the victor belongs.'[46]

One could speculate that such winning of respect for the group had something to do with the popularity of the new team sports and the loyalties they inspired among spectators. As individual sporting heroes emerged, they took on characteristics that many men and boys felt they lacked and—like cowboys and soldiers—became icons of manliness. Such heroes had enormous appeal for city-bred men who could not assert their masculinity the way their forefathers had. 'Sport reaffirmed that strength, aggressiveness, and the will to win—*male* values—were the fundamentals of life.'[47]

The rising popularity of sports was assisted when newspapers began devoting more space to sports coverage and periodicals began promoting sports photos. Most of the larger newspapers reported sporting events by the 1880s, and some even had regular columns to cover local, provincial, and international (especially American) sport.[48] Sports reports celebrated manliness and competition, pointing out specific achievements and lauding personal success.[49]

The increasing time, specialization, organization, and money involved in various sporting activities produced a gap between amateurs and professionals. The profit orientation of professional sport continues in sports such as hockey and baseball to this day.[50] Professionals and amateurs were governed by completely separate organizations, and at the higher levels sports organizations began to be run in the interest of profits rather than moral uplift.

Heroes of Manhood

Given the right guidance and the right role models, young boys will be 'eager to exercise their social consciousness and emulate their heroes by becoming ministers or missionaries or slum workers or men of achievement.'[51] So wrote William Byron Forbush in his book *The Boy Problem* (1902). The realities of hero-worship tell a different story.

A culture's heroes reflect its values.[52] For Canadians during the last quarter of the nineteenth century, the definitive hero was Ned Hanlan, the rowing champion who for the first time demonstrated that Canada could produce the best in the world.[53]

From a working-class background, Hanlan was world champion for four years. Challengers came from all over to race him, Sigmund Samuel recalled, but 'inevitably they lost'; 'we lionized him.'[54] He was so much better than his rivals that he gave his fans a true feeling of superiority. Hanlan's renown was enhanced by the fact that one of his managers was Canada's first full-time sportswriter, H.J.P. Good. Sporting heroes seem to have held more attraction for newspaper readers than political leaders. Readers of the press at this time were often more knowledgeable and more interested in sports than politics. Ned Hanlan held more appeal for most Canadians than did John A. Macdonald.[55]

In the US, the settlement of the West and the closing of the frontier resulted in a nostalgia for life as it was thought to have been lived in the 'Wild West'.[56] The American historian Frederick Jackson Turner, who in 1893 proclaimed the demise of frontier America, put great stock in the character of the men who embodied the spirit of the West. He celebrated all their 'heroic, masculine traits even as he lamented the passing of the conditions that produced them.' In the process the myth of the 'Wild West' was born.[57]

The complexity of that myth is staggering. As Jane Tompkins explains, the West functions as a symbol 'of freedom and of the opportunity for conquest. It seems to offer escape from the conditions of life in modern industrial society: from mechanized existence, economic dead ends, social entanglements, unhappy personal relations, political injustice.'[58] In particular, the image of the lone cowboy captivated many young minds, especially after the advent of pulp westerns in magazine and book form. And there were other manifestations of this ethos.

Published in 1902, Owen Wister's groundbreaking cowboy novel *The Virginian* was a best-seller in both the United States and Canada.[59] Jane Tompkins points out that the novel's hero, a chivalrous cowboy, is a 'lineal descendant of the Anglo-Saxon Knight-at-arms'. According to Tompkins, Wister's popular novel also suggests that 'the attributes of heroic-manhood—courage, toughness—are closely bound up with race.'[60]

The western mystique centred on violence, much of it racially motivated. Yet the slaughter of Native people is portrayed as noble, and those who perpetrated it are lauded as heroes, supreme examples of manliness.[61] While a student at Columbia Law School, Theodore Roosevelt had been inspired by 'the drama of racial expansion'. Richard Hofstadter demonstrates that in Roosevelt's historical work, *The Winning of the West*, he 'drew from the story of the Frontiersman's struggle with the Indians, the conclusion that the coming of the whites was not to be stayed and a racial war to the finish was inevitable.'[62] Roosevelt's heroes embody the toughness, strength of character, and ruthlessness that were thought necessary for success. In general, the message imparted was that if one was not manly, then one would not succeed in any undertaking. The same message would soon be translated into terms appropriate to the battlefield.

Toys and Games

In her study of materialism and children, Karen Calvert examined objects that belonged to children and the impact those objects had on the culture in which those children lived. What is significant about such objects is that 'they have always met more than the simple needs of the children. They have also met the parents' need to mold their infants into the accepted cultural image of the time.'[63] Because games and toys are usually made by adults for other adults to buy for children, they tend to reveal at least as much about parents' culture as that of their children.[64] The toys produced between 1867 and 1914 suggest that the period was one of increasing concern over boys' masculinity: 'parents preferred toys that they believed fostered the manliness of their sons and the femininity of their daughters.' In an examination of 325 portraits of boys under the age of seven, painted between 1830 and 1870, Calvert found that almost 20 per cent of the children posed with toys or clothing of a military nature, 'including little swords, guns, military costumes, bugles, drums, cannons, and toy soldiers'. These toys, like boys' games in general, were 'supposed to develop basic skills and encouraged such socially desirable traits as courage, leadership, teamwork, and competitiveness.'[65]

Childhood was increasingly divided into separate spheres, one for boys and one for girls. Girls were raised to take over from their mothers, to be kept away from all that was masculine, unstable, and aggressive. Boys had to be taught to be both 'assertive and individualistic' in order to develop properly into men.[66] Toys were employed in further delineating these roles, most often for the benefit of the parents concerned over the future of their children.

The proliferation of catalogues, books on child-rearing, articles in magazines for parents, and toy shops suggested not only that adults were taking a new interest in children, but also that toys were regarded as important pedagogical tools.[67] A desire to reach children at an impressionable age was one of the main reasons that parents approved of toys with a military theme. From the mid-nineteenth century until 1914, toy soldiers were more popular than virtually any other kind of toy for boys. In the United States, BB guns were much-cherished gifts, although by 1900, safety concerns were reducing their popularity. Children would have to be content with physically harmless—yet emotionally and iconographically powerful—simulated soldiers.

In turn-of-the-century Ontario, children and their parents had become accustomed to the school system and all the related effects of mass schooling. As a consequence of institutional schooling, children's play and play life changed. Thomas E. Jordan states that 'the form and content of play shifted as toys evolved. Early in the century toys were simple and allowed a fluid reality to change them in marvellous ways. With metal fabrication, toys became less ambiguous and more representational, which was probably a loss for creativity.' There can be no mistaking the intention of such 'literalness', even for those boys with active imaginations. A toy soldier was a soldier. And yet, as Erik Erickson recognized, this ready-made toy world allowed children to demonstrate that they knew what to do with the toys, in essence, 'making something', emulating, by creating little worlds. At the same time, these kinds of toys tended to 'habituate children to solitary, impersonal activity', which, according to Brian Sutton-Smith, was (and is) a 'forecast of their years to come as solitary professionals'.[68]

Boys have played with model soldiers since the classical period and have continued to do so ever since. Toy soldiers had been around in their modern forms since the days of Frederick the Great, who had them designed to commemorate his victories. Such toy soldiers were quickly put to use as playthings for affluent youngsters. Twenty years before World War I, a new method of casting the figures brought the price down, making them affordable for all classes.[69] Meanwhile, 'the growing public awareness of professional standing armies in Europe' served to 'widen considerably the toy soldier market'.[70] Toys in general, and toy soldiers in particular, were imported from England, Germany, and the United States to Canada and were found in a variety of castings, packages, and models to appeal to virtually every budget. It was no secret that manufactured toys had just as potent an appeal for adults.[71] As Roland Barthes has observed, 'they are all reduced copies of human objects, as if in the eyes of the public the child was, all told, nothing but a smaller man, a homunculus to whom must be supplied objects of his own size.'[72] Miniatures, whether of animals, vehicles, or soldiers, had become standard toys for children by the late nineteenth century. Smaller versions of adult themes take on added importance for the young child and in many cases become imbued with a 'totemic appeal'.[73]

Since militarism pervaded most aspects of public life and manliness had almost become a religion, perhaps it is not surprising to see that toys carried the same ideas and themes. Historian George L. Mosse has written that 'before the First World War, some thought them [toy soldiers] indispensable for educating youth in warfare.' Mosse goes on to suggest that, as a consequence of the popularity of these toys, 'war was woven into the fabric of daily life in a way that was irreconcilable with war as an extraordinary experience—and yet its trivialization helped people confront war, just as its glorification did.'[74] Boys in Ontario, too, spent a significant amount of time indoors during the cold winter months, and like their counterparts in Britain, occupied themselves with

> organizing sets of tin soldiers into battle formation on bedroom floors and table tops. By 1907 more than a hundred different military units were offered, with tents, guns, tanks and forts for the model fighting force. The Boer War, the arms race with German and the spread of amateur war-gaming in such movements as the Boy Scouts led to an increasing interest in miniature armies.[75]

By 1860, toys with a militaristic flavour were a significant part of 'the standard boy's arsenal'. A variety of guns—cap, pop, and air— were available by mail order from the United States. One catalogue featured six pages of guns and pistols, many of them sold with target games. As the Great War loomed closer, toy manufacturers and toy sellers often associated pop and air rifles with 'training for manhood'.[76] For Christmas of 1900, the Canadian department store

Eaton's offered boys' soldier suits, cannons with springs, and toy forts. The Christmas 1909 Eaton's catalogue featured 'War', described as a 'very interesting game, 17.5 × 23 inches, [which] consists of a number of soldiers mounted on horses, with two machine guns and ammunition. Guns are repeaters (a new departure in toy guns), are perfectly harmless and will make a good safe toy.'[77]

Toy soldiers were regarded as educational toys in some circles and, like adventure novels, could provide a certain sense of history. The tactile nature of toy soldiers allowed for the possibility of bringing history to life, but it was a historical representation that focused on military struggle.[78]

Toys—whether trains, Froebel building blocks, Erector sets, or model armies—'and the industrial culture mirrored each other.'[79] As socializing devices, toys are 'part of the paraphernalia which facilitate the process by which children prepare and are prepared for the performance of various social roles.' Toys are important shapers of the self in childhood, while pretend play often lays the groundwork for adult lives.[80] H.G. Wells wrote of using the floor as a sea, 'where we land and alter things and build and rearrange and hoist paper flags on pins, and subjugate populations and confer all the blessings of civilisation upon these lands.'[81]

Board games provide an interesting barometer for measuring changing values and important ideas, as well as the emphasis on manliness and militarism. New advances in technology improved their design and durability, reduced their cost, and increased appeal so that by the last quarter of the nineteenth century, board games were imported to Canada in increasing numbers. Already by the 1850s, 'Themes from popular culture and current events had largely replaced the earlier instructional and moral themes for board games.'[82] By the late 1890s catalogues from such companies as Parker and Bradley began to feature more and more games with subjects and titles that reflected a growing interest in the militaristic arts. 'The War in Cuba', 'The Siege of Havana', and 'The Philippine War' are just some of the names of games available. Death and destruction proved 'nearly as irresistible to games players as accumulating a pile of fantasy money'.[83] 'Russia Versus Turkey' was a British-made battle game in which the players raced in a double spiral across the board and tried to take possession of each other's home port. The Crimean War was commemorated in this game, in which 'victory is obtained by a majority of whichever side [takes] possession of the enemy's port. The victors are entitled to divide the pool as prize money.' The board is dotted with forts, ports, gunboats, strategic harbours, and all the central trappings of a good naval battle. 'The Invasion of Europe', released in 1910 and subtitled 'The Great War Game', 'was only one of a number of strategic war games produced in the years leading up to the Great War.' Reflecting the principles of modern warfare, this game featured co-ordinated efforts by the army and navy to secure possession of Europe 'by placing all members of their respective forces on squares containing ringed cities'.[84]

Board games were thought to serve a variety of important purposes, not the least of which was to 'give children an opportunity to practice possible future roles.' The various games available reflected the cultural values of the adults who purchased them. Games were popular with parents because of their educational value in teaching children how to take turns, how to follow rules, and how to win and lose.[85]

Thus, toys and games became influential conveyors of patterns and expectations for later life and reinforced the society's general emphasis on manliness and militarism.[86] As with dress and reading, there was a bifurcation of toys that split them up into specifically gendered spheres. 'Toys were increasingly marketed as appropriate only for boys or for girls.'[87] Like so much else, toys and play were becoming completely different pursuits for boys and girls.

Theorizing Childhood and Play

The concept of play itself took on a whole new dimension in the last years of the nineteenth century and the early years of the twentieth century. Play began to be associated more and more with modern theories of child-rearing:

> Writers and educators of the time began to extol play as having three advantages in socializing the young: play was a way of harmlessly releasing energy, of rehearsing the skills necessary for adulthood through enjoyable practice, and of working and mastering maturational problems through recapitulation in fantasy.[88]

According to David Cohen, educators like Froebel and Montessori 'did not see play as a good in itself so much as a means through which the child could better be taught formal skills.' Above all, play was valued as a way of controlling the child.[89] The literature on childhood at this time was saturated with words like 'regulated' and 'ordered', suggesting 'a deliberate, organized and widespread effort to rationalize and direct the play of children'.[90]

Group play exploited boys' 'naturally aggressive tendencies'. According to one turn-of-the-century expert, 'Boys must be watched for evidence of a tendency to effeminacy, or a fondness for girlish games.' Play in general seemed to offer boys natural outlets for their excessive energy and was far less restricted than girls' activities.[91] The suggestion that boys' play became 'rougher' as the new century began reflects the close interaction of diverse groups of urban children, which made them 'more visible to others'. The 'enforced attendance at school and the segregation of sexes created a male subculture dominated by older, larger boys.'[92]

G. Stanley Hall was one of the most influential authorities on child psychology and pedagogy in the late Victorian and Edwardian periods. Hall did not shy away from controversy, and many of his ideas attracted considerable criticism. Like many males of his era, he was concerned about how boys were being raised. From his position of power and influence, he spoke out about his worries, especially his concern that 'overcivilization' would lead boys to effeminacy. To counteract this trend, Hall felt it essential that boys be subject to a rigorous course of manliness and that 'they receive a virile education'. Hall began to view the strains and stresses of Victorian gentility as restraints on the development of manliness. As more and more comforts entered the home, the risk increased that boys would lose their primal masculinity. Hall was a strong believer that boys' 'primitive savagery' should be encouraged through education. The physical courage learned through fighting as a youth would lead to moral manliness in adulthood.[93]

Many of the play theorists, and particularly Stanley Hall, believed that boys had a 'natural' inclination to behave in an aggressive manner. Far from trying to smother this natural inclination, Hall and others recommended capitalizing on it. In Hall's view, every individual developed through a series of stages that mirrored human biological evolution, 'from savagery to civilization'. Throughout this 'recapitulation process', the boy should be guided in specific forms of play harmonious with each stage. To ensure that the child passed through each stage at precisely the right time, the appropriate form of organized play should be introduced at the appropriate time.[94]

Members of the playground movement, which was powerful in the United States and influential in Canada, were fully committed to controlling children's play, especially in the urban centres. In Canada, the playground movement was appealing to both working-class and middle- and upper-class organizers. For the working class, it brought access to green spaces and urban resources; for the dominant classes it promised to promote public awareness of the 'codes of the prevailing social order'.[95]

James L. Hughes was involved in the development of the playground movement in Toronto. As a rapidly growing city trying to accommodate more and more children, Toronto needed recreational space, as Hughes recognized. As well, Hughes felt that the school should begin to take more interest in children outside the hours of instruction. The playgrounds and the numerous facilities for baseball, soccer, rugby, and lacrosse that were added to the Toronto park system by Mayor J.S. Hocken were inspired by the American playground movement.[96] The social workers, psychologists, and educators behind the playground movement hoped that by transplanting play 'from city streets, where it was ... unorganized and uncontrolled, onto supervised playgrounds' they would be able to shape 'the moral and cognitive development of young people'.[97]

The playground, properly organized, was thought to be one of the most important parts of any educational institution. According to one authority, 'It is there [on the playground] that many of the highest virtues are awakened.' The playground, properly organized, would foster habits of self-control, co-operation, and leadership.[98]

At the same time, 'play organizers' were especially fond of team sports for adolescents. Team sports were viewed as an 'ideal means of integrating the young into the work rhythms and social demands of a dynamic and complex urban industrial civilization'—and, one might add, the militaristic values of such a civilization.[99] The general line of thinking was that, during adolescence, the 'instinct' to engage in teamwork comes to the fore. Play is no longer a solitary pursuit. According to the author of a paper presented in Toronto, American football was the 'most striking illustration' of such teamwork:

> while in ordinary competitive games each member plays for his own glory and advantage, in teamwork he subordinates his interests to those of the team. Behind football there is a strong heredity instinct. The game is nothing more nor less than the reproduction of tribal warfare. The captain is the chief, and the team his soldiers.... This type of game develops ... the military virtues— loyalty to the group, courage, fortitude, and so on.[100]

This argument is extreme in some points and crude in others, but it was not out of line with the thinking of the day. Varda Burstyn and Donald Mrozek both see a direct connection in this period between organized sport and organized violence or combat. Sport proved to be an ideal way of socializing young men in a militaristic mode and acquainting them with combat.[101]

Play theorists, with their interest in moral education and military values, attempted to co-opt team sport and free play for very specific purposes.[102] An influential article by a disciple of Stanley Hall made the link between play and war even more direct. In 'Play as a Moral Equivalent of War' George Johnson explained that a child's instincts were echoes of the 'historic activities of the race', and that among them was an instinct for war.[103] Play moved from being 'recreational' to being 'educational' and was intimately 'related to physical and psychological development', with a particular emphasis on political socialization. 'Impulses' were directed to tangible moral ends.[104] Desires and energies had to be channelled by those 'made anxious by the need to maintain traditional standards in the face of rapid change'.[105]

Certainly children did not simply give up their traditional spirit of play, and often they bridled under the imposition of 'a cohesive moral order'. In fact, many of the games and toys available were often in contradiction to the theories of Hall and Froebel. Instead, manufacturers relied on their 'personal knowledge of children's desire to compete, to imitate, to create and to exercise'.[106] In any case, the psychologists' theories and the knowledge of the toy manufacturers led to the same conclusion. Competition and imitation had very specific connotations between 1867 and 1914.

'Every child is . . . an unconscious imitator', wrote George A. Dickinson in his manual, *Your Boy: His Nature and Nurture*. It was thus vital to give the child the 'proper' models to imitate. What was significant about play for Dickinson was that 'the boy does in play, or tries to do, nearly everything he see others do.' In line with other thinkers of the time, Dickinson advised that play should be scrutinized, controlled, and made an integral part of every boy's education.[107] Whatever the young boy was doing could be seen to have some importance for the future:

> The boy that plays in the sand and makes a collection of pebbles from the beach is learning elementary lessons in geology. He who has a garden of flowers, and discusses the beauty, care, and habits of plants is beginning the study of botany. The boy who makes windmills, boxes, boats, carts, and kites, is beginning a course in mechanics. The boy who has a dog and trains him to docility and usefulness is on the way to mental progress: he is doing the things that make for patience and prudence. Moreover, play is a sure index of character, and as a general rule children play at the thing which later in life they are to do well.[108]

In the same way, playing with toy soldiers would train boys to be good soldiers themselves.[109]

Without doubt, boys were increasingly being trained to become manly men. Whatever they did—joining the Boy Scouts, hunting, camping, engaging in (or watching) sports, or playing with toy soldiers, little was left to chance. They were trained in every way possible to conform to society's needs and dictates.

8

Conclusion

Most accounts of Canadian history talk about the euphoria that came with the outbreak of World War I. Some accounts are more restrained, yet all suggest that there was enthusiasm and a marked willingness to defend Britain.

This enthusiasm evaporated as the war dragged on. Expectations of a short war gave way to the reality of a long, horror-filled nightmare. By 1916, maintaining a steady supply of volunteers had become so difficult that conscription was forced onto the Canadian people. As news of what was happening in France and Belgium reached Canada, the once unflinching support began to disappear. As losses mounted, so did criticism about the conduct of the war.

Prior to 1914, concern had been expressed about the militarization of Ontario society. To suggest that no one opposed the dominant trends and the dominant ideals of the era would be to close one's eyes to the realities of the time. However, the power, organization, and support behind the forces in favour of war were simply overwhelming. On every level, institutional or individual, the militarists prevailed. The pacifist point of view could not combat the tidal wave of pro-war sentiment, especially in places like Toronto. Those opposed to the war simply did not have the resources to convey their message effectively.

The Protestant churches in Canada have never held back from involvement in political, moral, and social causes. Their activism has often led them to initiate programs and make known views critical of government. Yet the same churches that had espoused pacifist beliefs were at the forefront of war support in 1914.[1]

One can speculate that the Protestant churches jumped on the pro-war bandwagon to compensate for their previous lack of enthusiasm.

However, the war was re-evaluated for them, by the press, personal accounts, and government reports. As John S. Moir has remarked, the war was recast in terms they could relate to: it became a holy war. 'Throughout the First World War', he writes, 'the Christian churches found no difficulty in supporting the "holy" wars against the "Huns". It was generally and confidently assumed that God was on the side of the big guns of the allies, and few individuals questioned the righteousness of the slaughter in Flanders' fields.'[2]

Pacifism was not acceptable to the middle- and upper-middle-class citizens of Ontario. It was a foreign notion that appeared to represent a rejection of everything a manly man was supposed to be. Moreover, even if one did have doubts about motives and aims of a war, a proper British gentleman was supposed to keep that opinion to himself. In *Tapestry of War*, Sandra Gwyn notes that Sir Wilfrid Laurier, then leader of the opposition, 'was as close to being a pacifist as it was possible to be in those times, even though he dared not say so out loud.'[3] For Laurier to have done so would have been political suicide. It was simply not acceptable to voice such a 'radical' view. What might have been acceptable to the labour journalist, the farmer, or the Methodist minister was not for a man of Laurier's stature.

Throughout the early years of the twentieth century, the main opponents of increasing militarization were the various churches, farm organizations, and labour representatives. The idea of pacifism was central to various European religious sects—Anabaptists, Quakers, Mennonites, Hutterites—who had settled in Canada in the eighteenth and nineteenth centuries.[4] But they were marginalized by the preponderance of British settlers. They may have been protected in numerous legal ways from military service, but this did not mean that they were welcome to express their views to the majority of Ontarians. The dominance of the British influence in Ontario suggests that no serious consideration could be given to such a radical ideal as pacifism. Imperial ideals simply reigned supreme. Upper and middle classes came together in the public arena and entrenched these beliefs within the layers of Ontario society.[5] Anyone voicing too strong an anti-militarist stand ran the risk of being labelled disloyal.[6]

Throughout the decade prior to World War I, all the major Protestant denominations (particularly the Methodists and Presbyterians), as well as many labour, farm, and women's organizations, took steps to promote peace. The task was daunting if not impossible. The introduction of cadet training in the school system was particularly alarming to those involved in the peace movement. Some peace advocates even went so far as to suggest that the increasing militarization of

Canadian society was designed to counter the enormous inroads that pacifist ideals had been making. The simple lack of a coherent foundation, as well as a failure to take stock of both the realities of the world situation and the Canadian attachment to Britain, prevented the pacifists from ever moving beyond the situation of preaching to the converted.[7] Although the efforts of various pacifist leaders were admirable, the power of the dominant militaristic paradigm seemed to elude them.

It was no secret that a manly performance in a major war would greatly enhance Canada's image. Like struggling adolescents, English Canadians desperately needed to demonstrate their capabilities. Lacking confidence on the stage of international affairs, many believed a war would be the young country's chance to flex its muscles as well as to demonstrate to Mother Britain that it could fight by her side as an equal. For Ontario's male citizens, a war would provide the opportunity to prove their manliness.

As it turned out, World War I would have an enormous impact on the image of Canada both at home and abroad. As Kathryn M. Bindon writes:

> Canada earned recognition as a sovereign state by her massive military contribution, a contribution made clear to the world by brilliant participation in such battles as Ypres, Vimy Ridge, Passchendaele as well as the liberation of Mons and the march to the Rhine. . . . Canada would emerge from the Great War with a heightened national identity, a tradition of military excellence and a lasting international reputation.[8]

When the war did end, in 1918, it was victory, not peace, that was celebrated. The archetypes of manliness and the examples of militarism that had been used to attract young men to the army were inscribed on the memorials erected in every community, large and small, after the war.[9] The continuing power of the ideals of manliness and militarism after 1918 reflects the intensity of the sentiment surrounding them. At the same time, the ongoing emphasis on the symbolism of manliness and militarism suggests that such symbolism was an intimate part of Ontario's cultural fabric. As David Gilmore explains in his cross-cultural survey of masculinity, the concepts and ideals of masculinity 'are not simply a reflection of individual psychology but a part of public culture, a collective representation.'[10]

As we have seen, what a boy was to become and how he conducted himself were intimately related to the idea of the nation at this time. Much was made of the 'pure Canadian type' shaped by the rigours of the Canadian climate for the ultimate test of true masculine character. The public culture of Ontario thus required a demonstration of both military attributes and manly bearing.[11] In the period from Confederation to World War I, war was consistently presented as the definitive test of manhood. War, in all its manifestations, served as an antidote to the crisis of masculinity, the fear of being perceived as effeminate, the plague of luxury and materialism, the changes brought about by industrialism, and the feminization of society. There is no doubt that the Great War was 'a masculine event'.[12] In the world—a fantasy world perhaps—constructed around the notions of loyalty, heroism, and manliness, war was not only moral and patriotic, it was simply 'good'. A romantic commitment to war had entrenched itself as a pseudo-religion in the province, indoctrinating young boys with a glamorized notion of sacrifice.

The notion of war as a romantic activity was extremely powerful in the years prior to the Great War. War offered experiences fundamentally different from those of everyday life. It offered a chance for those reared on adventure stories, team play, and patriotism to see their fantasies come true. The chance to participate in war was presented and perceived as exciting and desirable. This attraction of war as romance is described by Samuel Hynes: 'Those imaginary wars, however vivid and violent they may be, are romances; they are war turned into fictions, into shapely untruths. They feed our imaginations with the big abstractions of war—Heroism, Fame, Valour, Glory; they make death sentimental and battle melodramatic. Above all, they make war "familiar".'[13]

As the preceding pages have argued, many aspects of Ontario's culture worked together to inculcate in young boys the notions of masculinity and militarism that would create soldiers. At the same time war itself was also portrayed as an exciting adventure that would bring glory to those who participated and shame to those who did not. Commenting on the dichotomy between real war and the fictional unreal war that a young enlistee carried to the front, Hynes writes, 'it was not a war but a dream of war that drew that green boy on.' For a young man raised on popular novels, notions of manliness came from tales of dashing heroes 'for whom fighting was a personal matter'. The war that this young man and many like him were about to experience was profoundly different from those they had encountered through their reading. This war was not to be a war of personal courage and personal adventure.[14] Yet prior to the stagnation in the trenches, to the gassing and the mechanization, the idea of war had been full of romance and adventure.

Many attributes of the traditional masculine ideal can, at least in part, be traced to the fact that men have historically been hunters and warriors. In a modernizing society, which had for the most part done away with the need for these accepted and time-tested masculine roles, new ways of expressing manhood needed to be found. In the period 1867–1914 masculinity was once again given over to the idealized notion of the warrior. The Boer War served as an important rallying point for war sentiment. For those too young to fight, stories of that war provided an important spur to dreams of adventure. They carried with them the glory, heroism, and adventure of this conflict while growing up, just as many Vietnam enlistees carried the memory of World War II (or at least the John Wayne and Audie Murphy versions).

Parents in this increasingly regimented era now felt an obligation to bear children not just for personal or economic reasons, but for the state. They were producing patriots, citizens, and soldiers for whom the greatest honour was to serve their country as solders. For the nation to succeed and thrive, a certain quality of children—especially boys—had to be produced.

From its inception in the 1870s, formalized education had convinced children of the absolute necessity of obeying the commands of their teachers. On the playing field, the same message was conveyed by captains and coaches. From late infancy onward, children were instructed to obey; by late adolescence, many boys did so without hesitation. The implementation of drill in the school system was particularly useful in this regard because it instilled a mentality that would make boys receptive to obedience. Lads who went through cadet training were quick to follow orders. As one authority summed it up, 'It is a great thing to learn to obey. No man or boy is ever worth anything to the world until he has learned the great lessons of obedience.'[15]

The emphasis on bravery and courage that saturated many of the novels and stories for boys left little room for compassion or any other emotion that might cause a soldier to hesitate even for a moment. Rather, he should be prepared to follow any order, to go 'over the top' on command. Canadians were only too willing to obey.

Watching a group of soldiers embark on a boat to Britain, George Sterling Ryerson remarked:

> These young men were the cream of Canada's youth and chivalry, all volunteers, all willing to face the great adventure for King and country, for freedom and civilization. No conscripts were they, but freemen, glad and willing to demonstrate Canada's loyalty and to

make some return to England for the civil and religious liberty we had enjoyed under the protection of her flag for a hundred years or more.[16]

Training boys to be soldiers or cadets, one lieutenant colonel remarked shortly after the outbreak of war, was an 'instinctive working out of the national spirit in favour of building up character and physique, and at the same time incidentally providing for national self-defense'. The war was a rude awakening to some, but the nation, and Ontario in particular, like a good Boy Scout, was prepared:

> Where would have been the thousands of trained men offered by Canada for the defense of the Empire, and how would they have been officered and drilled in so short a time had it not been for the amount of military knowledge and enthusiasm stored up largely as a result of the cadet movement?[17]

At the same time the 'crisis of masculinity' prompted numerous efforts to ensure that boys were raised to be manly. As children came increasingly to be seen as the future of the nation, increasing emphasis was placed on order, moral training, and character education to ensure that they would grow up with the desired values.

The all-male fraternal culture that developed at this time was problematic. On the one hand, it offered opportunities for male camaraderie; on the other, it attracted males away from the home. The lure of the tavern and the pool hall worked against the rational and organized recreation that social controllers and reformers sought to implement. With fathers at work all day, it became urgent to ensure that young boys had the proper moral guidance and masculine influences. Boys' clubs sprang up to fill this need; of particular importance were the Boy Scouts with their joint emphasis on militarism and manliness. Hunting was another activity promoted as a way back to premodern manliness that at the same time would train young men to shoot and get them accustomed to shedding blood. At the same time the outdoor life was promoted not simply as a healthy alternative to city life, but also as a way for boys to experience the primal force of nature and, through camping, canoeing, scouting, and hiking, to acquire not only useful masculine skills but many military virtues.

Sports helped to reclaim manliness and at the same time to instil habits of discipline, obedience to authority, and teamwork. Sport/war analogies were commonplace, and those who encouraged sports often saw such activities as surrogates for war. Sports of all kinds provided abundant male role models. Whether watching or participating, boys would learn the value of courage, coolness under pressure, and the capacity to give and take punishment. Rough sports such as boxing, hockey, and football offered the added thrill of real physical danger. Particularly appealing by contrast to the tedious routines of school and work, sports also created all-male fraternities in which—free from the smothering tendencies of wives and mothers—violence and aggression were glorified. Moreover, sports offered a context in which heroes could rise. Toys and games were also co-opted to promote manliness and an interest in things military. From toy soldiers to board games to the playground, parents and educators attempted to produce a very specific result.

It is not too much to claim that, by 1914, most aspects of young men's lives were oriented towards the military. Their naturally aggressive tendencies were co-opted by the state to ensure the production of manly patriotic men who would willingly go to war.

As if in response to the threats to masculinity that men were facing, the society intensified its celebration of all things male even to the point of embracing the ultimate test of manliness: war. War was what young men and boys had been trained for, and when it came they embraced it with enthusiasm.

Even after the horrors became known, the conflict ended, and the survivors came home, manliness and militarism remained central elements of English-speaking Ontario's culture. For those too young to have served, the idea of the Great War became steeped in adventure, and many dreamed of another chance to serve.[18] For some, the dream would become a reality.

Notes

Chapter 1

1. Cited in Thomas P. Socknat, *Witness Against War: Pacifism in Canada, 1900–1945* (Toronto, 1987), 23.
2. Bruce McCall, *Thin Ice: Coming of Age in Canada* (Toronto, 1997), 73.
3. Enlistments in the CEF totalled 465,984 under the voluntary system and 83,355 under the Military Service Act. According to the Department of Militia, the total missing and dead for the country as a whole, not including injured, was 62,928. See J. Castell Hopkins, ed., *Canadian Annual Review of Public Affairs—1919* (Toronto, 1920), 19, 23, 24. According to Robert Bothwell, *A Short History of Ontario* (Edmonton, 1986), 'By June 1918 Ontario, out of a population of 2.5 million, 31 per cent of the Canadian total, had recruited 231,191 young men, or 43 per cent of Canada's enlistments—and the war had still five months to run.' Also see Desmond Morton, *Canada and War—A Military and Political History* (Toronto, 1981), 81; Desmond Morton, *When Your Number's Up—The Canadian Soldier in the First World War* (Toronto, 1993), 61; G.P. de T. Glazebrook, *Life in Ontario: A Social History* (Toronto, 1971), 225; Joseph Schull, *Ontario Since 1867* (Toronto, 1978), 214.
4. Eric Hobsbawm defines an invented tradition as a 'set of practices, normally governed by overtly or tacitly accepted rules of a ritual or symbolic nature, which seek to inculcate certain values and norms of behaviour by repetition, which automatically implies a continuity with the past. In fact, where possible, they normally attempt to establish continuity with a suitable historic past.' Eric Hobsbawm, 'Introduction', in Hobsbawm and Terrence Ranger, eds, *The Invention of Tradition* (Cambridge, 1983), 1. On instilling values and patriotism, especially in the schools, see Nancy

M. Sheehan, 'Philosophy, Pedagogy, and Practice: The IODE and the Schools in Canada, 1900–1945', *Historical Studies in Education* 2, 2 (1990): 307–9; Bernd Baldus and Meenaz Kassam, 'Make Me Truthful, Good, and Mild': Values in Nineteenth-Century Ontario Schoolbooks', *Canadian Journal of Sociology* 21, 3 (Summer 1996): 327–55.

5. Sergeant Harold Baldwin, *Holding The Line* (Chicago, 1918), vii. For a survey of enlistment motivations, see Michael Howard, 'Patriotism at a dead end', *The Times Literary Supplement*, 6 Jan. 1995, 5.

6. George Sterling Ryerson, *Looking Backward* (Toronto, 1924), 158.

7. On duty, see H.V. Nelles, 'Introduction', in Grace Morris Craig, *But This Is Our War* (Toronto, 1981), xi. For commentary on peer pressure and regular pay, see Alan R. Young, ' "We Throw the Torch": Canadian Memorials of the Great War and the Mythology of Heroic Sacrifice', *Journal of Canadian Studies*, 24, 4 (Winter 1990): 6; J.M. Bumsted, *The Peoples of Canada: A Post-Confederation History* (Toronto, 1992), 61; Morton, *When Your Number's Up*, 50. On the moral outrage factor, see Samuel Hynes, *The Soldier's Tale: Bearing Witness to Modern War* (New York, 1997), 44. For Canada, out of 515,456 soldiers, 228,751 were British-born and 286,705 Canadian-born. Ontario had 205,808 volunteers, Quebec, 52,993, Alberta, 36,013, BC and Yukon, 43,652. Hopkins, ed., *Canadian Annual Review of Public Affairs, 1919*, 23, 24.

8. For example, Geoffrey Best writes, 'The war began with exaltation and rejoicing. The nations that plunged into war gave an appearance of doing so gladly and enthusiastically.' Best, 'The Militarization of European Society, 1870–1914', in J.R. Gillis, ed., *The Militarization of the Western Mind* (New Brunswick, NJ, 1989), 13. For Europe in general, also see Brian Bond, *War and Society in Europe, 1870–1970* (London, 1984), 100; Modris Eksteins, *Rites of Spring: The Great War and the Birth of the Modern Age* (Toronto, 1989), 56; Keith Robbins, *The First World War* (Oxford, 1993), 1. On the situation in Canada, see R. Bothwell, I. Drummond and J. English, *Canada 1900–1945* (Toronto, 1987), 119; Robert Craig Brown and Ramsay Cook, *Canada 1896–1921: A Nation Transformed* (Toronto, 1991), 212; R. Matthew Bray, ' "Fighting as an Ally": The English Canadian Patriotic Response to the Great War', *Canadian Historical Review* 61, 2 (June 1980): 142; John H. Thompson, *The Harvests of War* (Toronto, 1978), 30; David Bourdon, 'Sportsmen's Patriotic Response to the First World War: The Calgary Experience', in *Proceedings of the 5th Canadian Symposium on the History of Sport and Physical Education* (Toronto, 26–9 Aug. 1982), 392; J.W. St G. Walker, 'Race and Recruitment in World War I: Enlistment of Visible Minorities in the Canadian Expeditionary Force', *Canadian Historical Review* 70, 1 (March 1989): 3. Arguably, this was the

dominant view. For the small but vocal pacifist response, see Thomas P. Socknat, *Witness Against War—Pacifism in Canada, 1900–1945* (Toronto, 1987). According to Donald Creighton, although Canada was ready and prepared in spirit the country was certainly deficient in material and organization. The CEF was to be 'the greatest collective enterprise that Canada had ever attempted'. See Creighton, *Canada's First Century, 1867–1967* (Toronto, 1970), 129, 130.

9. See William D. Mathieson, *My Grandfather's War: Canadians Remember the First World War, 1914–1918* (Toronto, 1981), 5; Leslie M. Frost, *Fighting Men* (Toronto, 1967), 15.

10. In 1896, the principal of a local public school wrote, 'Patriotism is defined to be "Love and devotion to one's country; the spirit that prompts to obedience to its laws, to the support and defence of its existence, rights and institutions, and to the promotion of its welfare."' W. Irwin, 'National Patriotism', *Canada Educational Monthly and School Magazine* 25, 10 (October 1896): 281. Elie Kedourie writes that 'Patriotism, affections for one's country, or one's group, loyalty to its institutions and zeal for its defense, is a sentiment known among all kinds of men.' *Nationalism* (London, 1960), 71.

11. Neil McDonald, 'Forming the National Character: Political Socialization in Ontario Schools, 1867–1914', Ph.D. thesis (OISE, U of T, 1980), 22. McDonald's highly significant work is essential in understanding the political nature of schooling during the period under examination here. For more on the idea of schooling and citizenry, see Barry M. Franklin, *Building the American Community: The School Curriculum and the Search for Social Control* (Philadelphia, 1986).

12. See David Ralph Spencer, 'An Alternate Vision: Main Themes in Moral Education in Canada's English-Language Working-Class Press, 1870–1910', Ph.D. thesis (University of Toronto, 1990), 161.

13. See, respectively, R. Gordon Kelly, 'Social Factors Shaping Some Late Nineteenth Century Children's Periodical Fiction', in James H. Fraser, ed., *Society and Children's Literature* (Boston, 1978), 37; Barrie Stacey, *Political Socialization in Western Society* (London, 1978), 2–3.

14. Spencer, *An Alternate Vision*, 9, 161, 162–5.

15. R. Gordon Kelly, *Mother Was a Lady: Self and Society in Selected American Children's Periodicals, 1865–1890* (Westport, Connecticut, 1974), xv, xvi; Neil McDonald, 'Egerton Ryerson and The School as an Agent of Political Socialization', in Neil McDonald and Alf Chaiton, eds, *Egerton Ryerson and His Times* (Toronto, 1978), 81.

16. See Fred I. Greenstein, 'Political Socialization', *Encyclopedia of the Social Sciences*, 1968, 551, quoted in Stacey, *Political Socialization*, 3, 4, 9.

17. For commentary on the state control of the family, especially through a Foucaltian framework, see Jacques Donzelot, *The Policing of Families*, translated by Robert Hurley (New York, 1979), 6–7. On social control in general, see F.M.L. Thompson, 'Social Control in Victorian Britain', *The Economic History Review*, Second Series, 34, 2, (May 1981): 199, 200, 206; Gareth Stedman Jones, *Languages of Class: Studies in English Working Class History, 1832–1982* (Cambridge, 1983), 79; and Stanley Cohen and Andrew Scull, 'Introduction: Social Control in History and Sociology', in Cohen and Scull, eds, *Social Control and the State: Historical and Comparative Essays* (Oxford, 1983), 4. Cohen and Scull based their argument on David Rothman's ideas. For the very important connection between social control and leisure, see Peter Bailey, *Leisure and Class in Victorian England: Rational Recreation and the Contest for Control, 1830–1885* (London, 1987), 137. F.M.L. Thompson suggests that the 'commercialization of leisure and the growth of an entertainment industry did more to transform leisure behaviour than all the efforts of reforming groups to substitute forms of approved rational recreation for what they saw as the licentious, abandoned, drunken, brutal, futile, degenerate, or even subversive forms of traditional amusements.' 'Social Control in Victorian Britain', 200. While commercialization was undoubtedly effective at transforming leisure, those with the power, finances, and control to commercialize often came from the same background as the reformers.

18. See Thompson, 'Social Control in Victorian Britain', 200–1; John A. Mayer, 'Notes Towards A Working Definition of Social Control in Historical Analysis', in Cohen and Scull, eds, *Social Control and the State*, 17.

19. Mayer, 'Notes Towards a Working Definition of Social Control in Historical Analysis', in *Social Control and the State*, 17–19, 22–23.

20. See Morris Janowitz, 'Sociological Theory and Social Control', *American Journal of Sociology* 81, 1 (July 1975): 82–108; Mayer, 'Notes Towards a Working Definition of Social Control', 24, 25, 27, 28.

21. See E.P. Thompson, *The Making of the English Working Class* (London 1991), 8; Anthony Giddens, *The Constitution of Society: Outline of the Theory of Structuration* (Cambridge, 1984), xxii; Anthony Giddens, *Social Theory and Modern Sociology* (Stanford, 1987), 204; Susan Desan, 'Crowds, Community and Ritual in the Work of E.P. Thompson and Natalie Davis', in Lynn Hunt, ed., *The New Cultural History* (Berkeley, 1989), 55; Keith McClelland, 'Introduction', in Harvey J. Kaye and McClelland, eds, *E.P. Thompson: Critical Perspectives* (Cambridge, 1990), 4.

22. Giddens, *Social Theory*, 220; Anthony Giddens, *New Rules of Sociological Method* (New York, 1976), 121.

23. Stephen Hardy and Alan Ingham, 'Games, Structures, and Agency: Historians on the American Play Movement', *Journal of Social History* No. 17 (Winter 1983): 286.

24. Antonio Gramsci, *Selections from the Prison Notebooks*, ed. and trans. Quentin Hoare and G. Nowell Smith (New York, 1987), 12.

25. T.J. Jackson Lears, 'The Concept of Cultural Hegemony: Problems and Possibilities', *American Historical Review* 90 (1985): 569, 570.

26. Ibid., 571, 573, 577.

27. Keith Walden, 'Speaking Modern: Language, Culture, and Hegemony in Grocery Window Displays, 1887–1920', *Canadian Historical Review* 70, 3 (1989): 299.

28. See C.P. Stacey, *Canada and the Age of Conflict*, vol. 1 (Toronto, 1977), 52; Douglas L. Cole, 'Imperialism and Nationalism in English Speaking Canada', in J.M. Bumsted, ed., *Documentary Problems in Canadian History*, vol. 2, *Post-Confederation* (Georgetown, Ont., 1968), 69, 72; Robert J.D. Page, 'Carl Berger and the intellectual origins of Canadian imperialist thought, 1867–1914', *Journal of Canadian Studies* 5, 3 (August 1970): 40. Feelings for Britain were extremely strong during the first real test of imperial allegiance, the Crimean War. See A.W. Rasporich, 'Imperial Sentiment in the Province of Canada during the Crimean War, 1854–1856', in W.L. Morton, ed., *The Shield of Achilles: Aspects of Canada in the Victorian Age* (Toronto, 1968).

29. See A.B. McKillop, *A Disciplined Intelligence: Critical Inquiry and Canadian Thought in the Victorian Era* (Montreal and Kingston, 1979), x; William Westfall, *Two Worlds: The Protestant Culture of Nineteenth-Century Ontario* (Montreal and Kingston, 1989), 9–11. The Catholic population, according to Westfall, was approximately 17 per cent. On the importance of Methodism and child-rearing, Neil Semple writes: 'Methodism aspired to help civilize and Christianize the entire nation and much of the world beyond.... The greatest protection that society could offer to children was religion itself, just as the Church could be a powerful ally for the young in the secular world.' ' "The Nurture and Admonition of the Lord": Nineteenth-Century Canadian Methodism's Response to Childhood', *Social History* 14, 27 (May 1981): 158.

30. According to Lynne Marks, 'In the early 1880s the editor of the *Campbellford Herald* claimed that no more than one-fifth of the inhabitants of the village could be found in church on a Sunday morning. If true, this would put Campbellford's religious participation lower than Toronto's, since the *Globe*'s 1882 survey found 45 per cent of Torontonians in

church on a given Sunday. The *Herald*'s estimate may have been unreasonably low, but other evidence suggests that churchgoing was a far from universal practice in small communities.' Marks, *Revivals and Roller Rinks: Leisure and Identity in Late-Nineteenth-Century Small-Town Ontario* (Toronto, 1996), 25. For more on the idea of Christianity evolving into a 'social religion', see Ramsay Cook, *The Regenerators: Social Criticism in Late Victorian English Canada* (Toronto, 1985), 4. The Houston quote is from Neil Sutherland, 'Introduction: Towards A History of English-Canadian Youngsters', in Michael B. Katz and Paul H. Mattingly, eds, *Education and Social Change: Themes from Ontario's Past* (New York, 1975), xxiii.

31. Westfall, *Two Worlds*, 14.

32. Perhaps the most telling indication of the differences between Quebec and Ontario arose during the South African or Boer War. If the Boer War was the high-water mark of imperialism, massive support from English Canadians was juxtaposed against virtually no support from French Canadians. The war was an adventure for the few who went, but, significantly, it was also a chance for them to demonstrate their allegiance to Britain and to reaffirm their ties to the Empire. As J.L. Granatstein and David J. Bercuson write, It could even be termed an 'emotional response to the British imperial spirit' so rampant at the time. J.L. Granatstein and David J. Bercuson, *War and Peacekeeping* (Toronto, 1991), 1.

On the other hand, Henri Bourassa, editor of *Le Devoir*, and the voice of French Canada, used it as an opportunity to warn of the dangers of imperialism. 'While Quebeckers sympathized with Bourassa's contention that Canada should not be called upon to fight the Empire's wars outside North America, English Canadians identified Canada's interests with the Empire. Many English Canadians were therefore eager to assert the country's nationhood through active participation in imperial affairs.' Ramsay Cook, 'The Triumph of Materialism', in Craig Brown, ed., *The Illustrated History of Canada* (Toronto, 1991), 402, 403.

33. Douglas L. Cole, 'Canada's "Nationalistic" Imperialists', *Journal of Canadian Studies* 5, 3 (August 1970): 45; John T. Saywell, 'The 1890s', in J.M.S. Careless and R. Craig Brown, eds, *The Canadians: 1867–1967* (Toronto, 1967), 120. Saywell writes, 'Many English Canadians in their search for a meaningful nationality adopted the pan-Anglo-Saxonism that afflicted late Victorian England. In a nation so defined and among a majority firm in the belief in racial superiority there was little room for French Canadians.'

34. On modernity and change in general, see Keith Walden, *Becoming Modern in Toronto: The Industrial Exhibition and the Shaping of a Late*

Victorian Culture (Toronto, 1997), 4. For specific references to the displacement of masculinity, see Andrew Tolson, *The Limits of Masculinity: Male Identity and Women's Liberation* (New York, 1977); Robert L. Griswold, *Fatherhood in America: A History* (New York, 1993), 32.

35. Westfall, *Two Worlds*, 8.

36. See E. Anthony Rotundo, 'Body and Soul: Changing Ideals of American Middle-Class Manhood, 1770–1920', *Journal of Social History* 4, 16 (1983): 32.

37. David I. Macleod, *Building Character in the American Boy: The Boy Scouts, YMCA, and Their Forerunners, 1870–1920* (Madison, 1983), xiv.

38. See Michael Kimmel, *Manhood in America: A Cultural History* (New York, 1996), 157. On the increased emphasis on athletics and the connection between games and war, see Peter McIntosh, *Fair Play: Ethics in Sport and Education* (London, 1979), 34; Arthur R.M. Lower, *Canadians in the Making*, 323. Lower writes, 'The team games are plainly sublimated warfare. Each team represents a tribe, or nation.'

39. R. Tait Mackenzie, MD, 'Canada's Opportunity in Physical Education', in *Addresses Delivered Before The Canadian Club of Montreal, 1911–1912*, 23 Feb. 1912.

40. An extensive literature discusses the connections between national characteristics, climate, and 'breeding'. See Carl Berger, 'Canadian Nationalism', in J.M. Bumsted, ed., *Interpreting Canada's Past*, vol. 2, *Post-Confederation*, 2nd edn (Toronto, 1993), 215–36; Berger, *The Sense of Power. Studies in the Ideas of Canadian Imperialism, 1867–1914* (Toronto, 1970), 128–30; Gerald Redmond, 'Viceregal Patronage: The Governors-General Canada and Sport in the Dominion, 1867–1909', in J.A. Mangan, ed., *The Cultural Bond: Sport, Empire, Society* (London, 1992), 159. For Canada's unique ability to instil vigour, see Leila G. Mitchell Mckee, 'Nature's Medicine: The Physical Education and Outdoor Recreation Programmes of Toronto's Voluntary Youth Organizations, 1880–1930', in *Proceedings of the Fifth Canadian Symposium on the History of Sport and Physical Education*, 130. For games and sports and their role in character-building, see Nancy B. Bouchier, 'Idealized Middle-Class Sport for a Young Nation: Lacrosse in Nineteenth-Century Ontario Towns, 1871–1891', *Journal of Canadian Studies*, 29, 2 (Summer 1994): 89; Jean Barman, 'Sports and the Development of Character', in Morris Mott, ed., *Sports in Canada: Historical Readings* (Mississauga, Ont., 1989), 234–46; Dominick Cavallo, *Muscles and Morals: Organized Playgrounds and Urban Reform, 1880–1920* (Philadelphia, 1981), 94.

41. For the evolution of thinking on children and childhood, see Philip Aries, *Centuries of Childhood: A Social History of the Family* (New

York, 1962); John Sommerville, *The Rise and Fall of Childhood* (Beverly Hills, 1980).

42. Macleod, *Building Character in the American Boy*, xv.

43. Lynne Segal, *Slow Motion: Changing Masculinities/Changing Men* (London, 1990), 111. Also see Edward N. Saveth, 'Theodore Roosevelt: Image and Ideology', *New York History* (January 1991); Joe L. Dubbert, *A Man's Place: Masculinity in Transition* (Englewoods Cliffs, NJ, 1979), 75.

44. See Peter G. Filene, *Him/Her/Self: Sex Roles in Modern America*, 2nd edn (Baltimore, 1986), 94, 98; Peter G. Filene, 'In Time of War', in Elizabeth and Joseph Pleck, eds, *The American Man* (Englewood Cliffs, NJ, 1980), 323.

45. The Lieutenant Governor's speech is quoted in both the *Toronto Mail*, 14 October 1892, and the *Toronto Globe*, 14 October 1892.

46. Peter Gay, *The Cultivation of Hatred*, vol. 3 of *Bourgeois Experience: Victoria to Freud* (New York, 1993), 3; Steven Mintz, *A Prison of Expectations: The Family in Victorian Culture* (New York, 1983), 24–5. Also see Asa Briggs, *Victorian Things* (London, 1988), 1; T.J. Schlereth, *Victorian America: Transformations in Everyday Life, 1876–1915* (New York, 1991), xii. Schlereth writes that 'the period ended not at the English monarch's death in 1901 but with the outbreak of World War I in 1814.'

47. See Brown and Cook, *Canada 1896–1921*, 5–6.

48. McKillop, *A Disciplined Intelligence*, ix.

49. Allan Smith, *Canada—An American Nation? Essays on Continentalism, Identity and the Canadian Frame of Mind* (Montreal and Kingston, 1994), 268, 30, 31, 32, 41. The Duncan quotes are cited by Smith. Peter Desbarats, 'The Special Role of Magazines in the History of Canadian Mass Media and National Development', in Benjamin D. Singer, ed., *Communications in Canadian Society*, 4th edn (Toronto, 1995), 77, notes that reprints from US periodicals were available to Canadian magazines at little or no cost. This availability is part of the reason that 'American ideas' reached such a wide audience in Canada. But this situation changed in the early 1890s, prompting Goldwyn Smith to write: 'In the field of periodical literature what chance can our Canadian publishers have against an American magazine with a circulation of a hundred and fifty thousand, and a splendour of illustration such as only a profuse expenditure can support?' Paul Rutherford states that, according to the trade journal *Printer and Publisher* (Aug. 1895: p. 1), most major newspapers, including the *Toronto Globe*, 'took much of their world news from American papers or news agencies and often subscribed to American syndication services which supplied feature material, humour

and fiction and even sermons. According to a survey taken in 1895, thirty-three newspapers subscribed to the United Press Service and fourteen to the rival Associated Press.' Some years later, this situation led to the creation of the Canadian Press. Rutherford, 'Made in America: The Problem of Mass Culture in Canada', in David H. Flaherty and Frank E. Manning, eds, *The Beaver Bites Back? American Popular Culture in Canada* (Montreal and Kingston, 1993), 263.

50. Smith, *Canada—An American Nation?* 42, 43.
51. Ibid., 44.

Chapter 2

1. W.L. Morton, 'Victorian Canada', in Morton, ed., *The Shield of Achilles: Aspects of Canada in the Victorian Age* (Toronto, 1968), 312, 321.
2. Heather Reilly, 'Attitudes to Women in Sport in Eastern Ontario: The Early Years, 1867–1885', in *Proceedings of the 5th Canadian Symposium on the History of Sport and Physical Education* (Toronto, 26–9 Aug. 1982), 380.
3. See Denis Judd, *Empire: The British Imperial Experience from 1765 to the Present* (London, 1996), 50–7; John Gooch, *Armies in Europe* (London, 1980), ch. 5; Desmond Morton, *Ministers and Generals: Politics and the Canadian Militia, 1868–1904* (Toronto, 1970), 3; Stephen J. Harris, *Canadian Brass: The Making of a Professional Army, 1860–1939* (Toronto, 1988), 11.
4. Morton, *Ministers and Generals*, vii, 3, 4; Harris, *Canadian Brass*, 11, 12.
5. Harris, *Canadian Brass*, 12.
6. See Granatstein and Bercuson, *War and Peacekeeping*, 1; George Woodcock, *The Century That Made Us: Canada 1814–1914* (Toronto, 1989), 51, 53.
7. Barbara M. Wilson, ed., *Ontario and the First World War, 1914–1918: A Collection of Documents* (Toronto, 1977), xvii; Randall White, *Ontario 1610–1985* (Toronto, 1985), 157. Of course, by 'society' White meant the ruling élite. For an example of one sector of this society, see Hereward Senior, 'Orangeism in Ontario Politics, 1872–1896', in Donald Swainson, ed., *Oliver Mowat's Ontario* (Toronto, 1972), 136–53. Also see D.F. Macdonald, 'The Great Migration', in C.J. Bartlett, ed., *Britain Pre-eminent: Studies of British World Influence in the Nineteenth Century* (London, 1969), 54–75; Creighton, *Canada's First Century*, 90. Perhaps the most obvious and influential indicator of sympathy towards Britain was the Empire Club of Canada. According to J. Castell Hopkins, 'The Empire Club of Canada, with its 600 members and a series of addresses by prominent men during the season of 1910 (for example),

was a considerable factor in the presentation of Imperial and patriotic ideas to the people—partly through the ordinary medium of press reports, partly through verbatim reports of the speeches in *Toronto Saturday Night*, partly through the publication of a yearly volume containing these addresses.' Hopkins, ed., *Canadian Annual Review of Public Affairs—1910* (Toronto, 1911), 125, 126. Speeches to the Empire Club in the years just prior to World War I reflected the élite view of the essential place of Canada in the British Empire and the need to maintain these ties. See, for example, Rev. Father Bernard Vaughan, 'Empire Citizenship', 15 Sept. 1910; A. Monro Grier, KC, 'Toronto and Her Place in the British Empire', 16 May 1912; 'How and Why is Canada British?', 23 Oct. 1912; W.H. Hearst, 'Ontario's Place in the Empire', 28 Nov. 1912; Rev. C.S. Eby, 'Imperial Citizenship', 28 Jan. 1909.

8. Barbara M. Wilson, 'Introduction', in Wilson, ed., *Ontario and the First World War*, ix; Frost, *Fighting Men*, 11.

9. Gwynne Dyer and Tina Viljoen, *The Defense of Canada: In the Arms of the Empire, 1760–1939* (Toronto, 1990), 199; Robert Bothwell, *A Short History of Ontario* (Edmonton, 1986), 112; Arthur R.M. Lower, *My First Seventy-five Years* (Toronto, 1967), 17.

10. See R.G. Moyles and Doug Owram, *Imperial Dreams and Colonial Realities: British Views of Canada, 1880–1914* (Toronto, 1988), 15; Schull, *Ontario Since 1867*, 109.

11. Patrick A. Dunae, *Gentlemen Emigrants: From the British Public Schools to the Canadian Frontier* (Toronto, 1981), 1, 8. Robert Bothwell (*A Short History of Ontario*, 99) writes that 'The largest ethnic group, if it can be called that, was "English"—701,413 out of the 1901 total of 2.2 million. Then followed "Irish", north and south, and Scots, 400,000 of them. . . . Methodists were the largest religious sect (666,000), followed by Presbyterians (477,000).' Consequently, 'the racial and religious complexion of the province, together with traditions and memories inherited from struggling forefathers, shaped its politics.'

12. Ross McCormack, 'Immigration and Ethnicity', in J.M. Bumsted, ed., *Interpreting Canada's Past*, vol. 2, *Post-Confederation*, 2nd edn (Toronto, 1993), 337.

13. Eric J. Hobsbawm, *Nations and Nationalism Since 1870* (Cambridge, 1990), 88.

14. For more on this point, see Liah Greenfeld, *Nationalism: Five Roads to Modernity* (Cambridge, Mass., 1992), 3.

15. See Berger, *The Sense of Power*, 99; Robert Lanning, 'Mapping the Moral Self: Biography, State Formation and Education in Ontario, 1820–1920', Ph.D. thesis (University of Toronto/OISE, 1990), 175.

16. Brown and Cook, *Canada 1896–1921*, 26–8.

17. Alan R. Young, ' "We Throw the Torch"—Canadian Memorials of the Great War and the Mythology of Heroic Sacrifice', *Journal of Canadian Studies* 24, 4 (Winter 1990): 5. See Mike O'Brien, 'Manhood and the Militia Myth: Masculinity, Class and Militarism in Ontario, 1902–1914', *Labour/Le Travail* 42 (Fall 1998): 115. For a fascinating look at militarism and its encroachment into Edwardian society that is applicable to Ontario as well, see Anne Summers, 'Edwardian Militarism', in R. Samuel, ed., *Patriotism*, vol. 1 (London, 1989). After listening to an enlistee reminisce about his experience in the Great War, Summers wondered, 'what on earth possessed him to join up; what was the connection, if any, between his initial enthusiasm for the war and the fact that before 1914 he had been active in the Boy Scouts?' Summers concludes that a wide and persistent range of military or militaristic modes of thinking must have developed during this period. See Anne Summers, 'Militarism in Britain Before WWI', *History Workshop* 2 (Autumn 1976): 104, 105.

18. Desmond Morton and J.L. Granatstein, *Marching to Armageddon: Canadians and the Great War, 1914–1918* (Toronto, 1989), 7. According to Gwynne Dyer and Tina Viljoen, 'Canada wasn't alone in being drawn into the *vortex of militarism*, of course. In Australia, New Zealand and South Africa too, entire national communities of European descent were being psychologically prepared to sacrifice their young men in huge numbers in the forthcoming struggle between the European great powers.' Dyer and Viljoen, *The Defense of Canada*, 180. On drill and rifle associations and Egerton Ryerson's support, see Garry J. Burke, 'Good for the Boy and the Nation: Military Drill and the Cadet Movement in Ontario Public Schools, 1865–1911', Ed.D. thesis (University of Toronto/OISE, 1995), 8. On the impact of the American Civil War, see Martin Green, *The Great American Adventure* (Boston, 1984), 16. On the rise of organizations, see O'Brien, 'Manhood and the Militia Myth', 118.

19. Brian Bond, *War and Society in Europe: 1870–1970* (London, 1984), 63.

20. *The Shorter Oxford English Dictionary*, 1973, 1323. Also see John Gillis, 'Introduction', in Gillis, ed., *The Militarization of the Western Mind* (New Brunswick, NJ, 1989), 1; C. Frederick Hamilton, 'Militarism', *The University Magazine* 9, 4 (1910): 524–41; C.B. Otley, 'Militarism and Militarization in the Public Schools, 1900–1972', *British Journal of Sociology* 29, 3 (Spring 1978): 322; Volker R. Berghahn, *Militarism: The History of an International Debate, 1861–1976* (n.p.: Great Britain, 1981), 2, 7, 9, 11. For a recent and wide-ranging discussion on this topic, see Charles Townshend, 'Militarism and Modern Society', *Wilson Quarterly* (Winter 1993): 71–82; Berger, *The Sense of Power*, 233.

21. See Berghahn, *Militarism*, 9; Jeffrey Richards, 'With Henty to Africa', in Richards, ed., *Imperialism and Juvenile Literature* (Manchester, UK,

1989), 81; John Mackenzie, *Propaganda and Empire: The Manipulation of British Public Opinion, 1880–1960* (Manchester, UK, 1984).

22. See Donna H. Felger, comp., *Boy's Fashions—1885 to 1905* (Cumberland, 1984); G. de T. Glazebrook, Katherine B. Brett, and Judith McErvel, *A Shopper's View of Canada's Past—Pages from Eaton's Catalogues, 1886–1930* (Toronto, 1969), 13; *Toronto Globe*, 20 Mar. 1891; Christina Bates, '"Beauty Unadorned": Dressing Children in Late Nineteenth-Century Ontario', *Material History Bulletin* 21 (Spring 1985): 31, 32.

23. Sheet music was extremely popular before the invention of the gramophone. See the entry 'Patriotic Music' in Helmut Kallman, Gilles Potvin, and Kenneth Winters, eds, *Encyclopedia of Music in Canada* (1981), 729–30, cited in Carman Miller, *Painting the Map Red: Canada and the South African War, 1899–1902* (Montreal and Kingston, 1993), 460, n. 14. The drill editorial is from *Toronto Globe*, 27 Feb. 1875. The mock battles are mentioned in *Toronto World*, 7 Nov. 1890. On the Industrial Exhibition military re-enactments, see *Toronto World*, 1 Sept. 1897; *Toronto Mail*, 18 Sept. 1888, 8 Sept. 1938; also Keith Walden, *Becoming Modern in Toronto: The Industrial Exhibition and the Shaping of a Late Victorian Culture* (Toronto, 1997), 267–8. On the positive attitudes to war, see John M. Mackenzie, 'Introduction', in Mackenzie, ed., *Popular Imperialism and the Military, 1850–1950* (Manchester, UK, 1992), 2. Even when organizations and individuals weren't completely overwhelmed by the militarization of society, positive attributes could always be found. Mike O'Brien observes that 'While Ontario clergymen were split on the question of military service, many lauded it for teaching men obedience, respect and reverence for authority.' O'Brien, 'Manhood and the Militia Myth', 199.

24. Gwynne Dyer, *War* (New York, 1985), 14. The information on this rather sweeping and heavily debated subject is as vast as it is contentious. See, for example, William Arkin and Lynne R. Dobrofsky, 'Military Socialization and Masculinity', *Journal of Social Issues* 34, 1 (1978): 154: 'Until recently, young males have either been lured or drafted into the military with the promise of becoming a man: "Join the army, Be a man"; "The army will make a man out of you"; or from the marines: "We only take a few good men." In general, the military has been defined as an opportunity to grow up, a belief that youth leaving home will return as men. Because there has been evidence enough in the form of medals, honors, recognition, jobs, education and success for those who have served, popular expectations have reinforced the military's role as a patriarch under whose influence and discipline a doubtless man emerges.'

25. Ray Raphael, *The Men from the Boys: Rites of Passage in Male America* (Lincoln, Neb., 1988), x. For commentary on various rites of passage in diverse cultural settings, see David D. Gilmore, *Manhood in the Making: Cultural Concepts of Masculinity* (New Haven, 1990). Commenting on Gilmore's work, Helen Kanitkar writes that this period (1870–1914) 'was a time when, as Gilmore has put it, "manhood was an artificial product coaxed by austere training and testing."' Linking the public school ethos with popular fiction, Kanitkar continues: 'As elsewhere, manhood was defined in terms of the received notions of the social environment and the age: To achieve it boys underwent rites of passage which separated them from home and the familiar, most particularly from their mothers' care and influence. They passed into the charge of men unrelated to them and were to suffer the dominance of older boys with authority over them. They were expected to stand on their own feet until the time came for them to exercise authority and power in their turn. The aim was to make "big men of little boys" as the Boy Scout manuals of the day put it.' Helen Kanitkar, ' "Real True Boys": Moulding the Cadets of Imperialism', in Andrea Cornwall and Nancy Lindisfarne, eds, *Dislocating Masculinity: Comparative Ethnologies* (New York, 1994), 184, 185.

26. Raphael, *The Men from the Boys*, x, xvi, 6, 10, 19.

27. Ibid., 19. On the obsessive interest in defining and promoting manliness, see Robyn Cooper, 'The Fireman: Immaculate Manhood', *Journal of Popular Culture* 28, 4 (Spring 1995): 146. Two among many works that address the concerns centring on feminization are Michael Roper and John Tosh, 'Introduction: Historians and the Politics of Masculinity', in Roper and Tosh, eds, *Manful Assertions: Masculinities in Britain Since 1800* (London, 1991), 19; David G. Pugh, *Sons of Liberty: The Masculine Mind in Nineteenth-Century America* (Westport, Conn., 1983), 116–17. According to Margaret Marsh, an influential essay by John Higham— 'The Reorientation of American Culture in the 1890s', in Higham, ed., *Writing American History* (Bloomington, Ind., 1970)—'triggered an interest in the historical meaning of masculinity.' Higham argued that beginning in the 1890s, 'the country witnessed a national urge to be young, masculine and adventurous, when Americans rebelled against the frustrations, the routine, and the sheer dullness of an urban-industrial culture. He cited the growing popularity of boxing and football, a disaffection from genteel fiction, and, not least, the rise in the level of national bellicosity, as important indicators of a new public mood.' Margaret Marsh, 'Suburban Men and Masculine Domesticity, 1870–1915', in Mark C. Carnes and Clyde Griffen, eds, *Meanings For Manhood: Constructions of Masculinity in Victorian America* (Chicago, 1990), 111.

28. See Raphael, *The Men from the Boys*, 19, 20, 110; Dyer, *War*, 8. Varda Burstyn is much more direct when it comes to linking sports and war: 'sport crafted a streamlined, abstracted, quantifiable version of the manly, antifeminine warrior and succeeded in creating a form of male ritual with great cathecting power and historical adaptability.' Burstyn sees a direct connection between sport, combat, and organized violence. Like John Keegan (whose *A History of Warfare* she cites), Burstyn recognizes the European notion of conscription as an important rite of passage that gave young men a tangible notion of manhood and, most importantly, placed more emphasis on the inevitable militarization of society. Burstyn, *The Rites of Men: Manhood, Politics and the Culture of Sport* (Toronto, 1999), 65-7.

29. See Angus McLaren, *The Trials of Masculinity: Policing Sexual Boundaries, 1870–1930* (Chicago, 1997), 33; Kim Townsend, *Manhood at Harvard: William James and Others* (New York, 1996), 17; Gail Bederman, *Manliness and Civilization: A Cultural History of Gender and Race in the United States, 1880–1917* (Chicago, 1995), 18; Michael Kimmel, *Manhood in America: A Cultural History* (New York, 1996), 119–20; Elliot J. Gorn, *The Manly Art: Bare-Knuckle Prize Fighting in America* (Ithaca, NY, 1986), 193; Joseph Kett, *Rites of Passage: Adolescence in America, 1790 to the Present* (New York, 1977), 173.

30. Morris Mott, 'One Solution to the Urban Crisis: Manly Sports and Winnipeggers, 1900–1914', *Urban History Review* 12, 2 (Oct. 1983): 58; Gillian Avery, *Childhood's Pattern: A Study of Heroes and Heroines of Children's Fiction, 1770–1950* (London, 1975), 170; Bederman, *Manliness and Civilization*, 18. In his study of masculinity and honour in France, Robert A. Nye writes that 'Honour is a masculine concept. It has traditionally regulated relations among men, summed up the prevailing ideals of manliness, and marked the boundaries of masculine comportment.' Nye, *Masculinity and Male Codes of Honour in Modern France* (New York, 1993), vii.

31. See J.A. Mangan and James Walvin, eds, *Manliness and Morality: Middle Class Masculinity in Britain and America 1800–1940* (New York, 1987), 1; George L. Mosse, *Fallen Soldiers: The Memory of the World Wars* (New York, 1990), 59, 60; James Mangan, *The Games Ethic and Imperialism* (London, 1985), 18; Raphael, *The Men from the Boys*, x; Norman Vance, *The Sinews of the Spirit* (Cambridge, 1985), 8–10; Bruce Haley, *The Healthy Body and Victorian Culture* (Cambridge, Mass., 1978), 206; Filene, *Him/Her/Self*, 70; Gorn, *The Manly Art*, 140; Leonore Davidoff and Catherine Hall, *Family Fortunes: Men and Women of the English Middle Class, 1780–1850*, (Chicago, 1987), 108–13; Roper and Tosh, 'Introduction', in *Manful Assertions*, 2; Mott, 'One Solution to the Urban Crisis', 58; Reilly, 'Attitudes to Women in Sport in Eastern

Ontario', 380–1; Carnes and Griffen, eds, *Meanings for Manhood*, chs 1, 4, 7. For some further observations on the definition, use, and evolution of 'manliness', see Stefan Collini, ' "Manly Fellows": Fawcett, Stephen and the Liberal Temper', and Boyd Hilton, 'Manliness, Masculinity and the Mid-Victorian Temperament', both in Lawrence Goldman, ed., *The Blind Victorian: Henry Fawcett and British Liberalism* (Cambridge, 1989), 41–59, 60–79. In *A Manly Boy: A Series of Talks and Tales for Boys* (Toronto, 1900), 17, Reverend Louis Albert Banks writes: 'No quality is more admirable in a man or a boy than what we commonly call pluck. A plucky person does not easily give up the thing which seems desirable for him to do.' C. Frederick Hamilton, writing in 1910, said that 'courage is to a man what chastity is to a woman—the one indispensable thing.' Cited in O'Brien, 'Manhood and the Militia Myth', 119.

32. George L. Mosse, *Nationalism and Sexuality* (New York, 1985), 13.

33. Ibid., 23, 86.

34. E. Anthony Rotundo, 'Body and Soul: Changing Ideals of American Middle-Class Manhood, 1770–1920', *Journal of Social History* 16 (1983): 28. Rotundo (p. 23) suggests that American masculine ideals, not manliness per se, shifted from a 'standard rooted in the life of the community and the qualities of a man's soul to a standard of manhood based on individual achievement and the male body.' This doesn't contradict Mosse's emphasis, but suggests that divergent competing ideals of masculinity could function in the same sphere.

35. George L. Mosse, *The Image of Man: The Creation of Modern Masculinity* (New York, 1996), 3.

36. See Joseph H. Pleck, 'The Theory of Male Sex-Role Identity: Its Rise and Fall, 1936 to the Present', in Harry Brod, ed., *The Making of Masculinities: The New Men's Studies* (Boston, 1990), 22.

37. Kimmel, *Manhood in America*, 120.

38. On this reverence, see, for example, Richard Jenkins, *The Victorians and Ancient Greece* (Cambridge, Mass., 1980), 192–226. On the Greek perspective, see John Keegan, *A History of Warfare* (New York, 1993), 246–8; Yvon Garlan, 'War and Peace', in Jean-Pierre Vernant, ed., *The Greeks*, trans. Charles Lambert and Teresa Lavender Fagan (Chicago, 1995), 72–8. Varda Burstyn (*The Rites of Men*, 29) pulls no punches: 'Both symbolically and practically, Greek athletics were rehearsals for military action; in a phrase, they were "war games".'

39. Allen Guttmann, *The Erotic in Sports* (New York, 1996), 17, 38–9.

40. Richard Gruneau and David Whitson, *Hockey Night In Canada: Sport, Identities and Cultural Politics* (Toronto, 1993), 68.

41. See Nancy B. Bouchier, 'Idealized Middle-Class Sport for a Young Nation: Lacrosse in Nineteenth-Century Ontario Towns, 1871–1891',

Journal of Canadian Studies 29, 2 (Summer 1994): 93. A significant impetus for the Christian manliness movement may have stemmed from the fact that in the second half of the nineteenth century there was a strong association between religion and femininity.

42. David W. Brown, 'Social Darwinism, Private Schooling and Sport in Victorian and Edwardian Canada', in J.A. Mangan, ed., *Pleasure, Profit, Proselytism: British Culture and Sport at Home and Abroad 1700–1914* (London, 1988), 216, 217. Also see Olive Anderson, 'The Growth of Christian Militarism in Mid-Victorian Britain', *English Historical Review* 86 (1971): 46–72. This essay focuses on an earlier period than the one under discussion here, but it contains a number of valuable insights into the place of the British army in the eyes of the public. For a history of the British public school tradition and its Christian influences in early Ontario, see J.D. Purdy, 'The English Public School Tradition in Nineteenth-Century Ontario', in F.H. Armstrong, ed., *Aspects of Nineteenth-Century Ontario* (Toronto, 1974), 237–52.

43. David W. Brown, 'Prevailing Attitudes Towards Sport, Physical Exercise and Society in the 1870s: Impressions from Canadian Periodicals', *Canadian Journal of History of Sport* 17, 2 (Dec. 1986): 58; Alan Metcalfe, 'Some Background Influences on Nineteenth Century Canadian Sport and Physical Education', *Canadian Journal of History of Sport and Physical Education* 5, 1 (May 1974): 67.

44. Haley, *The Healthy Body and Victorian Culture*, 142.

45. Norman Vance, *The Sinews of the Spirit* (Cambridge, 1985), 1, 10.

46. Burke, 'Good for the Boy', 81.

47. Mark Girouard, *The Return to Camelot: Chivalry and the English Gentleman* (New Haven, 1981), 3–5, 8.

48. Ibid., 7.

49. John R. Gillis, *Youth and History: Tradition and Change in European Age Relations, 1770–Present* (New York, 1974), 111.

50. On the fire brigades, see Marks, *Revivals and Roller Rinks*, 117–18.

51. See Rotundo, 'Body and Soul', 28; *Toronto Globe*, 14 May 1895.

52. O'Brien, 'Manhood and the Militia Myth', 122, 126–8. In regard to women in the workforce, he writes: 'In 1911 work outside the home was largely a male preserve. 2,358,519 men were employed (86.5%) and 366,629 women (13.5%).' The latter figure, however, represents an increase in the number of working women over previous decades, and it does not account for the major increases in the teaching field. See Bill Freeman and Richard Nielsen, *Far From Home: Canadians in the First World War* (Toronto, 1999), 6.

53. F.J. Campbell, 'The Canadian Militia', *Queen's Quarterly* 10, 2 (Oct. 1902): 199; *Toronto Globe*, 7 Nov. 1890.

54. Marks, *Revivals and Roller Rinks*, 118, 119.

55. Ibid., 119–20.

56. See Miller, *Painting the Map Red*, 6, 7; E.A. Hardy and H.M. Cochrane, *Centennial Story: The Board of Education for the City of Toronto, 1850–1950* (Toronto, 1950), 224.

57. *Toronto Empire*, 14 May 1894; *Toronto Globe*, 4–18 Feb. 1899, 25 May 1899, cited in Bruce Carter, 'James L. Hughes and the Gospel of Education', Ed.D. thesis (University of Toronto/OISE, 1966), 343.

58. *Toronto Globe*, 24 May 1894.

59. Granatstein and Bercuson, *War and Peacekeeping*, 7; Desmond Morton, *A Military History of Canada* (Edmonton, 1990), 93, 94; Brown and Cook, *Canada, 1896–1921*, 165.

60. Brown and Cook, *Canada, 1896–1921*, 166–7; Granatstein and Bercuson, *War and Peacekeeping*, 16; Morton, *A Military History of Canada*, 106, 107; Cecilia Morgan, *Public Men and Virtuous Women: The Gendered Languages of Religion and Politics in Upper Canada, 1791–1850* (Toronto, 1996), 23–4, 48. Granatstein and Bercuson (p. 17) write: 'The idea that determined young farmers and merchants, clutching the Union Jack in one hand and a flintlock in the other hand, saved Canada for the Empire was all-pervasive.'

61. Morton, *A Military History of Canada*, 109, 110.

62. See Campbell, 'The Canadian Militia', 197, 208. Also see Lieutenant Colonel A.B. Cunningham, *Queen's Quarterly* 19, 4 (1912); Morton, *A Military History of Canada*, 96; Desmond Morton, *Canada and War* (Toronto, 1981), 9; Marks, *Revivals and Roller Rinks*, 118.

63. See John Springhall, Brian Fraser, and Michael Hoare, *Sure and Steadfast: A History of The Boys' Brigade—1893 to 1983* (London, 1983), 25–6. The literature on martyrdom is mentioned primarily in a British context, yet it has strong parallels to the Canadian situation. See J.A. Mangan, 'Duty unto Death: English Masculinity and Militarism in the Age of the New Imperialism', in Mangan, ed., *Tribal Identities: Nationalism, Europe, Sport* (London, 1996), 10. The power of the Loyalist myth still lingered even after the Great War. George Sterling Ryerson attributed the enthusiastic and patriotic response of young men to the CEF to the Loyalist legacy. In 1924 he wrote, 'The "spirit" of the Loyalists was demonstrated in the loyalty of Canada in the Great War, when nearly half a million Canadians voluntarily enlisted for service in defense of the Empire.' Ryerson, *Looking Backward*, 152.

Chapter 3

1. Daphne Read, ed., *The Great War and Canadian Society: An Oral History* (Toronto, 1978), 90, 99.

2. On the regime of the clock and the mechanization of society, see Alan Trachtenberg, *The Incorporation of America: Culture and Society in the Gilded Age* (New York, 1982), 7; Kimmel, *Manhood in America*, 83, 89.

3. T.J. Jackson Lears, *No Place of Grace: Antimodernism and the Transformation of American Culture, 1880–1920* (Chicago, 1981, 1994), 98.

4. See Read, ed., *The Great War and Canadian Society*, 14.

5. Ernest Renan, cited in Morton, *Canada and War*, 14; Miller, *Painting the Map Red*, 9; Sandra Gwyn, *Tapestry of War: A Private View of Canadians in the Great War* (Toronto, 1992), 50; Morton and Granatstein, *Marching to Armageddon*, 1; William James, 'The Moral Equivalent of War' (1910), in Leon Bramson and George W. Goethals, eds, *War: Studies from Psychology, Sociology, Anthropology* (New York, 1968), 23; Captain William Wood, 'In Case of War', *The Canadian Magazine* 11, 2 (June 1898): 93–5. The *Harper's* article is quoted in Lynne B. Iglizkin, 'War, Sex, Sports, and Masculinity', in L.L. Farrar, Jr, ed., *War: A Historical, Political and Social Study* (Santa Barbara, Calif., 1978), 64. Advertisements to subscribe to *Harper's Magazine* appeared in numerous Canadian journals. See, for example, *Canada Educational Monthly* 5, 11 (Nov. 1883): 3.

6. Miller, *Painting the Map Red*, 8, 9.

7. See Arthur R.M. Lower's comments on 'other' wars in his autobiography, *My First Seventy-five Years*, 15–17.

8. Norman Penlington, 'Ontario's Contribution to the South African War', *Ontario History* 42, 4 (1950): 171; Schull, *Ontario Since 1867*, 126. Penlington writes: 'For Canada as a whole the war provided a stage on which to demonstrate her political determination: for Ontario the war illustrated the influence of the province on federal policy.' This suggests how important and powerful Ontario had become in the Confederation, and how close its ties were to Britain.

9. Lower, *My First Seventy-five Years*, 17.

10. See Saywell, 'The 1890s', 134; Brown and Cook, *Canada 1896–1921*, 163; Miller, *Painting the Map Red*, xi; Granatstein and Bercuson, *War and Peacekeeping*, 1. See *The Canadian Magazine* 15, 4 (Aug. 1900), which contains 'The Maple Leaf in South Africa', by a Canadian Officer, 339–46, and 'A Short History of the Boer War', by Norman Patterson, 347–56.

11. Lower, *My First Seventy-five Years*, 117. For the tightening of the tie to Britain, see George F. Stanley, *Canada's Soldiers: The Military History of an Unmilitary People* (Toronto, 1960), 288.

12. Robert Shipley, *To Mark Our Place: A History of Canadian War Memorials* (Toronto, 1987), 41, 42; Desmond Morton, *A Military History of Canada* (Edmonton, 1999), 117.

13. Berger, *The Sense of Power*, 3, 4, 9; C.P. Stacey, *Canada and the Age of Conflict*, vol. 1, *1867–1921* (Toronto, 1977), 52; Woodcock, *The Century That Made Us*, 104.

14. Penlington, 'Ontario's Contribution', 172; Berger, *The Sense of Power*, 5, 9, 41.

15. Penlington, 'Ontario's Contribution', 172–3.

16. Berger, *The Sense of Power*, 15; Woodcock, *The Century That Made Us*, 105.

17. See Bumsted, *The Peoples of Canada*, 150–1; Berger, *The Sense of Power*, 233, citing C.F. Hamilton, 'Shall Canada Have a Navy', *University Magazine* 7 (Oct. 1909): 397.

18. Woodcock, *The Century That Made Us*, 105.

19. See Sheehan, 'Philosophy, Pedagogy, and Practice: The IODE and the Schools in Canada', 308–10; Brown and Cook, *Canada 1896–1921*, 42, 43.

20. Schull, *Ontario Since 1867*, 127; Brown and Cook, *Canada 1896–1921*, 31; Penlington, 'Ontario's Contribution', 173; *Toronto Mail and Empire,* 24 May 1894.

21. Berger, *The Sense of Power*, 236.

22. Page, 'Canada and the Imperial Idea in the Boer War Years', 34, 45. One could add Penlington's similar observations: 'the popularity of such works as *Deeds that Won the Empire* show that it was not hard for the young man of the late nineteenth century to see adventure in war. So lightheartedly did some volunteers of the first contingent enter the war that a war correspondent wrote that many of them believed that "they were going on one of the greatest outings of their lives,—a gigantic picnic." ' Penlington, 'Ontario's Contribution', 173. The idea of war as an adventure was extremely pervasive during this period and carried over completely intact to World War I.

23. James L. Hughes was an enthusiastic supporter of drill in the schools. His influence on Ontario education policy was enormous. In 1874 Hughes was made Inspector of Schools for Toronto, and he later became Chief Inspector. Organized play and the cadets were enterprises to which he devoted a great deal of energy. He was also known as an extreme patriot and worked hard to strengthen the bond of Empire. Hughes was active in the League of Empire and was one of the Canadian delegates when the Empire League was formed in 1894. Importantly, he regarded Colonel George T. Denison as one of the 'greatest Canadians'. See Carter, 'James L. Hughes and the Gospel of Education'; Hardy and Cochrane,

Centennial Story: The Board of Education for the City of Toronto; Lorne Pierce, *Fifty Years of Public Service: A Life of James L. Hughes* (Toronto, 1924). Pierce's flattering memoir paints a very rosy picture of Hughes.

24. Sigmund Samuel, *In Return: The Autobiography of Sigmund Samuel* (Toronto, 1963), 31; Ronald G. Haycock, *Sam Hughes: The Public Career of a Controversial Canadian, 1885–1916* (Ottawa and Waterloo, Ont., 1986), 1, 2, 9, 10, 13; J. Castell Hopkins, *Canadian Annual Review —1912* (Toronto, 1913), 284.

25. Page, 'Canada and the Imperial Idea in the Boer War Years', 48; Mariana Valverde, *The Age of Light, Soap, and Water: Moral Reform in English Canada, 1885–1925* (Toronto, 1991), 20; Anna Davin, 'Imperialism and Motherhood', *History Workshop* 5 (1978): 9, 12.

26. On the 'idea' of childhood, see Michelle Perrot, 'Roles and Characters', in Perrot, ed., *A History of Private Life: From the Fires of Revolution to the Great War*, vol. 4, general eds, Philippe Ariès and Georges Duby, trans. Arthur Goldhammer (Cambridge, Mass., 1990), 203. In early modern Europe, Ariès suggests in his often quoted work, the increasing survival rates for children led to greater investments in emotional attachment. Thus 'the character and development of childhood . . . could legitimately become of crucial significance to the entire community.' *Centuries of Childhood*, 38; also see Semple, ' "The Nurture and Admonition of the Lord:" ', 158. On how the family became linked to the state as well as the increasing mechanization of the family, see Robert L. Griswold, *Fatherhood in America* (New York, 1993), 31–3. On the move towards rule, professionals, and guidance, see Tannis Peikoff and Stephen Brickley, 'Creating Precious Children and Glorified Mothers: A Theoretical Assessment of the Transformation of Childhood', in Russell Smandych, Gordon Dodds, and Alvin Esau, eds, *Dimensions of Childhood: Essays on the History of Children and Youth in Canada* (Winnipeg, 1991), 29. Jacques Donzelot suggests that 'this transformation of the family was not effected without the active participation of women. In working class and bourgeois strata alike—women were the main point of support for all the actions that were directed toward the reformulation of family life. For example, the woman was chosen by the medical and teaching professions to work in partnership with them in order to disseminate their principles, to win adherence to the new norms, within the home.' Donzelot, *The Policing of Families*, trans. Robert Hurley (New York, 1979), xxiii.

27. Starr is quoted in Neil Sutherland, *Children in English Canadian Society: Framing the Twentieth Century Consensus* (Toronto, 1976), 17. On the social engineering of family agencies, see Christopher Lasch, *Haven in a Heartless World: The Family Besieged* (New York, 1977),

13, 14, 18; Hardyment, *Dream Babies: Child Care From Locke to Spock*, 95–100.

28. On the Boer War and military reform, see Carmen Miller, 'Sir Frederick William Borden and Military Reform, 1896–1911', *Canadian Historical Review* 50, 3 (Sept. 1969): 276. Here Miller implies that the performance of non-regular troops initiated contempt for a regular army, in contrast to a citizen army. On immigration and industrialization, see Susan E. Houston, ' "The Waifs and Strays" of a Late Victorian City: Juvenile Delinquents in Toronto', in Joy Parr, ed., *Childhood and Family in Canadian History* (Toronto, 1982), 132, 136; Ian Drummond, *Progress Without Planning: The Economic History of Ontario from Confederation to the Second World War* (Toronto, 1987), 167; J.M.S. Careless, *Toronto to 1918: An Illustrated History* (Toronto, 1984), 109; Keith Walden, *Becoming Modern in Toronto: The Industrial Exhibition and the Shaping of a Late Victorian Culture* (Toronto, 1997), 4, 8; Alvin Finkel and Margaret Conrad, with Veronica Strong-Boag, *History of the Canadian Peoples*, vol. 2, *1867 to the Present* (Mississauga, Ont., 1993), 94; Bothwell, *A Short History of Ontario*, 98; Donald H. Avery, *Dangerous Foreigners: European Immigrant Workers and Labour Radicalism in Canada, 1896–1932* (Toronto, 1979), 16; Donald H. Avery, *Reluctant Host: Canada's Response to Immigrant Workers, 1896–1994* (Toronto, 1995), ch. 1. Keith Walden, in *Becoming Modern*, 4, 8, calls the rate and extent of change in the urban environment 'staggering'. Walden correctly describes this process as one where 'the world seemed to have speeded up, to have become more complex.' Most of this change, especially in urban realms, focused in and on Toronto. Walden states that no other city had the same range of industrial activity as Toronto.

29. Bothwell, Drummond, and English, *Canada 1900–1945*, 14; Sutherland, *Children in English Canadian Society*, 156; Marilyn Barber, 'Canadianization Through the Schools of the Prairie Provinces Before World War I: The Attitudes and Aims of the English-Speaking Majority', in Martin L. Kovacs, ed., *Ethnic Canadians: Culture and Education* (Regina, 1978), 281; Careless, *Toronto to 1918*, 120; Walden, *Becoming Modern in Toronto*, 9; Valerie Knowles, *Strangers At Our Gates: Canadian Immigration and Immigration Policy, 1540–1990* (Toronto, 1992), 91, 92. Bothwell, Drummond, and English write, 'The cities to be sure were confusing. They were growing much too quickly and sanitation, public services and housing facilities could not keep up the pace. . . . Toronto proportionately grew even faster than Montreal.'

30. See David I. Macleod, 'Act Your Age: Boyhood, Adolescence and the Rise of the Boy Scouts of America', *Journal of Social History* 16, 2 (Winter 1992): 3.

31. Madge Merton and The Editor, 'Our Children and Their Reading', *Canadian Magazine* 6, 3 (Jan. 1896): 282. Merton discusses Bok's work.

32. Sutherland, *Children in English Canadian Society*, 17, 25, 26; Joy Parr, 'Introduction', in Parr, ed., *Childhood and Family in Canadian History*, 10; Davin, 'Imperialism and Motherhood', 10.

33. Sutherland, *Children in English Canadian Society*, 17. Also see Jane Lewis, 'Motherhood Issues During the Late Nineteenth and Early Twentieth Centuries: Some Recent Viewpoints', *Ontario History* 75, 1 (Mar. 1983): 5, 6.

34. Valverde, *The Age of Light, Soap, and Water*, 25.

35. Davin, 'Imperialism and Motherhood', 12, 13; Sutherland, *Children in English Canadian Society*, 20, 27.

36. On the training of boys and girls, see Sutherland, *Children in English Canadian Society*, 93; Carroll Smith-Rosenberg, *Disorderly Conduct: Visions of Gender in Victorian America* (New York, 1985), 212. In partial contrast to Smith-Rosenberg's view, Claudia Nelson suggests that the ideas surrounding motherhood changed little prior to 1914 because the necessity of a static maternal image depended on the ability of the mother to present herself as an 'icon'. 'Motherhood, actual or potential, was their stock in trade, and to divest themselves of the secular mariolatry that surrounded them during the high Victorian period would have been to destroy the fulcrum by means of which they expected to move the world.' Nelson, *Invisible Men: Fatherhood in Victorian Periodicals, 1850–1910* (Athens, Ga., 1995), 4.

37. See Carolyn Strange, *Toronto's Girl Problem: The Perils and Pleasures of the City, 1880–1930* (Toronto, 1995), 22, 28. The distinction between a public/masculine culture and a private/feminine sphere was never fully accepted. There has always been a mixing or blurring of the two, especially in Upper Canada. For more on this, see Cecilia Morgan, *Public Men and Virtuous Women: The Gendered Languages of Religion and Politics in Upper Canada, 1791–1850* (Toronto, 1996), 7, 8.

38. John Tosh, 'What Should Historians Do with Masculinity? Reflections on Nineteenth Century Britain', *History Workshop Journal* 38 (1994): 184; Seton cited in Gorn, *The Manly Art*, 183.

39. See Tosh, 'What Should Historians Do with Masculinity', 184; Allan Smith, 'The Myth of the Self-Made Man in English Canada, 1850–1914', *Canadian Historical Review* 59, 2 (1978): 198.

40. John Abbott, 'Accomplishing "a Man's Task": Rural Women Teachers, Male Culture, and the School Inspectorate in Turn of the Century Ontario', 50, and Susan Gelman, 'The "Feminization" of the High School: Women Secondary School Teachers in Toronto: 1871–1930',

77, both in Ruby Heap and Alison Prentice, eds, *Gender and Education in Ontario* (Toronto, 1991).

41. See Lears, *No Place of Grace*, 11; Smith-Rosenberg, *Disorderly Conduct*, 12.

42. S. Silcox, 'Sexless Schools', *Proceedings of the Fortieth Annual Convention of the Ontario Educational Association* (Toronto, 1901), 392.

43. Craig Heron, *The Canadian Labour Movement: A Short History* (Toronto, 1989), 10, 11; Tosh, 'What Should Historians Do with Masculinity', 186.

44. Tosh, 'What Should Historians Do with Masculinity', 188.

45. Desmond Morton, cited in David W. Brown, 'Militarism and Canadian Private Education: Ideal and Practice, 1861–1918', *Canadian Journal of History of Sport* 17, 1 (May 1986): 48.

46. Richard Hofstadter, *Social Darwinism in American Thought* (New York, 1965), 171.

47. Walter Houghton, *The Victorian Frame of Mind* (New Haven, 1957), 209, 210.

48. See David W. Brown, 'Sport, Darwinism and Canadian Private Schooling to 1918', *Canadian Journal of History of Sport* 16, 1 (May 1985): 32; Page, 'Canada and the Imperial Idea', 38, 39.

49. See Angus McLaren, *Our Own Master Race: Eugenics in Canada, 1885–1945* (Toronto, 1990), 9, 49; Pearson cited in Daniel Pick, *War Machine: The Rationalization of Slaughter in the Modern Age* (New Haven, 1993), 81.

50. James and Simmel cited in Peter Gay, *The Cultivation of Hatred*, vol. 3 of *Bourgeois Experience, Victoria to Freud* (New York, 1993), 4; Freud cited in Pick, *War Machine*, 2.

51. See Mackenzie, 'Introduction', in *Popular Imperialism and the Military*, 2; Michael Howard, 'Empires, Nations and Wars', in Howard, *The Lessons of History* (New Haven, 1991), 39; Pick, *War Machine*, 158; George L. Mosse, *The Culture of Western Europe* (London, 1963), 54, 57.

52. See Paul Thompson, *The Edwardians: The Remaking of British Society* (London, 1992), 180; Robert Coles, *The Political Life of Children* (New York, 1986), 61; Howard, 'Empires, Nations and Wars', 39, 40; Richard Gwyn, *Nationalism Without Walls* (Toronto, 1995); Granatstein and Bercuson, *War and Peacekeeping*, 7.

53. Eric Hobsbawm, 'Mass-Producing Traditions: Europe, 1870–1914', in Hobsbawm and Ranger, eds, *The Invention of Tradition*, 263, 264, 271.

54. See Benedict Anderson, *Imagined Communities* (London, 1983); Pick, *War Machine*, 158; James Mayo, *War Memorials as Political Landscape* (New York, 1988), xvi.

55. Coles, *The Political Life of Children*, 60, 61. Also see Michael C.C. Adams, *The Great Adventure: Male Desire and the Coming of World War I* (Bloomington, Ind., 1990), chs 3, 4. This will be expanded on in Chapter 7.
56. See Robert Hughes, *Culture of Complaint* (New York, 1993), 148; Zelinsky, *Nation Into State*, 13.
57. Many of the ideas here have come from the work of Richard Slotkin. See Slotkin, *Regeneration Through Violence: The Mythology of the American Frontier, 1600–1800* (Middletown, Conn., 1973), 3; Slotkin, *Gunfighter Nation: The Myth of the Frontier in Twentieth Century America* (New York, 1992), 13. For the impact of print on glorification, see Zelinsky, *Nation Into State*, 30–1, 41; Robert L. McDougall, 'Public Image Number One: The Legend of the Royal Canadian Mounted Police', in McDougall, *Totems: Essays on the Cultural History of Canada* (Ottawa, 1990), 129. On the popularity of American and British heroes in Canada, see W.H. Kesterton, *A History of Journalism in Canada* (Toronto, 1979), 183.
58. See Cooper, 'The Fireman', 161.
59. See Wendy R. Katz, *Rider Haggard and the Fiction of Empire* (Cambridge, 1987), 28; Vance, *The Sinews of the Spirit*, 1.
60. See Katz, *Rider Haggard and the Fiction of Empire*, 61.
61. Zelinsky, *Nation Into State*, 28, 53.
62. Thomas Carlyle, *Heroes and Hero-Worship* (New York and Boston, 1840), 235; Mangan, 'Duty Unto Death: English Masculinity and Militarism', 15.
63. See Graham Dawson, *Soldier Heroes: British Adventure, Empire, and the Imagining of Masculinities* (London, 1994), 1.
64. Renan cited in John Hutchinson and Anthony D. Smith, eds, *Nationalism* (New York, 1994), 18.
65. See Harvey Green, *Fit For America: Health, Fitness, Sport and American Society* (New York, 1986), 237; Jeffrey Richards, 'Introduction', in Richards, ed., *Imperialism and Juvenile Literature*, 7. Bernard Porter writes, 'Jingoism fed on heroes and wars, and it just so happened that most of Britain's heroes murdered then were murdered in the cause of empire, and most of her wars and quarrels were over colonies.' Porter, *The Lion's Share: A Short History of British Imperialism, 1850–1983*, 2nd edn (London, 1984), 115.
66. See Vance, *The Sinews of the Spirit*, 13; Adams, *The Great Adventure*, 41, 45.
67. See Mosse, *The Image of Man*, 101; Rotundo, *American Manhood*, 5–6; Jeffrey Hantover, 'The Boy Scouts and the Validation of Masculinity', *Journal of Social Issues* 34, 1 (1978): 185.

68. See Haley, *The Healthy Body and Victorian Culture*, 3, 207, 208; Roberta J. Park, 'Biological Thought, Athletics and the Formation of a "Man of Character" 1830–1900', in Mangan and Walvin, eds, *Manliness and Morality*, 7; Theodore P. Greene, *America's Heroes: The Changing Models of Success in American Magazines* (New York, 1970), 127–31. Also see Rotundo, *American Manhood*, 223; Hantover, 'The Boy Scouts', 186. For an interesting comparison, see Leo Lowenthal, 'The Triumph of Mass Idols', in Lowenthal, *Literature, Popular Culture and Society* (Palo Alto, Calif., 1968), 109–40.

69. See Green, *Fit For America*, 203; Rotundo, *American Manhood*, 200, 241; Kett, *Rites of Passage*, 13; Rupert Wilkonson, *American Tough: The Tough Guy Tradition and the American Character* (Westport, Conn., 1984), 116.

70. The 'self-made' man—the entrepreneur or robber baron—holds special appeal in Western society and subsequently in Ontario. See Trachtenberg, *The Incorporation of America*, 5; Lears, *No Place of Grace*, 18; Pugh, *Sons of Liberty*, xix; Harvey Green, *Fit For America*, 203. In an article on the British public school ethos in Ontario, J.D. Purdy writes, 'The barons of Bay and St. James Streets were as heroic to Canadian boys as the imperial demi-gods of Rudyard Kipling or G.A. Henty. To be a leading industrialist or businessman in a small Ontario community was a more honourable (and more profitable) career than to be a political figure.' Purdy, 'The English Public School Tradition in Nineteenth-Century Ontario', 247.

71. Keith A.P. Sandiford, 'The Victorians at Play: Problems in Historical Methodology', *Journal of Social History* 15, 2 (Winter 1981): 277.

72. See Brown, 'Sport, Darwinism and Canadian Private Schooling', 28; David W. Brown, 'Prevailing Attitudes Toward Sport, Physical Exercise and Society in the 1870s: Impressions from Canadian Periodicals', *Canadian Journal of History of Sport* (Dec. 1986): 58–60; Purdy, 'The English Public School Tradition in Nineteenth Century Ontario'.

73. Brown, 'Social Darwinism, Private Schooling and Sport in Victorian and Edwardian Canada', 217.

74. See J.A. Mangan, *Athleticism in the Victorian and Edwardian Public School* (Philadelphia, 1986), 9; J.A. Mangan, *The Games Ethic and Imperialism* (London, 1985), 18. James L. Hughes cited in Sutherland, *Children in English Canadian Society*, 191.

75. Brown, 'Social Darwinism, Private Schooling and Sport in Victorian and Edwardian Canada', 217, 219; Peter Parker, *The Old Lie: The Great War and the Public School Ethos* (London, 1987), 18, 32, 33.

76. See Brown, 'Social Darwinism, Private Schooling and Sport in Victorian and Edwardian Canada', 226; Rotundo, *American Manhood*, 240, 241.

77. Filene, 'In Time of War', 322; Myriam Miedzian, *Boys Will Be Boys* (New York, 1991), 56, 34–6. Filene, of course, is referring to the American situation, but this is relevant (almost identical) to the Canadian case.

78. David Jackson, *Unmasking Masculinity* (London, 1990), 217. On advertising, see Jane Pettigrew, *An Edwardian Childhood* (Boston, 1993), 80; Mackenzie, *Propaganda and Empire*; Jackson Lears, 'American Advertising and the Reconstruction of the Body, 1880–1930', in Kathryn Grover, ed., *Fitness in American Culture* (Amherst, Mass., 1989); William R. Hunt, *Body Love: The Amazing Career of Bernarr Macfadden* (Bowling Green, Ohio, 1996); Gruneau and Whitson, *Hockey Night In Canada*, 62.

79. Robert Wohl, *The Generation of 1914* (Cambridge, Mass., 1979), 23. Also of relevance here is Hugh Cunningham, 'The Language of Patriotism, 1750–1914', *History Workshop Journal* 12 (1981). For the importance of cultural symbolism, see Jackson, *Unmasking Masculinity*, 218. On sports as a metaphor, see Thompson, *The Edwardians*, 185; Paul Fussell, *The Great War and Modern Memory* (New York, 1975), 9. This was taken to the extreme with the incident initiated by one Captain Nevill who kicked a football as the signal to advance. In this case, the mingling of sport and war was complete. See Colin Veitch, ' "Play Up! Play Up! and Win the War!" Football, the Nation and the First World War, 1914–1915', *Journal of Contemporary History* 20 (1985): 363–4. Michael Adams relates that in 'Harold Begbie's book for boys, The Story of Baden-Powell, sports are a paradigm for life. Three officers killed at Mafeking "had run a great race". Baden-Powell holding that city against the Boers is "the intrepid goalkeeper".' Adams, *The Great Adventure*, 38.

Chapter 4

1. Cited in Paul Fussell, *The Boy Scout Handbook and Other Observations* (New York, 1982), 177.

2. See R.G. Moyles, 'A "Boy's Own" View of Canada', *Canadian Children's Literature* 34 (1984): 42.

3. This story has been masterfully documented in Peter Buitenhuis, *The Great War of Words: British, American, and Canadian Propaganda and Fiction, 1914–1933* (Vancouver, 1987), esp. 1. Buitenhuis (p. xviii) writes that, after the horrific war, 'The reading public no longer had the trust in important authors that they had in the days before the Great War. The prestige and power of authorship dwindled significantly.' This suggests that from the period under examination here until approximately 1917, authors wielded enormous influence.

4. See George Parker, *The Beginnings of the Book Trade in Canada* (Toronto, 1984), 13.

5. Ibid.

6. See H. Pearson Gundy, *Book Publishing and Publishers in Canada before 1900* (Toronto, 1965), 31; Parker, *The Beginnings of the Book Trade*, 25.

7. Paul Rutherford, *The Making of the Canadian Media* (Toronto, 1978), 3–4; Parker, *The Beginnings of the Book Trade*, 29; H. Pearson Gundy, 'The Development of Trade Book Publishing in Canada', *Royal Commission on Book Publishing* (Toronto, n.d.), 4.

8. See Parker, *The Beginnings of the Book Trade*, 25, 26, 30; Rutherford, *The Making of the Canadian Media*, 3. The quotation is from Rutherford.

9. Rutherford, *The Making of the Canadian Media*, 3; Parker, *The Beginnings of the Book Trade*, 52.

10. See Gundy, 'The Development of Trade Book Publishing', 22, 24. Commenting on the quality of literacy in relation to the working classes, David Ralph Spencer writes that 'compulsory school attendance did assist in transforming an illiterate society into a literate one. But it is not only literacy but the degree of literacy which is important to this discussion. Labour journalists were aware that a functional ability to read and write existed in the working classes.' Spencer, 'An Alternate Vision', 47.

11. Benedict Anderson, *Imagined Communities* (London, 1991), 36, 38, 44; Lucien Febvre and Henri-Jean Martin, *The Coming of the Book* (London, 1976), 259–60.

12. Stephen Kline, *Out of the Garden* (Toronto, 1993), 80. Also see Neil Postman, *Amusing Ourselves to Death* (New York, 1985), 42; Robert Darnton, 'Towards a History of Reading', *Wilson Quarterly* (Autumn 1989): 93; Neil Postman, *The Disappearance of Childhood* (New York, 1982), 18.

13. See Kline, *Out of the Garden*, 81, on schooling and literacy. For the importance of books as gifts and prizes, see Dorothy Entwistle, 'Embossed Gilt and Moral Tales: Reward Books in English Sunday Schools', *Journal of Popular Culture* 28, 1 (Summer 1994): 81–96; Hardy and Cochrane, *Centennial Story: The Board of Education for the City of Toronto*, 74.

14. See Kline, *Out of the Garden*, 81, 82; and James Walvin, *A Child's World: A Social History of English Childhood, 1800–1914* (London, 1984), 127. The quotation on oral culture is from Susan Houston and Alison Prentice, *Schooling and Scholars in Nineteenth Century Ontario* (Toronto, 1988), 190.

15. Richards, 'Introduction', in Richards, ed., *Imperialism and Juvenile Literature*, 1.

16. Joan Rockwell, *Fact In Fiction: The Use of Literature in the Systematic Study of Society* (London, 1974), 4, 43, 65.

17. See John Cawelti, *Adventure, Mystery and Romance* (Chicago, 1976), for an examination of the intricacies of formula fiction.

18. Anne Scott Macleod, 'Children's Literature and American Culture, 1820–1860', in James H. Fraser, ed., *Society and Children's Literature* (Boston, 1978), 14; R. Gordon Kelly, *Mother Was a Lady*, 4.

19. See Claudia Nelson, *Boys Will Be Girls: The Feminine Ethic and British Children's Fiction: 1857–1917* (New Brunswick, NJ, 1991), 1; Macleod, 'Children's Literature', 15–16; and, especially, Daniel T. Rodgers, 'Socializing Middle-Class Children: Institutions, Fables, and Work Values in Nineteenth-Century America', *Journal of Social History* 13, 3 (Spring 1980): 357.

20. See Dennis Butts, 'The Adventure Story', in Butts, ed., *Stories and Society: Children's Literature in its Social Context* (London, 1992), 67, 68.

21. Rodgers, 'Socializing Middle-Class Children', 356.

22. See Elizabeth Segel, ' "As the Twig is Bent . . .": Gender and Childhood Reading', in Elizabeth A. Flynn and Patrocino P. Schweickart, eds, *Gender and Reading: Essays on Readers, Texts, and Contexts* (Baltimore, 1986), 170, 171; Kimberley Reynolds, *Girls Only? Gender and Popular Children's Fiction in Britain, 1880–1910* (London, 1990), 50.

23. See Segel, ' "As the Twig is Bent . . ." ', 171; Reynolds, *Girls Only?*, 51; Rodgers, 'Socializing Middle-Class Children', 360; Nelson, *Boys Will Be Girls*, 107. Nelson writes, 'Henty's boys are concerned not with what they feel but with what they do.'

24. See Segel, ' "As the Twig is Bent . . ." ', 172–4; Sally Allen McNall, 'American Children's Literature, 1880-Present', in Joseph M. Hawes and N. Ray Hiner, *American Childhood: A Research Guide and Historical Handbook* (Westport, Conn., 1985), 383; Nelson, *Boys Will Be Girls*, 1. Leslie Fiedler has written that at this time American novels were often about 'adventure and isolation plus escape at one point or another, or a flight from society to an island, a woods, the underworld, a mountain fastness—some place, at least, where mothers do not come.' Fiedler, *Love and Death in the American Novel* (New York, 1966), 181. According to Alison Lurie, Mark Twain's *Tom Sawyer* was written in reaction to the moralizing tales of the early part of the century. It is subversive and remarkable in a number of ways. Tom succeeds by lying, stealing, and sneaking around and he is rewarded with gold. See Lurie, *Don't Tell the Grown-ups: Subversive Children's Literature* (Boston, 1990), 4.

25. Reynolds, *Girls Only?*, 59. Varda Burstyn has described 'an exaggerated ideal of manhood linked mythically and practically to the role of the

warrior' as 'hypermasculinity'. Burstyn, *The Rites of Men: Manhood Politics and the Culture of Sport* (Toronto, 1999), 4.

26. See Peter N. Stearns, *American Cool: Constructing a Twentieth-Century Emotional Style* (New York, 1994), 31, 32, 44. Stearns (pp. 32–3) makes an important distinction between fear and anger. 'Fear differed from anger, of course, in that its role in character development was more indirect. Whereas anger could be usefully channelled, fear had no direct utility. Its role was more subtle, providing the test that allowed males to learn their own moral and emotional courage. The links between fear and anger were nevertheless real. Both emotions provided moments of great intensity vital to effective living. Both could be used for motivation and moral development, if properly mastered. The spirited Victorian boy was one who did not avoid fear, but faced it and triumphed over it, while using anger as a spur to action.'

27. Reynolds, *Girls Only?*, 59.

28. See Stanley S. Blair, ' "What are you going to make out of this boy?": The Role of Poetry in the "Management" of Boys, 1875–1900', in Harry Eiss, ed., *Images of the Child* (Bowling Green, Ohio, 1994), 308–9.

29. Joel. Dubbert, *A Man's Place: Masculinity in Transition* (Englewood Cliffs, NJ: Prentice-Hall, 1979), 36.

30. See Blair, ' "What are you going to make out of this boy?" ', 311–15.

31. E. Hershey Sneath and George Hodges, *Moral Training in the School and Home: A Manual for Teachers and Parents* (New York, 1913), 5.

32. Nicholas Tucker, *The Child and the Book: A Psychological and Literary Exploration* (Cambridge, 1990), 123.

33. See F.J. Harvey Darton, *Children's Books in England: Five Centuries of Social Life*, 3rd edn, revised by Brian Alderson (Cambridge, 1982), 302; Mackenzie, *Propaganda and Empire*, 18; Peter Hunt, *An Introduction to Children's Literature* (New York, 1994), 56; Robert H. MacDonald, 'Signs from the Imperial Quarter: Illustrations in *Chums*, 1892–1914', *Children's Literature* 16 (1988): 33; Sheehan, 'Philosophy, Pedagogy, and Practice', 309.

34. Richard Phillips, *Mapping Men and Empire: A Geography of Adventure* (London, 1997), 46.

35. MacDonald, 'Signs from the Imperial Quarter', 31–3.

36. Quoted by Oliver Warner, 'Introduction', in Captain Marryat, *Mr. Midshipman Easy* (London, 1967), xvi–xvii, cited in Hunt, *An Introduction to Children's Literature*, 56, 57.

37. MacDonald, 'Signs from the Imperial Quarter', 33.

38. Eric Quale, *The Collector's Book of Boy's Stories* (London, 1973), 96; Hunt, *An Introduction to Children's Literature*, 60.

39. J.S. Bratton, 'Of England, Home and Duty: The Image of England in Victorian and Edwardian Juvenile Fiction', in John Mackenzie, ed., *Imperialism and Popular Culture* (Manchester, 1986), 76; Richards, 'Introduction', in Richards, ed., *Imperialism and Juvenile Literature*, 1; Kelly, *Mother Was a Lady*, 35.

40. Phillips, *Mapping Men and Empire*, 53; Kline, *Out of the Garden*, 81.

41. Mintz, *A Prison of Expectations*, 22, 23.

42. For concerns over the new mass culture, see Houston and Prentice, *Schooling and Scholars*, 191. The authors write that the 'market for pulp fiction and pictorial periodicals proved insatiable.' Dee Garrison, *Apostles of Culture: The Public Librarian and American Society, 1876–1920* (New York, 1979), 68.

43. See Carole Gerson, *A Purer Taste: The Writing and Reading of Fiction in Nineteenth-Century Canada* (Toronto, 1989), 4; F. Henry Johnson, *A Brief History of Canadian Education* (Toronto, 1968), 72; Sutherland, *Children in English Canadian Society*, 19; Jane Pettigrew, *An Edwardian Childhood* (Boston, 1993), 84. Sutherland (p. 19) writes that 'Parents were enlisted in the battle to prevent poisonous literature from being distributed on railway cars or by newsboys, and from being imported from the United States. They were also asked to encourage the reading and writing of good books and magazines for young people, to buy such literature for their youngsters, and to ensure that it was in school libraries.'

44. S.J. Radcliff, 'History in the Public Schools', *Proceedings of the Forty-Eighth Annual Convention of the Ontario Educational Association* (Toronto, 1909), 268.

45. Bruce Curtis, ' "Littery Merrit", "Useful Knowledge", and the Organization of Township Libraries in Canada West, 1840–1860', *Ontario History* 78, 4 (Dec. 1986): 285; William A. McKeever, *Training the Boy* (Toronto, 1913), 130.

46. See Michael Denning, *Mechanic Accents: Dime Novels and Working-Class Culture in America* (London, 1987), 48; Lorne Bruce, *Free Books For All: The Public Library Movement in Ontario, 1850–1930* (Toronto, 1994), x, xii. On the noble sentiments on how important access to the right kinds of books is, see Rev. W.H. Withrow, 'Public Libraries', *Canada Educational Monthly and School Magazine* 6, 5–6 (May/June 1884): 193.

47. See Paul Rutherford, *A Victorian Authority: The Daily Press in Late Nineteenth-Century Canada* (Toronto, 1982), 34; Murray G. Ross, *The Y.M.C.A. in Canada* (Toronto, 1951), 84, 85; Samuel, *In Return*, 39; 'What the People of Toronto Read', *Canadian Bookman* 1, 2 (Feb. 1909): 20; Mary Vipond, 'Best Sellers in English Canada, 1899–1918:

An Overview', *Journal of Canadian Fiction* 24 (1979): 100. Robert Darnton says that by the late nineteenth century, 'Borrowing patterns in German, English, and American libraries had fallen into a strikingly similar pattern: 70 to 80 per cent of the books came from the category of light fiction (mostly novels).' Darnton, 'Towards a History of Reading', 90.

48. Education Department of Ontario, *Catalogue of Books for Public Libraries, Ontario 1895* (Toronto, 1895), 6–9, 16–18, 20–7, 30–42, 78, 96, 103.

49. Denning, *Mechanic Accents*. In his introduction to readers of his *Kingston's Magazine* in 1859, W.H.G. Kingston expressed a rather different view: 'My great aim is to give you a periodical which you will not throw aside as soon as read, but which you will value and look over years hence as an old familiar friend, when you may be battling with the realities of life under the suns of India, in the backwoods of Canada or in the United States.' Maurice Rooke-Kingsford, *The Life, Work and Influence of William Henry Giles Kingston* (Toronto, 1947), 185, cited in Margery Fisher, *The Bright Face of Danger* (London, 1986), 52.

50. See Darnton, 'Towards a History of Reading', 94; Christopher Wilson, 'The Rhetoric of Consumption: Mass-Market Magazines and the Demise of the Gentle Reader, 1880–1920', in Richard W. Fox and T.J. Jackson Lears, eds, *The Culture of Consumption* (New York, 1983), 41; Richard L. Bushman, *The Refinement of America* (New York, 1992), 280–7, 483–8; Louis Dudek, *Literature and the Press* (Toronto, 1960), 66, 110; Denning, *Mechanic Accents*, 71; Brantlinger, 'How Oliver Twist Learned To Read, and What He Read', in Patrick Scott and Pauline Fletcher, eds, *Culture and Education in Victorian England* (London, 1990), 60, 62; Jan Cohn, *Creating America: George Horace Lorimer and The Saturday Evening Post* (Pittsburgh, 1989), 21–59; Burton Bledstein, *The Culture of Professionalism* (New York, 1976), 77; Fredric Jameson, 'Reification and Utopia in Mass Culture', *Social Text* 1, 130 (1979): 148, cited in Denning, *Mechanic Accents*.

51. See Parker, *The Beginnings of the Book Trade in Canada*, x: Fraser Sutherland, *The Monthly Epic: A History of Canadian Magazines* (Markham, Ont., 1989); Mary Vipond, *The Mass Media in Canada*, rev. edn (Toronto, 1992), ch. 1; W.H. Kesterton, *A History of Journalism in Canada* (Toronto, 1967), 39; Sandro Contenta, *Rituals of Failure: What Schools Really Teach* (Toronto, 1993), 13; Douglas Fetherling, *The Rise of the Canadian Newspaper* (Toronto, 1990), 68.

52. Lower, *My First Seventy-five Years*, 17. Douglas Fetherling writes, 'The War was soon consuming the public's attention as few events outside the country had ever done, but the *Brantford Expositor* was typical

when, in devoting its whole front page to the relief of Mafeking, it used as illustration a sketch of Baden-Powell and a crudely drawn map.' Fetherling, *The Rise of the Canadian Newspaper*, 68–9.

53. See Margaret Beckman, Stephen Langmead, and John Black, *The Best Gift: A Record of the Carnegie Libraries in Ontario* (Toronto, 1984), 31; Gerson, *A Purer Taste*, 4, 7, 67–9; Curtis, ' "Littery Merrit" '; E.C. Bow, 'The Public Library Movement in Nineteenth Century Ontario', *Ontario Library Review* 66 (1982); Bruce, *Free Books For All*, 48, 66; Glazebrook, *Life in Ontario: A Social History*, 195; Schull, *Ontario Since 1867*, 200; Glazebrook, Brett, and McErvel, *A Shopper's View of Canada's Past*, 44, 146; Parker, *The Beginnings of the Book Trade*, ix, 147; V. Merrill Distad with Linda M. Distad, 'Canada', in J. Don Vann and R.T. VanArsdel, eds, *Periodicals of Queen Victoria's Empire* (Toronto, 1996), 103; Vipond, 'Best Sellers in English Canada', 99, 108; Vipond, 'What the People of Toronto Read', 20, 21. According to Beckman, Langmead, and Black, *The Best Gift*, 31: 'By 1904 there were 10 [Carnegie] Libraries in Chatham, Stratford, Windsor, Sarnia, Brantford, Paris, Brockville, Berlin, Smiths Falls, and Lindsay.'

54. Dubbert, *A Man's Place*, 64, 65.

55. Ibid., 73.

56. Graham Dawson, *Soldier Heroes: British Adventure, Empire and the Imagining of Masculinities* (London, 1994), 1–2; Carolyn Steedman, *The Radical Soldier's Tale: John Pearman, 1819–1908* (London, 1988), 37–9, cited in Dawson, *Soldier Heroes*, 2. Peter Buitenhuis writes of Tennyson's 'The Charge of the Light Brigade' that it 'did more to glorify and thus in part to justify the blunders of the Crimean War than any other piece of writing:

> Theirs not to reason why,
> Theirs but to do or die.'

Buitenhuis, *The Great War of Words*, 5–6. Commenting on the connection between boys' youth groups, the military, and adventure novels, John Springhall, Brian Fraser, and Michael Hoare write: 'popular fiction for boys, such as G.A. Henty's *With Kitchener in the Soudan* (1903) or his *By Sheer Pluck: A Tale of the Ashanti War* (1884), brought to many young lives that were drab and ordinary the splendour of military and imperial adventure, and possibly created a frame of mind receptive to uniformed organizations.' Springhall, Fraser, and Hoare, *Sure and Steadfast*, 21.

57. See Richards, 'Introduction', in Richards, ed., *Imperialism and Juvenile Literature*, 1; J.S. Bratton, 'Of England, Home, and Duty: The Image of England in Victorian and Edwardian juvenile fiction', in Mackenzie, ed., *Imperialism and Popular Culture*, 73–93.

58. Mackenzie, *Propaganda and Empire*, 208–9.

59. Vancouver City Archives, 255, vol. 191, *IODE in B.C., 1900–1925*, 24, cited in Sheehan, 'Philosophy, Pedagogy, and Practice', 309.

60. See Martin Green, *Dreams of Adventure, Deeds of Empire* (London, 1979), xi; Dawson, *Soldier Heroes*, 235; Paul Zweig, *The Adventurer* (New York, 1974), vii, 4, 9; Phillips, *Mapping Men and Empire*, 51. George L. Mosse (*The Image of Man*, 114–15) writes: 'Many of the so-called war stories are primarily tales of courage and iron devotion to duty in which a spirit of adventure is also present. Nevertheless, masculinity from the very start was fascinated by adventure, even if this was not consciously expressed. The spirit of adventure was easily co-opted by governments once the war started, used by recruiting posters and war propaganda, or expressed by volunteers eager to serve their country.' Eric Hobsbawm discusses the changing content of fiction during the period under observation here. He calls much of what was written 'exoticism'. Hobsbawm, *The Age of Empire* (London, 1987), 80. On the rise of spy stories, see David Stafford, 'Spies and Gentlemen: The Birth of the British Spy Novel, 1893–1914', *Victorian Studies* (Summer 1981). For an American view of similar literature, see J. Frederick Mac-Donald, ' "The Foreigner" in Juvenile Series Fiction, 1900–1945', *Journal of Popular Culture* 3, 3 (Winter 1974).

61. See C.D. Eby, *The Road to Armageddon: The Martial Spirit in English Popular Literature, 1870–1914* (Durham, NC, 1987), 73; Fisher, *The Bright Face of Danger*, 52; Walvin, *A Child's World*, 128.

62. John M. Mackenzie, 'Introduction', in Mackenzie, ed., *Popular Imperialism and the Military, 1850–1950* (Manchester, UK, 1992), 14.

63. Nelson, *Boys Will Be Girls*, 107.

64. E. Wendy Saul and R. Gordon Kelly, 'Christians, Brahmins and other Sporting Fellows: An Analysis of School Sports Stories', *Children's Literature in Education* 15, 4 (1984): 234; Patrick Howarth, *Play Up and Play the Game: The Heroes of Popular Fiction* (London, 1973), 16; Marjory Macmurchy, 'Tom Brown's School', *Canadian Educational Monthly* 24, 12 (Dec. 1901): 378–80; Rev. Herbert Symonds, 'Arnold of Rugby', *Canadian Educational Monthly* 25, 4 (Apr. 1902); H.W. Auden, 'The Work of the Great English Public Schools, Pt.1', *Educational Monthly of Canada: A Journal of Education* 27, 5 (May 1904): 190–3; Adams, *The Great Adventure*, 16; Eby, *The Road to Armageddon*, 93.

65. Rider Haggard, *Allan Quatermain* (London, 1990 [1887]), 93.

66. Martin Green, *Seven Types of Adventure Tale* (Philadelphia, 1991), 41. Also see Green's other volumes on adventure: *Dreams of Adventure, Deeds of Empire*, xi; *The Great American Adventure* (Boston, 1984), 4; *The Adventurous Male: Chapters in the History of the White Male Mind* (Philadelphia, 1993).

67. Green, *The Great American Adventure*, 6.

68. Hunt, *An Introduction to Children's Literature*, 5.

69. Quoted ibid., 3.

70. Green, *The Great American Adventure*, 1, 2.

71. Lower, *My First Seventy-five Years*, 6.

72. Joseph Bristow, *Empire Boys: Adventures in a Man's World* (London, 1991), 30. Also see Butts, 'The Adventure Story', 67.

73. Cate Haste, *Keep the Home Fires Burning* (London, 1977), 6, 7; Eby, *The Road to Armageddon*, 9. Also see Anne Summers, 'Edwardian Militarism', in Raphael Samuel, ed., *Patriotism*, vol. 1 (London, 1989), 238. For a thorough treatment of literature relating to war during this period, see I.F. Clarke, *Voices Prophesying War* (London, 1966). 'War is fun' is from W.J. Reader, *'At Duty's Call': A Study in Obsolete Patriotism* (Manchester, UK, 1988), 20, 28. On the martial spirit, see Jeffrey Richards, 'Popular Imperialism and the Image of the Army in Juvenile Literature', in Richards, *Popular Imperialism and the Military*, 81, 82. The magazine's role is discussed in Eby, *The Road to Armageddon*, 73. Robert MacDonald, ' "Calling All Chums—And Speaking of Squissies": The Construction of Gender in the British Boys' Periodicals, 1890–1918', lecture draft, 6 Apr. 1989, 1.

74. See Bernard Porter, *The Lion's Share: A Short History of British Imperialism, 1850–1983*, 2nd edn (New York, 1984), 128–9.

75. John Gooch, 'Attitudes to War in Late Victorian and Edwardian England', in Brian Bond and Ian Roy, eds, *War and Society: A Yearbook of Military History* (London, 1975), 91; Peter Parker, *The Old Lie: The Great War and the Public School Ethos* (London, 1987), 17.

76. Eby, *The Road to Armageddon*, 6.

77. Phillips, *Mapping Men and Empire*, 51. What this may suggest is a further blanket of shared ideas and values about what boys/men should be doing in society, for themselves and for their nation.

78. Quoted in Morton, *When Your Number's Up*, 52.

79. Quoted in Read, ed., *The Great War and Canadian Society: An Oral History*, 90.

80. According to Joseph McAleer, *Popular Reading and Publishing in Britain, 1914–1950* (Oxford, 1992), 7, the co-founder of Mass Observation, Tom Harrison, and his colleagues found that 'popular fiction could promote specific attitudes (such as patriotism) and stereotypes . . . through repetition.'

81. Wendy R. Katz, *Rider Haggard and the Fiction of Empire* (Cambridge, 1987), 1, 4; Patrick Dunae, 'Boy's Literature and the Idea of Empire', *Victorian Studies* 24, 1 (Autumn 1980): 111; Guy Arnold, *Held Fast for*

England: G.A. Henty, Imperialist Boy's Writer (London, 1980), 19; Reynolds, *Girls Only?*, 69.

82. See Howarth, *Play Up and Play the Game*, 78; Merton, 'Our Children', 283; Nelson, *Boys Will Be Girls*, 107; John Cargill Thompson, *The Boys' Dumas: G.A. Henty: Aspects of Victorian Publishing* (Cheadles, Cheshire, UK, 1975), 8; Roy Turnbaugh, 'Images of Empire: George Alfred Henty and John Buchan', *Journal of Popular Culture* 9 (1975): 734, cited in J.A. Mangan, 'Duty unto Death: English Masculinity and Militarism in the Age of the New Imperialism', in Mangan, ed., *Tribal Identities: Nationalism, Europe, Sport* (London, 1996), 25.

83. Darton, *Children's Books in England*, 297; Gail S. Clark, 'Imperial Stereotypes: G.A. Henty and the Boys' Own Empire', *Journal of Popular Culture* 18, 4, 5; (Spring 1985); Tucker, *The Child and the Book*, 154. According to Clark, 'All the racial groups Henty treats do share one trait in common—an inferiority to the British. The universal failure of any group to withstand the British provided the clearest demonstration of their inferiority. Clearly, Henty's descriptions thus amounted to a justification of British dominance on the basis of racial superiority.' Also see Patrick Brantlinger, 'Victorians and Africans: The Genealogy of the Myth of the Dark Continent', in Henry Louis Gates, Jr, ed., *Race, Writing, and Difference* (Chicago, 1985), 185, 194, 198, 207–9; Eric Cheyfitz, *The Poetics of Imperialism* (New York, 1991), 4; Louis James, 'Tom Brown's Imperialist Sons', *Victorian Studies* 17 (1973): 89, 97; Patrick A. Dunae, 'Boy's Literature and the Idea of Race: 1870–1900', *Wascana Review* (Spring 1977): 84. According to Richard Phillips, 'Victorian ideas about race, guided by Darwinian evolutionary theory, filtered through to adventure stories in settings and stories in which whites encounter stock "savages" and members of "degenerate" races. Clashes between white heroes and non-white beliefs, customs, and bodies generally left whites in better shape and confirmed white superiority.' Americans also had deep racial elements in their stories, most notably the Tarzan series, which was written by an American and featured a lost English nobleman who rises above his 'savage environment' due to his superior heredity. See John Newsinger, 'Lord Greystoke and Darkest Africa: The Politics of the Tarzan Stories', *Race and Class* 28, 2 (1986): 60–2.

84. Katz, *Rider Haggard*, 61; Samuel Hynes, *The Soldier's Tale: Bearing Witness to Modern War* (New York, 1997), 11, 12.

85. David A.T. Stafford, 'Spies and Gentlemen', *Victorian Studies* (Summer 1981): 509. During the height of the Cold War (with 'alienation' a key concept being applied to society) the popularity of Ian Fleming's James Bond soared. One can draw parallels between the two periods, espe-

cially in regard to their depictions of manliness and militarism, which in the later period culminated with the debacle of the Vietnam War.

86. Phillips, *Mapping Men and Empire*, 63–4.

87. Quoted in Arnold, *Held Fast for England*, 31, 63.

88. Richards, 'Popular Imperialism and the Image of the Army in Juvenile Literature', 83. Also see Stuart Hannabuss, 'The Henty Phenomenon', *Children's Literature in Education* 14, 2 (Summer 1983): 85. Gail S. Clark writes that 'Henty himself intended that his books serve two functions: teach history and inculcate moral character.' Clark, 'Imperial Stereotypes: G.A. Henty and the Boys' Own Empire', 49. Peter Hunt (*An Introduction to Children's Literature*, 67–8) comments, 'Perhaps the most important genre in fiction was still the "empire-building" novel, led by G.A. Henty and W.H.G. Kingston, and followed by the mass-market "manly boy" cult in which Christianity and the rights of Empire (and the right to plunder the Empire) were more or less conterminous.'

89. R.G. Moyles and Doug Owram, *Imperial Dreams and Colonial Realities: British Views of Canada, 1880–1914* (Toronto, 1988), 39, 43. For one interpretation of the image of the Mountie, see Robert L. McDougall, 'Public Image Number One: The Legend of the Royal Canadian Mounted Police', in McDougall, *Totems: Essays on the Cultural History of Canada* (Ottawa, 1990), 125–42.

90. See Samuel Hynes, *The Edwardian Turn of Mind* (London, 1991), 18; Peter Keating, *The Haunted Study: A Social History of the English Novel, 1875–1914* (London, 1991), 355; Carole Scott, 'Kipling's Combat Zones: Training Grounds in the Mowgli Stories, Captains Courageous, and Stalky & Co.', in Francelia Butler, Barbara Rosen, and Judith A. Plotz, eds, *Children's Literature* #20 (New Haven, 1992), 53; D.H. Stewart, 'Stalky and the Language of Education', in Butler, Rosen, and Plotz, eds, *Children's Literature* #20, 36, 44, 48; Bristow, *Empire Boys*, 40. Bristow is referring for the most part to the *Boy's Own Paper*. For an interesting comparison on the animal theme, see Robert H. MacDonald, 'The Revolt Against Instinct', *Canadian Literature* 84 (1980): 18–29.

91. See Dave Brown, 'Images of Sport in Canadian Fiction: The Contribution of Ralph Connor', in *Proceedings of the 5th Canadian Symposium on the History of Sport and Physical Education* (Toronto, 26–9 Aug. 1982), 24–7.

92. Daniel Francis, *National Dreams: Myth, Memory and Canadian History* (Vancouver, 1997), 30–5; Pierre Berton, *Why We Act Like Canadians* (Toronto, 1982), 43; Ralph Connor, *Corporal Cameron of the North West Mounted Police* (Toronto, 1912). Both Berton and Connor are quoted in Francis.

93. See McAleer, *Popular Reading and Publishing in Britain*, ch. 7; Darton, *Children's Books in England*, 299; Peter Keating, *The Haunted Study: A Social History of the English Novel, 1875–1914* (London, 1991), 36–7; Jack Cox, *Take a Cold Tub, Sir: The Story of The Boy's Own Paper* (Surrey, UK, 1982), 62. Advertisements for the *Boy's Own Paper* and the *Boy's Own Annual* appeared in Canadian magazines. For the *Boy's Own Paper*, see, for example, *Canada Educational Monthly and School Magazine* 1, 10 (Oct. 1879). On page 1, a half-page advertisement for the Canadian edition of the *Boy's Own Paper* listed stories by R.M. Ballantyne ('The Red Man's Revenge'), W.H.G. Kingston, and Jules Verne. The advertisement also stated, 'And for sale by all Booksellers in the Dominion'. *Canadian Educational Monthly and School Magazine* 4, 9 (Sept. 1882): 3, stated in its advertisement that the periodical was addressed to 'Parents, Pupils, Teachers, Trustees, Ministers'. The advertisements appear in consecutive issues. For the *Boy's Own Annual*, see *The Canadian Bookman* 1, 10 (Oct. 1909): 155.

94. The American magazines for children, *St. Nicholas, Pluck and Luck* and *Brave and Bold*, were greatly influenced by the content of boys' manuals and their moral ideas. Like the *Boy's Own Paper*, they also featured 'action-packed' stories in which a boy hero finds the courage and moral fibre to resolve a situation that turns out well. Frank Merriwell and Fred Fearnot were two of the most popular boy heroes. See Dubbert, *A Man's Place*, 36, 37; Kelly, *Mother Was a Lady*, 11–12, 18–19.

95. See Richards, 'Introduction', in Richards, ed., *Imperialism and Juvenile Literature*, 5; Kirsten Drotner, *English Children and Their Magazines, 1751–1945* (New Haven, 1988), 66, 67; Eby, *The Road to Armageddon*, 6; Parker, *The Old Lie*, 127, 135; Kelly Boyd, 'Knowing Your Place— The Tensions of Manliness in Boys' Story Papers, 1918–1939', in M. Roper and J. Tosh, eds, *Manful Assertions* (London, 1991), 146; Macdonald, 'Calling All Chums', 2, 3, 8, 9; Gillian Avery, *Childhood's Pattern: A Study of the Heroes and Heroines of Children's Fiction, 1770–1950* (London, 1975), 194; Reader, *'At Duty's Call'*, 29; Bristow, *Empire Boys*, 14. On the move from didacticism to entertainment, see Drotner, *English Children*, 66, 67. On Jack Harkaway as a model for boys, see MacDonald, 'Calling All Chums', 4; E.S. Turner, *Boys Will Be Boys* (London, 1948), 91.

96. Samuel, *In Return*, 66–7.

97. Grace Morris Craig, *But This Is Our War* (Toronto, 1981), 10. Craig writes: 'From the time he and his friends had learned that Canada was at war, Ramsey's only ambition had been to take part in this great adventure' (p. 58).

98. Samuel Hynes, *A War Imagined: The First World War and English Culture* (London, 1990), 46.

99. See Avery, *Childhood's Pattern*, 194; Pettigrew, *An Edwardian Childhood*, 84. *Chums* 2, 72 (24 Jan. 1894): 352, for example, features two advertisements for air rifles, one that will 'kill birds, rats, rabbits, etc.', and a 'How to Develop Muscle and Improve the Physique' pamphlet available for boys.

100. 'Toronto Battalion: Boys' Brigade Welcomes Home Hon. G.W. Ross', *The Canadian Boy* (Guelph, Ont.) (Oct. 1901): 54–6.

101. John Foster, 'How British Sailors Are Trained; or Life on Board the Ocean Training Ship *Port Jackson*', *Boy's Own Paper* 29, 1450 (27 Oct. 1906): 60.

102. MacDonald, 'Signs from the Imperial Quarter', 35, 39, 43.

103. See, for example, Lord Mountmorres, 'Heroes of To-day: Captain Lord Charles Beresford', *Chums* 7, 51 (30 Aug. 1893): 9; *Young Canada Illustrated Annual 1902* (Toronto, 1902).

104. Arthur Temple, 'Our Great Living Generals: Field-Marshal Viscount Wolseley', *Young Canada Illustrated Annual 1897* (Toronto, 1897), 56–8.

105. Ibid., 97–9.

106. *Boy's Own Paper* 29, 1485 (29 June 1907): 618–19; ibid., 1482 (8 June 1907): 574.

107. Fampton Blewitt, 'A Chat About Armour', *Boy's Own Paper* 29, 1457 (15 Dec. 1906): 170.

108. H. Alexander Parsons, 'The Colonial Coins of the British Empire', *Boy's Own Paper* 29, 1466 (16 Feb. 1907): 317.

109. See, for example, A.P. Hatton, 'Bugle-Calls and Their Meanings' and J. Paul Taylor, 'The 'B.O.P.' Angler', *Boy's Own Paper* 29, 1474 (13 Apr. 1907): 442–3; W.M. Vardon, 'How and Why To Exercise: A Chat on Physical Culture', *Boy's Own Paper* 29, 1453 (17 Nov. 1906): 110.

110. See Moyles and Owram, *Imperial Dreams*, 43; *The Young Canadian* 1, 1 (Jan. 1891); *The Canadian Boy* 2, 6 (May 1901): 6, 8, 20, 26, 28, 35.

111. See Turner, *Boys Will Be Boys*, 78; MacDonald, 'Calling All Chums', 1; Richards, 'Popular Imperialism and the Image of the Army in Juvenile Literature', 81; Geoff Fox, 'Pro Patria: Young Readers and the "Great War"', *Children's Literature in Education* 16, 4 (1985): 238; Eby, *The Road to Armageddon*, 75; Bristow, *Empire Boys*, 20, 21; George Orwell, 'Boys' Weeklies', in *The Collected Essays, Journalism & Letters of George Orwell*, vol. I, *'An Age Like This', 1920–1940*, Sonia Orwell and Ian Angus, eds (London, 1968), 460–85. David I. Macleod writes, 'The motto, "Be Prepared", called for careful preparation for the sort of sudden heroics which now filled boys' stories.' *Building Character In the American Boy* (Madison, 1983), 18.

Chapter 5

1. The School Act of 1871 created what was a codified, modern school system in the province of Ontario, providing free education and initiating compulsory schooling for children between ages seven and 12. According to Paul Axelrod, Ontario was the first province to legislate compulsory attendance. See Alison Prentice, *The School Promoters* (Toronto, 1977), 16; Paul Axelrod, *The Promise of Schooling: Education in Canada, 1800–1914* (Toronto, 1997), 35.

2. See Samuel Bowles and Herbert Gintis, *Schooling in Capitalist America* (New York, 1977), 9; Houston and Prentice, *Schooling and Scholars in Nineteenth Century Ontario*, x; Sutherland, 'Introduction: Towards a History of English-Canadian Youngsters', xx; Neil McDonald, 'Egerton Ryerson and the School as an Agent of Political Socialization', in Neil McDonald and Alf Chaiton, eds, *Egerton Ryerson and His Times* (Toronto, 1978), 84, 98; Andy Green, *Education and State Formation* (London, 1990), 1; Edward R. Tannenbaum, *1900: The Generation before the Great War* (New York, 1976), 31; Bruce Curtis, *Building the Educational State: Canada West, 1836–1871* (London, Ont., 1988); Robert Lanning, 'Moral Character: John Millar and the Educational System in Ontario, 1890–1905', MA thesis (OISE, 1986), 11, 16.

3. Francis, *National Dreams*, 52–6.

4. 'His *Report on a System of Public Elementary Instruction for Upper Canada*, published in 1846, was based on observations he had made in Holland, Belgium, Germany, Switzerland, and Britain in 1844–5, and in the United States, where various systems of physical education already existed.' Don Morrow et al., *A Concise History of Sport in Canada* (Toronto, 1989), 72. See also James L. Gear, 'Factors Influencing the Development of Government Sponsored Physical Fitness Programmes in Canada from 1850 to 1972', *Canadian Journal of History of Sport and Physical Education* 4, 2 (Dec. 1973): 2; Axelrod, *The Promise of Schooling*, 40; Hardy and Cochrane, *Centennial Story: The Board of Education for the City of Toronto*, 187. Friedrich Froebel (1782–1852) was a German philosopher of education who was the originator of the kindergarten. See Robert Ulich, *History of Educational Thought* (New York, 1950). Friedrich Ludwig Jahn was a 'fervent German nationalist (who) believed the heroic qualities needed to unify Germany could be instilled in young people through rigorous physical discipline and gymnastics.' See Dominick Cavallo, *Muscles and Morals: Organized Playgrounds and Urban Reform, 1880–1920* (Philadelphia, 1981), 19. George L. Mosse (*The Image of Man*, 43) writes that Friedrich Jahn 'called gymnastic exercise the "lifeline of the German people"

because it alone would lead to youthfulness and manliness.... Jahn from the very first saw gymnastics as shaping true manliness and also as a preparation for military skills.' Also see Peter McIntosh, *Fair Play: Ethics in Sport and Education* (London, 1979), 47, 48.

5. Axelrod, *The Promise of Schooling*, 25.

6. George S. Tomkins, *A Common Countenance: Stability and Change in the Canadian Curriculum* (Scarborough, Ont., 1986), 36; Axelrod, *The Promise of Schooling*, 25, 26; Green, *Education and State Formation*, 1. Also see E. Brian Titley and Peter J. Miller, eds, *Education in Canada: An Interpretation* (Calgary, 1982), 1. On the 'moulding influence', see Marvin Lazerson, 'Canadian Educational Historiography: Some Observations', in McDonald and Chaiton, eds, *Egerton Ryerson and His Times*, 4–5. On learning being synonymous with state knowledge, see Bruce Curtis, 'Schoolbooks and the Myth of Curricular Republicanism: The State and the Curriculum in Canada West, 1820–1850', *Histoire Sociale/Social History* 16, 32 (1983): 305, 306; Lanning, 'Mapping the Moral Self', 145. On theories of training and socializing children, see Lloyd de Mause, *The History of Childhood* (New York, 1974), 51–3; McDonald, 'Forming the National Character', 34, 35; Rodgers, 'Socializing Middle-Class Children', 358.

7. On patriotism in the school, see, for example, Miss E.J. Preston, 'The Spirit of Patriotism', *Canada Educational Monthly and School Magazine* 14, 3 (Mar. 1892): 85–9; 'Patriotism in Text Books', *Canada Educational Monthly and School Magazine* 18, 3 (Mar. 1896): 102–3; Irwin, 'National Patriotism', 281–4. On citizenship, see Sheehan, 'Philosophy, Pedagogy, and Practice', 307–10; A.A. Jordan, 'The Teaching of Citizenship in the Public School', *Proceedings of the Forty-Sixth Annual Convention of the Ontario Educational Association*, 2–4 Apr. 1907 (Toronto, 1907), 293; A.C. Todd, 'Patriotism, As It Should Be Taught in Our Schools', *Proceedings of the Forty-Sixth Annual Convention of the Ontario Educational Association*, 383, 386. Bruce also said that 'any person who has made his country better for having lived in it is a patriot.' E.W. Bruce, 'Teaching Patriotism', *Proceedings of the Thirty-Seventh Annual Convention of the Ontario Educational Association* (Toronto, 1898), cited in Edwin C. Guillet, *In the Cause of Education* (Toronto, 1960), 182. Paul Axelrod (*The Promise of Schooling*, 56) writes that 'English-Canadian educators sought to instil in schoolchildren a passionate commitment to their Anglo-Saxon heritage and identity. The "Loyalist Cult", which was especially influential in Ontario, spread to other regions by the turn of the century.'

8. C.E. Kelly, 'The Public School and Our National Life', *Proceedings of the Forty-Sixth Annual Convention of the Ontario Educational*

Association, 288; D.D. Moshier, 'The School in the State and the State in the School', *Proceedings of the Forty-First Annual Convention of the Ontario Educational Association* (Toronto, 1902), 384; Joseph G. Elliot, 'Citizen-Making, the Mission of the School', *Proceedings of the Forty-Fifth Annual Convention of the Ontario Educational Association*, 17–19 Apr. 1906 (Toronto, 1906), 331; Lanning, 'Moral Character', 36.

9. Irwin, 'National Patriotism', 282.
10. Preston, 'The Spirit of Patriotism', 86–88.
11. Irwin, 'National Patriotism', 281, 283.
12. W. Irwin, 'National Patriotism' (part II), *Canadian Educational Monthly and School Magazine* 18, 11 (Nov. 1896): 324–6.
13. McDonald, 'Forming the National Character', 54.
14. See Supt. C.B. Gilbert, 'Character and School Education', *Canada Educational Monthly* 21, 2 (Feb. 1898): 48; J.E. Wells, 'The Teacher as a Moulder of Character', *Canada Educational Monthly and School Chronicle* 11, 10 (Oct. 1880): 29.
15. See Lanning, 'Moral Character', 10, 18; John Millar, *School Management* (Toronto, 1897), 58.
16. Millar, *School Management*, 13.
17. Ibid., 12, 26, 27.
18. Neil McDonald, 'Canadianization and the Curriculum: Setting the Stage, 1867–1890', in Titley and Miller, eds, *Education in Canada*, 100. For a similar viewpoint, see Bumsted, *The Peoples of Canada*, 19. For a typical example of indoctrination directed to teachers in regard to the glorification of England, see Prof. Wm Dale, 'The Greatness of England', *Canadian Educational Monthly* 23, 4 (Apr. 1900): 136–8.
19. See Robert M. Stamp, 'Empire Day in the Schools of Ontario: The Training of Young Imperialists', *Journal of Canadian Studies* 8, 3 (1973): 38; McDonald, 'Forming the National Character', 194–6.
20. McDonald, 'Forming the National Character', 194, 196, 197; Sanford Evans, 'Empire Day: A Detailed History of Its Origin and Inception', *Canadian Magazine* 13, 3 (July 1899): 275; Stamp, 'Empire Day in The Schools of Ontario', 32–5. McDonald (p. 195) writes that 'Harcourt vigourously defended the certain advantages of patriotic endeavour like Empire Day against those who warned about jingoism and the emergence of militaristic attitudes.' According to the Department of Education *Annual Report* for 1899, Harcourt felt that 'This exposure imbued the minds of students with "the highest kind of patriotism".'
21. Cited in McDonald, 'Forming the National Character', 224–6.
22. Anne Bloomfield, 'Drill and Dance as Symbols of Imperialism', in J.A. Mangan, ed., *Making Imperial Mentalities: Socialization and British Imperialism* (Manchester, UK, 1990), 74.

23. Ibid., 74, 75; Stamp, 'Empire Day in the Schools of Ontario', 32, 34, 38; Todd, 'Patriotism, As It Should Be Taught in Our Schools', 386.

24. Stamp, 'Empire Day in the Schools of Ontario', 38.

25. See Sheehan, 'Philosophy, Pedagogy, and Practice', 311.

26. Frank Wise, comp., *The Empire Day By Day—A Calendar Record of British Valour and Achievement on Five Continents and on the Seven Seas*, Prepared for the Minister of Education in Connection with Empire Day (Toronto, 1910), 5.

27. *Empire Day in Ontario*, Friday May 22, 1914 (pamphlet), Department of Education, Legislative Assembly of Ontario, 1914.

28. McDonald, 'Forming the National Character', 230.

29. Address by J.L. Hughes, Public School Inspector of Toronto, before the Empire Club of Canada, 2 Nov. 1905, *Empire Club Speeches*, 1906.

30. Dr J.E. Hett, 'The Benefits Derived from Physical Training and Medical Inspection', *Proceedings of the Forty-Eighth Annual Convention of the Ontario Educational Association*, 13–15 Apr. 1909 (Toronto, 1909), 347. Borden is quoted in Sutherland, *Children in English Canadian Society*, 191. Merritt is cited in Berger, *The Sense of Power*, 246.

31. Berger, *The Sense of Power*, 235, 192; Frank Cosentino and Maxwell L. Howell, *A History of Physical Education in Canada* (Toronto, 1971), 28.

32. J. Thomas West, 'Physical Fitness, Sport and the Federal Government: 1909 to 1954', *Canadian Journal of History of Sport and Physical Education* 4, 2 (Dec. 1973): 29.

33. Desmond Morton, 'The Cadet Movement in the Moment of Canadian Militarism, 1900–1914', *Journal of Canadian Studies* 13, 2 (Summer 1978): 57; Houston and Prentice, *Schooling and Scholars in Nineteenth Century Ontario*, 251; Axelrod, *The Promise of Schooling*, 56. Houston and Prentice write, ' "A few parents have objected", the local superintendent honestly admitted, "but generally, the drill has been quite acceptable and beneficial." ' On Canadianization, see Kelly, 'The Public School and Our National Life', 289. Kelly states that 'The public school is the greatest Canadianizing power that is making for the unifying of all our people into a Canadian race with common aspirations for the future greatness of our country.'

34. J.R. Lumby, 'The Stranger Within Our Gates', *Proceedings of the Fifty-First Annual Convention of the Ontario Educational Association*, 9–11 Apr. 1912 (Toronto, 1912), 351, 356; George S. Tomkins, *A Common Countenance: Stability and Change in the Canadian Curriculum* (Scarborough, Ont., 1986), 123.

35. John Herald, 'Sport in Our Schools', *Canada Educational Monthly and School Chronicle* 11, 9 (Sept. 1880): 380, 389; Prof. Archibald

Cuthbertson, 'Physical Culture in Schools and Colleges', *Canada Educational Monthly and School Magazine* 11, 10 (Oct. 1889): 297, 298.

36. James L. Hughes, *Manual of Drill and Calisthenics* (Toronto, 1879), 2, cited in Carter, 'James L. Hughes and the Gospel of Education', 46, 47.

37. Archibald Cuthbertson, 'Physical Culture in Schools and Colleges', 300, and W.B.T. Macaulay, 'Physical Culture in the Public Schools', 230–1, both in *Dominion Educational Association: The Minutes of Proceedings, with Addresses, Papers, and Discussions of the First Convention of the Association*, 1892 (Montreal, 1893).

38. President Hyde, 'The Social Mission of the Public School', *Canadian Educational Monthly and School Magazine* 18, 11 (Nov. 1896): 330.

39. On the challenge to manliness, see David G. Pugh, *Sons of Liberty: The Masculine Mind in Nineteenth Century America* (Westport, Conn., 1983), 150; Macleod, *Building Character in the American Boy*, 52; Anne Douglas, *The Feminization of American Culture* (New York, 1977). On the growing numbers of female teachers, see Robert M. Stamp, 'Evolving Patterns of Education: English-Canada from the 1870's to 1914', in J.D. Wilson, R. Stamp, and L.P. Audet, eds, *Canadian Education: A History*, (Scarborough, 1970), 317.

40. S. Silcox, 'Sexless Schools', *Proceedings of the Fortieth Annual Convention of the Ontario Educational Association* (Toronto, 1901), 390.

41. Susan Gelman, 'The "Feminization" of the High School: Women Secondary School Teachers in Toronto, 1871–1930', in Ruby Heap and Alison Prentice, eds, *Gender and Education in Ontario* (Toronto, 1991), 78. In the same volume, also see John Abbott, 'Accomplishing "A Man's Task": Rural Women Teachers, Male Culture, and the School Inspectorate in Turn of the Century Ontario'. Abbott (p. 49) states that women were paid lower wages than men and that as more women came into the system, it was the men who were elevated to the higher ranks.

42. Silcox, 'Sexless Schools', 392.

43. F.J. Campbell, 'Relation of Our Educational System to Practical Life', *Queen's Quarterly* 10, 2 (Oct. 1902): 214.

44. Maurice Hutton, 'The Strathcona Trust', *Proceedings of the Fifty-First Annual Convention of the Ontario Educational Association*, 9–11 Apr. 1912 (Toronto, 1912), 328, 329.

45. S. Truman, 'Military Training in Schools', *Proceedings of the Forty-Eighth Annual Convention of the Ontario Educational Association*, 13–15 Apr. 1909 (Toronto, 1909), 314; W. Scott, 'The Value of Deportment', *Proceedings of the Thirty-Fourth Annual Convention of the Ontario Educational Association in Session with the Dominion Educational Association*, 16–18 Apr. 1895 (Toronto, 1895), 346; Sandro

Contenta, *Rituals of Failure: What Schools Really Teach* (Toronto, 1993), 25; W.F. Moore, 'The Boy Best Equipped for the Duties of Life', *Proceedings of the Forty-First Annual Convention of the Ontario Educational Association* (Toronto, 1902), 294, 295.

46. See Tomkins, *A Common Countenance*; Contenta, *Rituals of Failure*, 16–18; Axelrod, *The Promise of Schooling*, 57.

47. W.E. Groves, 'Physical Training: Its Value and Necessity', *Proceedings of the Forty-Fifth Annual Convention of the Ontario Educational Association*, 17–19 Apr. 1906 (Toronto, 1906), 285, 292, 293.

48. Burke, 'Good for the Boy', 92, 107–10, 111, 114.

49. Morton, 'The Cadet Movement', 59; Hardy and Cochrane, *Centennial Story: The Board of Education for the City of Toronto*, 159. Minister Ross constantly sought to equate sport and drill with self-control, self-defence, and other manly notions. See Lanning, 'Mapping the Moral Self', 285, 349.

50. D.M.L. Farr, *The Canadian Encyclopedia*, Second Edition, vol. 3, (Edmonton, 1988), 2015.

51. The Trinity College circular is cited in David W. Brown, 'Militarism and Canadian Private Education: Ideal and Practice, 1861–1918', *Canadian Journal of History of Sport* 17, 1 (May 1986): 46; J.J. Findlay, 'The British Army and the British Schoolboy', *Canada Educational Monthly* 23, 10 (Oct. 1900): 302, 306.

52. Pierce, *Fifty Years of Public Service*, 70.

53. On the interest and acceptance of the cadets, see Lieut.-Col. E.W. Haggerty, 'History of the Cadet Movement in Canada', *Proceedings of the Fifty-Fourth Annual Convention of the Ontario Educational Association*, 5–8 Apr. 1915 (Toronto, 1915), 158. Sam Hughes is quoted in Robert M. Stamp, *The Schools of Ontario, 1876–1976* (Toronto, 1982), 93–5. Like many of his generation and place, Hughes saw drill and the trappings of militarism as a panacea for all that was wrong with society. A lad who received military training would no doubt be superior in virtually every way to one who did not. Not only would he be 'highly cultured, open-hearted, level-headed', or in a word, manly, but he would 'be less likely to yield to the temptations besetting the pathway in life'. See Hughes, 'The Relationship between the School and the Empire', 301. On the numbers who had drilled, see Morton, *When Your Number's Up*, 4; Berger, *The Sense of Power*, 5.

54. See Cosentino and Howell, *A History of Physical Education in Canada* (Toronto, 1971), 14–16, 24–33; Sutherland, *Children in English Canadian Society*, 191; Marta Danylewycz and Alison Prentice, 'Canadian Education Before the Great War', in J.M. Bumsted, ed., *Interpreting Canada's Past*, vol. 2, *Post-Confederation*, 2nd edn (Toronto, 1993),

258; Gear, 'Factors Influencing the Development of Government Sponsored Physical Fitness Programmes in Canada', 11, 5.

55. See Morrow et al., *A Concise History of Sport in Canada*, 78; Carter, 'James L. Hughes and the Gospel of Education', 47.

56. Robert Lanning, *Dictionary of Canadian Biography*, vol. 13, *1901–1910* (Toronto, 1994), 703–5.

57. Morrow et al., *A Concise History of Sport in Canada*, 78; Millar, *School Management*, 31; A.H. Morrison, 'Physical Education', *Proceedings of the Twenty-First Annual Convention of the Ontario Education Association*, Apr. 1881, cited in Edwin C. Guillet, *In the Cause of Education* (Toronto, 1960), 93.

58. Don Morrow et al., *A Concise History of Sport in Canada*, 78, 80.

59. Helen Lenskyj, 'The Role of Physical Education in the Socialization of Girls in Ontario, 1830–1930', Ph.D. thesis (University of Toronto/OISE, 1983), 209.

60. Egerton Ryerson, 'Physical Training in Schools: Gymnastic Exercises No. 1', *Journal of Education* 5, 65 (May 1852), cited in Gear, 'Factors Influencing the Development of Government Sponsored Physical Fitness Programmes', 2; Moore, 'The Boy Best Equipped for the Duties of Life', 295.

61. Millar, *School Management*, 27.

62. Lanning, 'Mapping the Moral Self', 284.

63. See Alan Metcalfe, *Canada Learns To Play: The Emergence of Organized Sport, 1807–1914* (Toronto, 1987), 15, 16; Bailey, *Leisure and Class in Victorian England*, 133–7; Brown, 'Social Darwinism, Private Schooling and Sport in Victorian and Edwardian Canada', 219; Metcalfe, 'Some Background Influences on Nineteenth Century Canadian Sport and Physical Education', 69; Terry Roberts, 'The Influence of the British Upper Class on the Development of the Value Claim for Sport in the Public Education System of Upper Canada from 1830 to 1875', *Canadian Journal of History of Sport and Physical Education* 4, 1 (May 1973): 28; Peter Lindsay, 'The Impact of the Military Garrisons on the Development of Sport in British North America', *Canadian Journal of History of Sport and Physical Education* 1, 1 (May 1970): 33. According to Nancy Howell and Maxwell L. Howell, 'In 1872 the withdrawal of the Imperial troops left a gap in the social life of the people. Much of the sport and entertainment of the townsmen had centred around the local barracks and the soldiers had initiated many new games and entertainments.' Howell and Howell, *Sports and Games in Canadian Life, 1700 to the Present* (Toronto, 1969), 60.

64. See Roberts, 'The Influence of the British Upper Class', 36, 37; David W. Brown, 'Canadian Imperialism and Sporting Exchanges: The

Nineteenth-Century Cultural Experience of Cricket and Lacrosse', *Canadian Journal of History of Sport* 18, 1 (May 1987): 55; Brian Stoddart, 'Sport, Cultural Imperialism, and Colonial Response in the British Empire', *Comparative Studies in Society and History* 30, 4 (Oct. 1988): 650–4; Glazebrook, *Life in Ontario: A Social History*, 195.

65. Herald, 'Sport in Our Schools', 389.

66. Don Morrow, 'Lacrosse as the National Game', in Morrow et al, *A Concise History of Sport in Canada*, 55, 64.

67. Nancy B. Bouchier, 'Idealized Middle-Class Sport for a Young Nation: Lacrosse in Nineteenth-Century Ontario Towns, 1871–1891', *Journal of Canadian Studies* 29, 2 (Summer 1994): 90, 91, 92.

68. See James Mangan, *Athleticism in the Victorian and Edwardian Public School* (London, 1986), 192; John Nauright, 'Sport and the Image of Colonial Manhood in the British Mind: British Physical Deterioration Debates and Colonial Sporting Tours, 1878–1906', *Canadian Journal of History of Sport* 23, 2 (Dec. 1992): 58.

69. Howell and Howell, *Sports and Games in Canadian Life*, 60, 79.

70. Bailey, *Leisure and Class in Victorian England*, 137. Bailey, in reference to the general population, writes, 'Thus, the new model athletic sports boasted some impeccable credentials: they provided a regimen which brought physical fitness to the individual, toughening him against the debilities of city life and maintaining his readiness for armed service; they also provided an education in self-discipline and team work which acted as a moral police over the individual's life at large.' Also see Colin Veitch, ' "Play Up! Play Up! and Win the War!" Football, the Nation and the First World War, 1914–1915', *Journal of Contemporary History* 20 (1985): 365; Haley, *The Healthy Body and Victorian Culture*, 147, 171.

71. Parvin, *Authorization of Textbooks for the Schools of Ontario, 1846–1950*, 3; Michael W. Apple and Linda K. Christian-Smith, eds, *The Politics of the Textbook* (New York, 1991), 2, 3, 4; Lanning, 'Mapping The Moral Self', 150.

72. See A. McVicar, 'History and Canadian Citizenship', *Proceedings of the Forty-Eighth Annual Convention of the Ontario Educational Association*, 13–15 Apr. 1909 (Toronto, 1909), 193; McDonald, 'Forming the National Character', 343, 344; Young, ' "We Throw the Torch": Canadian Memorials of the Great War and the Mythology of Heroic Sacrifice', 7, 8.

73. Lanning, 'Mapping the Moral Self', 339, 341, 343. In his history of the Ontario Educational Association, *In the Cause of Education*, xix, Edwin C. Guillet states the British influence was enormous and cites Thomas Arnold, who makes a point similar to that of Lanning. 'He [Thomas Arnold] sought to prepare the minds of his students for further learning by instilling not only knowledge but the desire for it. His

emphasis upon biography sought to arouse in his boys a wish to emulate the great men of the past.'

74. Walter Scott, 'History', cited in J.J. Tilley, *Methods in Teaching* (Toronto, 1899), 242, cited in McDonald, 'Forming the National Character', 348; Lanning, 'Mapping the Moral Self', 348; Silcox, 'Sexless Schools', 392.

75. Baldus and Kassam, '"Make Me Truthful, Good, and Mild"', 336, 337–41.

76. Stamp, *The Schools of Ontario, 1876–1976*, 11, 92. In the Hodges Room at the Ontario Institute for Studies in Education, University of Toronto, one can see the readers that Stamp has examined. *The Ontario Public School History of Canada*, Authorized by the Minister of Education for Ontario (Toronto, 1910, 1916), 247, 250. Viola Parvin states that in 1846 Ryerson adopted the 'Irish National Series of Readers' because they were unaffected by American influences. After Confederation a new 'Canadian Series' was adopted and in the mid-1880s an official 'Ontario Reader' was finally sanctioned. Parvin, *Authorization of Textbooks*, 25–33, 68.

77. *The Ontario Public School History of Canada*, 249, 254.

78. George Wrong, *Ontario High School History of England*, Authorized by the Minister of Education for Ontario (Toronto, 1911, 1916), 5–9, 93, 488–509.

79. See McDonald, 'Forming the National Character', 342, 347.

80. Contenta, *Rituals of Failure*, 13.

81. Houston and Prentice, *Schooling and Scholars*, 191.

82. J.S. Deacon, 'Public School Libraries', *Proceedings of the Fortieth Annual Convention of the Ontario Educational Association* (Toronto, 1901), 413.

83. Miss Maud M. Hawkins, 'Teaching of Literature in the Lower School', *Proceedings of the Forty-Fifth Annual Convention of the Ontario Educational Association*, 149.

84. W.E. Macpherson, 'Supplementary Reading in the Lower School', *Proceedings of the Forty-Eighth Annual Convention of the Ontario Educational Association* (Toronto, 1909), 200, 201.

85. Jordan, 'The Teaching of Citizenship', 293.

86. See J.A. Mangan, 'Introduction', in Mangan, ed., *Making Imperial Mentalities: Socialisation and British Imperialism* (Manchester, UK, 1990), 2, 3; Timothy J. Stanley, 'White Supremacy and the Rhetoric of Educational Indoctrination: A Canadian Case Study', in Mangan, ed., *Making Imperial Mentalities*, 147; Robert Morgan, 'English Studies as Cultural Production in Ontario, 1860–1920', Ph.D. thesis (University of Toronto/OISE, 1987), 4, 14–17.

87. Paul W. Bennett, ' "Little Worlds": The Forging of Social Identities in Ontario's Protestant School Communities and Institutions, 1850–1930', Ed.D. thesis (University of Toronto/OISE, 1990), 2–5.
88. Richard B. Howard, *Upper Canada College, 1829–1979* (Toronto, 1979), 331.
89. Ibid., 315.
90. Angus Wilson, *The Strange Ride of Rudyard Kipling: His Life and Works* (St Albans, 1979), 339.
91. Arthur Lower, *Canadians in the Making* (Toronto, 1958), 352–3; Stamp, *The Schools of Ontario, 1876–1976*, 96.

Chapter 6

1. See Rotundo, 'Body and Soul', 23–8; Kimmel, *Manhood in America*, 121, 157–8; Michael A. Messner, *Power At Play: Sports and the Problem of Masculinity* (Boston, 1992), 13, 14; Semple, ' "The Nurture and Admonition of the Lord" ', 157; Dubbert, *A Man's Place*, 125; Bederman, *Manliness and Civilization*, 14–17; Gorn, *The Manly Art*, 192–4; Griswold, *Fatherhood in America*, 31–3; Tolson, *The Limits of Masculinity*; Filene, *Him/Her/Self*.
2. See Ronald D. Cohen, 'Child-Saving and Progressivism, 1885–1915', in Joseph M. Hawes and N. Ray Hiner, eds, *American Childhood: A Research Guide and Historical Handbook* (Westport, Conn., 1985), 274; Stamp, *The Schools of Ontario*, 53–89.
3. See Jo B. Paoletti, 'Clothes Make the Boy, 1860–1910', *Dress: Journal of the Costume Society of America* 9 (1983): 19; Christina Bates, ' "Beauty Unadorned": Dressing Children in Late Nineteenth-Century Ontario', *Material History Bulletin* 21 (Spring 1985): 32; Kimmel, *Manhood in America*, 160–1.
4. Pye Henry Chavasse, *Advice to a Mother on the Management of Her Children* (Toronto, 1880), 135–6.
5. David Macleod, 'A Live Vaccine: The YMCA and Male Adolescence in the United States and Canada, 1870–1920', *Histoire Sociale/Social History* 11, 21 (May 1978): 5, 6.
6. Ibid., 6, 7; Ernest Thompson Seton, 'Organized Boyhood: The Boy Scout Movement, Its Purposes and Its Laws', *Success Magazine* 13 (Dec. 1910): 804, cited in Betty Keller, *Black Wolf: The Life of Ernest Thompson Seton* (Vancouver, 1984), 161; Perrot, 'Roles and Characters', 203, 217, 218.
7. Semple, ' "The Nurture and Admonition of the Lord" ', 157.
8. See Gillis, *Youth and History*, 98. For some examples of recruiting

posters, see Peter Paret, Beth Irwin Lewis, and Paul Paret, *Persuasive Images: Posters of War and Revolution* (Princeton, NJ, 1992).

9. Dubbert, *A Man's Place*, 148.

10. Gorn, *The Manly Art*, 142. Gorn writes that 'In the saloon, the firehouse, or the gang, many working-class males found their deepest sense of companionship and human connectedness.' Also see Mark C. Carnes, 'Middle-Class Men and the Solace of Fraternal Ritual', in Carnes and Griffen, eds, *Meanings for Manhood: Constructions of Masculinity in Victorian America*, 37–52; Mark C. Carnes, *Secret Ritual and Manhood in Victorian America* (New Haven, 1989), 52–4, 109. In *Secret Ritual*, Carnes suggests that these ritualistic gatherings were outlets for the demonstration of manly virtues and could be significant arenas for young men coming of age to demonstrate their manliness. Lynne Marks calls these fraternal orders 'bastions of masculinity' and states that their appeal crossed class lines. Marks, *Revivals and Roller Rinks*, 109–10.

11. See Burstyn, *The Rites of Men*; Bruce Kidd, *The Struggle for Canadian Sport* (Toronto, 1996), 19; William A. McKeever, *Training the Boy* (Toronto, 1913), 111; Dubbert, *A Man's Place*, 148, 149. Valverde, *The Age of Light, Soap, and Water*, 78, argues that sobriety and clean living were often equated as supremely masculine qualities in the eyes of middle-class reformers.

12. See Burke, 'Good for the Boy', 95.

13. Marks, *Revivals and Roller Rinks*, 81.

14. Reverend Louis Albert Banks, *A Manly Boy: A Series of Talks and Tales For Boys* (Toronto, 1900), 15, 43.

15. Marks, *Revivals and Roller Rinks*, 82–3.

16. Ibid., 83.

17. C. Stanley Hall is quoted in Peter Stearns, *American Cool*, 31; J. Adams Puffer, *The Boy and His Gang* (Boston, 1912), 91, quoted in Kimmel, *Manhood in America*, 161.

18. Quoted in Stearns, *American Cool*, 31.

19. See Nelson, *Invisible Men: Fatherhood in Victorian Periodicals*, 45; Burstyn, *The Rites of Men*; Kidd, *The Struggle for Canadian Sport*, 19.

20. See E.C.H., 'Where Are the Fathers?', *Canadian Educational Monthly* 23, 11 (Nov. 1900): 340.

21. Ibid., 341. See 'Need of a Father's Influence', *Canada Educational Monthly and School Magazine* 15, 1 (Jan. 1893): 7, 8; Richard Sennett, *Families Against the City: Middle Class Homes of Industrial Chicago, 1872–1890* (Cambridge, Mass., 1970), 217; Nelson, *Invisible Men*, 15; John Demos, 'The Changing Faces of Fatherhood: A New Exploration in American Family History', in Stanley H. Cath, Alan R. Gurwitz, and

John Munder Ross, eds, *Father and Child: Developmental and Clinical Perspectives* (Boston, 1982), 425–45.

22. Burstyn, *The Rites of Men*, 52, 54.

23. Dubbert, *A Man's Place*, 33.

24. Bederman, *Manliness and Civilization*, 15. For a comprehensive description of this evolution, see Peter Gay, *The Tender Passion*, vol. 2 of *Bourgeois Experience, Victoria to Freud* (Oxford, 1986), 219–54.

25. On the concerns about masturbation, see G.J. Barker-Benfield, *The Horrors of the Half-Known Life: Male Attitudes Towards Women and Sexuality in Nineteenth-Century America* (New York, 1976), 179–81; Thomas Laqueur, *Making Sex: Body and Gender from the Greeks to Freud* (Cambridge, Mass., 1990), 28–9; Peter Gay, *Education of the Senses*, vol. 1 of *Bourgeois Experience, Victoria to Freud* (Oxford, 1984), 294–318; Kimmel, *Manhood in America*, 45, 129. On Hall, see R.P. Newman, 'Masturbation, Madness, and the Modern Concepts of Childhood and Adolescence', *Journal of Social History* 8 (1975): 9–15; Bederman, *Manliness and Civilization*, 79–80.

26. Dubbert, *A Man's Place*, 27–9.

27. Ibid., 27–32.

28. See Bederman, *Manliness and Civilization*, 15.

29. Gorn, *The Manly Art*, 134; Marks, *Revivals and Roller Rinks*, 117.

30. See Messner, *Power At Play*, 14. Although formed much later than the Boys' Brigade and the YMCA, the Boy Scouts wielded the most influence and was certainly the organization most oriented towards manliness and militarism.

31. Hynes, *The Edwardian Turn of Mind*, 26; Tim Jeal, *Baden-Powell* (London, 1989), 358; Victor Bailey, 'Scouting for Empire', *History Today* 32 (July 1982): 7; Summers, 'Edwardian Militarism', 241; Reader, *'At Duty's Call': A Study in Obsolete Patriotism*, 39, 77; Judd, *Empire*, 204–5; John Nauright, 'Sport and the Image of Colonial Manhood in the British Mind: British Physical Deterioration Debates and Colonial Sporting Tours, 1878–1906', *Canadian Journal of History of Sport* 23, 2 (Dec. 1992): 54–6. According to Nauright (p. 56), 'A plethora of books and articles appeared from 1901 onwards which addressed the question of whether the British race was in a state of permanent decline.' Also see Lt. Col. William H. Merritt, 'Patriotic Military Training', *Canadian Magazine* 28, 3 (Jan. 1907). Merritt makes a plea for citizen militia training along the lines of the Swiss system.

32. See Allen Warren, 'Sir Robert Baden-Powell, the Scout Movement and Citizen Training in Great Britain, 1900–1920', *English Historical Review* 101 (1986): 383; Allen Warren, 'Citizens of the Empire: Baden-

Powell, Scouts and Guides and an Imperial Ideal, 1900–1940', in Mackenzie, ed., *Imperialism and Popular Culture*, 237.

33. On 'imperial decline', see Hynes, *The Edwardian Turn of Mind*, 27; Donald Read, *Edwardian England, 1901–1905: Society and Politics* (London, 1972), 13.

34. For a discussion of the differences between the Boy Scouts and the other major non-affiliated youth group, the Woodcraft movement, as well as commentary on the supposed plagiarism of ideas, see Brian Morris, 'Ernest Thompson Seton and the Origins of the Woodcraft Movement', *Journal of Contemporary History* 5, 2 (1970): 183–94. Victor Bailey writes that 'We could do worse than to remind ourselves of the extent to which scouting was an authentic cultural expression of the pervasive Edwardian anxieties for the future of the British Empire.' Bailey, 'Scouting for Empire', 7.

35. Judd, *Empire*, 201–3. Ernest Thompson Seton, also known as Black Wolf, founded the League of Woodcraft Indians in 1901. The inspiration for this came from his travels and meetings with Aboriginals. Seton met Baden-Powell in 1906 and was shocked to find all his ideas incorporated and plagiarized in *Scouting for Boys*. 'What galled Seton most', according to Betty Keller, 'about his plagiarism was the fact that Baden-Powell had subverted his games and activities to militaristic ends. "My aim was to make a man," Seton wrote in his *History of the Boy Scouts*; Baden-Powell's was to make a soldier.' See Keller, *Black Wolf*, 164–5, 166, 169.

36. Hantover, 'The Boy Scouts and the Validation of Masculinity', 184. In a review of David I. Macleod's *Building Character in the American Boy*, Geoffrey Blodgett notes that Macleod 'stresses that city living, not females, posed the immediate threat to moral masculinity in the eyes of men concerned to guide their own kind through the crisis of adolescence.' 'Reviews', *Journal of Interdisciplinary History* 15, 2 (Autumn 1984): 362.

37. See Robert H. MacDonald, *Sons of the Empire: The Frontier Ethic and the Boy Scout Movement, 1890–1918* (Toronto, 1993), 3; and Lt.-General Sir R.S.S. Baden-Powell, 'The Boy Scout Movement', Address to the Empire Club of Canada, 31 Aug. 1910, 12.

38. David I. Macleod, 'Act Your Age: Boyhood, Adolescence and the Rise of the Boy Scouts of America', *Journal of Social History* 16, 2 (Winter 1982): 10. W.J. Reader (*'At Duty's Call'*, 77–8) writes that 'Scouting was just the sort of movement, with mass rallies, singing, camping, private ritual, group loyalties and discipline, which might have been deliberately set up to cultivate the bellicose patriotism which many people considered the country needed in its young men.'

39. Michael Rosenthal, *The Character Factory: Baden-Powell and the Origins of the Boy Scout Movement* (London, 1986), 1, 2, 7.

40. John Springhall, *Youth, Empire and Society: British Youth Movements, 1883–1940* (London, 1977), 16.

41. See Blodgett, 'Reviews', 363; MacDonald, *Sons of the Empire*, 8: Hynes, *The Edwardian Turn of Mind*, 27.

42. Baden-Powell, 'The Boy Scout Movement', 12. Baden-Powell's trip to Canada was given considerable publicity. See Hopkins, ed., *The Canadian Annual Review of Public Affairs*, vol. 10, 1910, 594, 595.

43. Allen Warren, 'Popular Manliness: Baden-Powell, Scouting and the Development of Manly Character', in Mangan and Walvin, eds, *Manliness and Morality*, 201. Elsewhere, Warren writes of Baden-Powell that 'His eccentricities and enthusiasms as a soldier are carried fully into *Scouting for Boys*, as is his hostility to the constraints of the contemporary educational system with its narrow syllabus, its rote learning and its failure to incorporate ideas of citizen training and character development.' Warren, 'Sir Robert Baden-Powell, the Scout Movement and Citizen Training', 387.

44. Hantover, 'The Boy Scouts', 190, 189.

45. See Wilkinson, *American Tough*, 7.

46. Hantover, 'The Boy Scouts', 185.

47. Michael Rosenthal, 'Recruiting for the Empire: Baden-Powell's Scout Law', *Raritan* 4 (Summer 1984): 39.

48. Ibid., 32, 45; MacDonald, *Sons of the Empire*, 5.

49. See Macleod, 'Act Your Age', 6, 9; Bailey, 'Scouting for Empire', 6.

50. R.S.S. Baden-Powell, *The Canadian Boy Scout* (Toronto, 1911), ix, quoted in Leila G. Mitchell McKee, 'Nature's Medicine: The Physical Education and Outdoor Recreation Programmes of Toronto's Voluntary Youth Organization's, 1880–1930', *Proceedings of the 5th Canadian Symposium on the History of Sport and Physical Education* (Toronto, 26–9 Aug. 1982), 130.

51. See G. Wall, 'Recreational Land Use in Muskoka', in G. Wall and J. Marsh, eds, *Recreational Land Use: Perspectives on Its Evolution in Canada* (Ottawa, 1982), 144.

52. Sigmund Samuel, *In Return: The Autobiography of Sigmund Samuel* (Toronto: University of Toronto Press, 1963), 63.

53. Hunting as a chance to demonstrate one's manhood is from Charles Bergman, *Orion's Legacy: A Cultural History of Man as Hunter* (New York, 1996), 212; Baden-Powell is quoted in John M. Mackenzie, 'The Imperial Pioneer and Hunter', in *Manliness and Morality*, 176, 178, and the transmission of manly qualities is found in Mackenzie on pp. 176

and 178. The idea of indifference to hunting putting one's manhood in doubt, is from Michael Rosenthal, 'Recruiting for the Empire', 46.

54. Matt Cartmill, *A View to a Death in the Morning: Hunting and Nature Through History* (Cambridge, Mass., 1993), 30.

55. See Steven Lonsdale, *Animals and the Origins of Dance* (London, 1981), 59, cited in Cartmill, *A View to a Death*, 30; Ray Raphael, *The Men from the Boys: Rites of Passage in Male America* (Lincoln, 1988).

56. J.K. Anderson, *Hunting in the Ancient World* (Berkeley, 1985), 29, cited in Bergman, *Orion's Legacy*, 69.

57. Bergman, *Orion's Legacy*, 67–9.

58. Cited in Cartmill, *A View to a Death*, 31.

59. See Bergman, *Orion's Legacy*, 137; K. Thomas, *Man and the Natural World: A History of the Modern Sensibility* (New York, 1983), 183, quoted in Cartmill, *A View to a Death*, 31.

60. Anthony Rotundo, *American Manhood—Transformations in Masculinity from the Revolution to the Modern Era* (New York, 1993), 35. A boy might sift through or read his father's magazines. Throughout issues of *Rod and Gun* and *Motor Sports in Canada*, there were articles on duck, deer, moose, and bear hunting, all kinds of fishing and climbing stories, and numerous advertisements for guns, powder, and pistols.

61. On boys and the desire to kill animals, see George A. Dickinson, MD, *Your Boy: His Nature and Nurture* (Toronto, 1909), 11. The quote on boys being fond of fighting comes from William A. McKeever, *Training the Boy*, 111.

62. By no means was this mentality the only one, yet it was surely the dominant one. Major conservation groups and projects were under way during this period, such as the Sierra Club, the national, provincial, and state parks, and the founding of various journals promoting a new appreciation of nature. Of course, this in turn coincided with the development of mass tourism. See W.R. Wadsworth, 'With Rifle and Rod in the Moose Lands of Northern Ontario', *The Canadian Magazine* 13, 3, (July 1899): 254, 256; T.J. Schlereth, *Victorian America—Transformations in Everyday Life, 1876–1915* (New York, 1991), 217; Alexander Wilson, *The Culture of Nature* (Toronto, 1991); Stephen Kern, *The Culture of Time and Space, 1880–1920* (Cambridge, Mass., 1983), 166; John A. Jackle, *The Tourist* (Lincoln, 1985). Interesting, though, was the situation in Britain. Land was transformed from its natural state into either a 'planned wilderness' or specific hunting grounds. Initiated by the Enclosure movement and culminating in the personal garden, the procedures focused on pleasure, profit, and power. See John Rennie Short, *Imagined Country: Society, Culture and Environment* (London, 1991), 34, 67.

63. Richard Hummel, *Hunting and Fishing for Sport: Commerce, Controversy, Popular Culture* (Bowling Green, Ohio, 1994), 11, 12.

64. See Bergman, *Orion's Legacy*, 214–15.

65. See Dubbert, *A Man's Place*, 124; Bederman, *Manliness and Civilization*, 174, 193.

66. Cartmill, *A View to a Death*, 137.

67. See Mackenzie, 'The Imperial Pioneer and Hunter', in *Manliness and Morality*, 179, 181; John M. Mackenzie, *The Empire of Nature: Hunting, Conservation and British Imperialism* (Manchester, 1988), 22. This symbolism of imperialism had tangible results. Many of the natural history museums, which in turn came to embody the spirit of imperialism, were heavily dependent upon imperial hunters for their artifacts. See Mackenzie, *The Empire of Nature*, 38; Inderpal Grewal, 'The Guidebook and the Museum: Imperialism, Education and Nationalism in The British Museum', in Patrick Scott and Pauline Fletcher, eds, *Culture and Education in Victorian England* (London, 1990), 199, 206, 214.

68. R.G. Moyles and Doug Owram, *Imperial Dreams and Colonial Realities: British Views of Canada, 1880–1914* (Toronto, 1988), 61.

69. Ibid., 63, 62.

70. Hummel, *Hunting and Fishing for Sport*, 21, 135. Fishing, as well, evolved during this time frame. Recreational fishing served as an outdoor retreat, a simple nostalgic activity, and a more accessible option for young boys than hunting. See Colleen J. Sheehy, 'American Angling: The Rise of Urbanism and the Romance of the Rod and Reel', in Kathryn Grover, ed., *Hard at Play: Leisure in America, 1840–1940* (Amherst, Mass., 1992), 77, 78.

71. Bergman, *Orion's Legacy*, 210–11.

72. Ibid., 211.

73. Mackenzie, 'The Imperial Pioneer and Hunter', 191.

74. See Mackenzie, *The Empire of Nature*, 45–7; J.S. Bratton, 'Of England, Home and Duty: The Image of England in Victorian and Edwardian Juvenile Fiction', in John M. Mackenzie, ed., *Imperialism and Popular Culture* (Manchester, 1986) 90. Ballantyne's work is quoted in Bruce Haley, *The Healthy Body and Victorian Culture* (Cambridge, Mass., 1978), 160.

75. MacDonald, *Sons of the Empire*, 26.

76. Gay, *The Cultivation of Hatred*, 3, 97.

Chapter 7

1. Thorstein Veblen, *The Theory of the Leisure Class* [1899], 170, cited in Pugh, *Sons of Liberty*, 116.

2. See Daniel Pick, *War Machine: The Rationalization of Slaughter in the Modern Age* (New Haven, 1993), 111–12.

3. Rotundo, *American Manhood*, 5, 6; Banks, *A Manly Boy*, 32; Sylvanus Stall, *What a Young Man Ought To Know* (Toronto, 1897), 158.

4. Alan Trachtenberg, *The Incorporation of America: Culture and Society in the Gilded Age* (New York, 1982), 7.

5. See McKee, 'Nature's Medicine', 129.

6. George Altmeyer, 'Three Ideas of Nature in Canada, 1893–1914', *Journal of Canadian Studies* 11, 3 (1976): 23. Also see Alan Smith, 'Farms, Forests and Cities: The Image of the Land and the Rise of the Metropolis in Ontario, 1860–1914', in David Keane and Colin Read, eds, *Old Ontario: Essays in Honour of J.M.S. Careless* (Toronto, 1990), 71–91.

7. See C.W. Saleeby, 'Worry: The Disease of the Age', *Canadian Magazine* 33 (Dec. 1906): 118–20, (Jan. 1907): 225–30, (Feb. 1907), 347–53, (Mar. 1907), 452–7, (Apr. 1907), 537–43; Mckee, 'Nature's Medicine', 129.

8. See J. Marsh and G. Wall, 'Introduction: Themes in the Investigation of the Evolution of Outdoor Recreation', in G. Wall and J. Marsh, eds, *Recreational Land Use*, 2.

9. Smith, 'Farms, Forests and Cities', 76.

10. See McKee, 'Nature's Medicine', 129, 130; R. Tait McKenzie, 'The University and Physical Efficiency', *University Magazine* 6 (Apr. 1907): 168.

11. Altmeyer, 'Three Ideas of Nature in Canada', 23.

12. J. Benidickson, 'Northern Ontario's Tourist Frontier', in Wall and Marsh, eds, *Recreational Land Use*, 158.

13. See Brian Morris, 'Ernest Thompson Seton and the Origins of the Woodcraft Movement', *Journal of Contemporary History* 5, 2 (1970): 13; Altmeyer, 'Three Ideas of Nature in Canada', 25.

14. See E.T. Seton, *The Book of Woodcraft and Indian Lore* (London, 1912), 3, quoted in McKee, 'Nature's Medicine', 130.

15. 'A Boys' Camp in Temagami', *Rod and Gun and Motor Sports in Canada* 10, 1 (June 1908): 49–51, quoted in Smith, 'Farms, Forests and Cities', 79. Also see Benidickson, 'Northern Ontario's Tourist Frontier', 165–6.

16. See G. Wall and R. Wallis, 'Camping for Fun: A Brief History of Camping in North America', in Wall and Marsh, eds, *Recreational Land Use*, 342; 'The Men with Hearts of Boys', *Outdoor Canada* 4, 8 (1908): 67; Trent University Archives, Ontario Camping Association Papers, vol. 7, folder no. 2, 'Camp Temagami, 1905', cited in Benidickson, 'Paddling for Pleasure: Recreational Canoeing as a Canadian Way of Life', in Wall and Marsh, eds, *Recreational Land Use*, 325–6.

17. McKee, 'Nature's Medicine', 132.

18. See Wall, 'Recreational Land Use in Muskoka', 142, 143.

19. M. Parkinson, 'Lake Temagami, a Northern Playground', *Canadian Magazine* (June 1914): 167, quoted in Benidickson, 'Northern Ontario's Tourist Frontier', 157.

20. Pye Henry Chavasse, *Advice to a Mother* (Toronto, 1880), 134.

21. Lord Mountmorres, 'Heroes of To-day: Captain Lord Charles Beresford', *Chums* 2, 51 (30 Aug. 1893): 9.

22. Kidd, *The Struggle for Canadian Sport*, 19.

23. Quoted in David Howell and Peter Lindsay, 'Social Gospel and the Young Boy Problem, 1895–1925', in Morris Mott, ed., *Sports in Canada: Historical Readings* (Toronto, 1989), 222–3.

24. Gruneau and Whitson, *Hockey Night In Canada*, 42–3.

25. See Bailey, *Leisure and Class in Victorian England*, 5. Most major sports had some form of organizational body in the period before World War I. See Metcalfe, *Canada Learns To Play*, 101.

26. Jobling, 'Urbanization and Sport in Canada', 75. This is not to suggest that the cities were all-powerful. Baseball, for example, was played in many parts of North America under many different rules. Each region, where the diverse styles were played, flourished in its own limited way. When championship teams went to play each other, one suitable set of rules had to be established and this eventually led to uniform codification. Civic pride was an important aspect of maintaining a unique style and rules for so long. When published guides were printed and broadly distributed, as with Spalding's rules for baseball and other sports, the effect was complete. Games were increasingly tied to equipment and this further sped up the 'commodification' of sport. See William Humber, 'Cheering for the Home Team: Baseball and Town Life in 19th Century Ontario, 1854–1869', in *Proceedings of the 5th Canadian Symposium on the History of Sport and Physical Education*, 189–90; Gunther Barth, *City People* (New York, 1980), 191; Kidd, *The Struggle for Canadian Sport*, 17–18.

27. Kidd, *The Struggle for Canadian Sport*, 18.

28. Ibid., 19; K.B. Walmsley, 'Cultural Signification and National Ideologies: Rifle Shooting in Late Nineteenth Century Canada', *Social History* 20, 1 (1995): 63–72.

29. Bruce Kidd writes that 'the acclaimed equation of sport and manliness was so pervasive that it led constables and magistrates to equivocate with the law. "I feel confident that it will be a long time before Parliament will think it wise to so hedge in young men and boys by legislation that all sports that are rough and strenuous or even dangerous must be given up. Virility in young men would soon be lessened and self-reliant manhood a thing of the past."' This was the response of one Judge

Snider of Hamilton in arguing for the acquittal of two men who had been arrested for prizefighting. Kidd, *The Struggle for Canadian Sport*, 26.

30. Gorn, *The Manly Art*, 107, 137.

31. Ibid., 141.

32. Ibid., 188–202.

33. See Lois Bryson, 'Sport and the Maintenance of Masculine Hegemony', *Women's Studies International Forum* 10 (1987): 349, quoted in Messner, *Power At Play*, 15.

34. 'In promoting dominance and submission, in equating force and aggression with physical strength, modern sport naturalized the equation of maleness with power, thus legitimizing a challenged and faltering system of male domination.' L. Komisar, 'Violence and the Masculine Mystique', in D.F. Sabo and R. Runfola, eds, *Jock: Sports and Male Identity* (Englewood Cliffs, NJ, 1980), quoted in Messner, *Power At Play*, 15.

35. See Peter N. Stearns, *American Cool* (New York, 1994), 72–3.

36. Kidd, *The Struggle for Canadian Sport*, 19, 26.

37. 'By 1914, 20 volunteer-led governing bodies claimed "national" jurisdiction in their respective sports'. Ibid., 21.

38. James Walvin, *A Child's World* (London, 1984), 81.

39. See Walter Camp and Lorin Deland, *Football* (Boston, 1896), 42–52, quoted in Roberta J. Park, 'Physiologists, Physicians, and Physical Educators: Nineteenth Century Biology and Exercise, "Hygienic" and "Educative"', *Journal of Sport History* 14, 1 (Spring 1987): 32; Roberta J. Park, 'Healthy, Moral and Strong—Educational Views of Exercise and Athletics in Nineteenth Century America', in Grover, ed., *Fitness in American Culture*, 125.

40. J.A. Mangan, 'Games Field and Battlefield: A Romantic Alliance in Verse and the Creation of Militaristic Masculinity', in Mangan, ed., *Making Men*, 140, 141. In his study of masculine culture in France, Robert A. Nye discusses the close association between sports and war, especially the fact that sports were the best way socially to create the moral and psychological conditions of the battlefield. After France's humiliating defeat by Prussia in 1870, Nye suggests that fencing and gymnastics organizations sought to instil in young men the mental and physical courage required for revenge. As well, traditional sports were revived, English sports introduced, and an association of sports with manliness officially encouraged, all for the specific purpose of teaching courage and martial sentiments to young men. Sport went beyond fitness and health concerns and became firmly entrenched as a character-building process. Nye, *Masculinity and Male Codes of Honor in Modern France* (New York, 1993), 219.

41. Metcalfe, *Canada Learns To Play*, 68, 69.

42. There is still a hidden agenda behind many organized team sports today. In his study of Little League baseball, Gary Allen Fine writes that 'Adults see Little League baseball as a distinctly moral endeavour, training boys to be upstanding citizens.' *With the Boys: Little League Baseball and Preadolescent Culture* (Chicago, 1987), 2.

43. Kidd, *The Struggle for Canadian Sport*, 27.

44. Gruneau and Whitson, *Hockey Night In Canada*, 17.

45. See Kidd, *The Struggle for Canadian Sport*, 28, 29; Gruneau and Whitson, *Hockey Night In Canada*, 34; Park, 'Healthy, Moral and Strong', 124.

46. Johan Huizinga, *Homo Ludens: A Study of the Play Element in Culture* (London, 1970), 70.

47. Elliot J. Gorn and Warren Goldstein, *A Brief History of American Sports*, 145; Kimmel, *Manhood in America*, 137.

48. Jobling, 'Urbanization and Sport', 70. Also see Gruneau and Whitson, *Hockey Night In Canada*, 82.

49. See Gruneau and Whitson, *Hockey Night In Canada*, 83; Rutherford, *The Making of the Canadian Media*, 60–1.

50. See Gruneau and Whitson, *Hockey Night In Canada*, 56. The authors (p. 36) also mention that the modernization of professional sports and of sports in general had an important and unique geographical element to it. This was directly related to the urban arena—the city and the desire to erect stadiums to draw in the fans. A 'new organization of space based on economic utility and value' was the consequence of the move to the developed urban areas. 'People interested in using land recreationally began to compete economically with other potential users for access. The competition for space and the capital requirements necessary for building facilities demanded the creation of formal organizations. At the same time, growing concerns about urban anonymity in an increasingly large and heterogeneous population created opportunities for sport to be promoted as a new form of civic identification and belonging.'

51. William Byron Forbush, *The Boy Problem: A Study in Social Pedagogy*, Introduction by G. Stanley Hall (Boston, 1902), 9, 20.

52. Sidney Hook, *The Hero in History* (Boston, 1943), 23, quoted in Don Morrow, 'The Myth of the Hero in Canadian Sport History', *Canadian Journal of History of Sport* 23, 2 (Dec. 1992): 72.

53. Metcalfe, *Canada Learns To Play*, 177.

54. Samuel, *In Return*, 21, 23.

55. See Kidd, *The Struggle for Canadian Sport*, 20; Alvin Finkel and Margaret Conrad, with Veronica Strong-Boag, *History of the Canadian Peoples, vol. 2, 1867–the Present* (Mississauga, Ont., 1993), 155.

56. See Marcus Klein, *Easterns, Westerns, and Private Eyes: American Matters, 1870–1900* (Madison, Wis., 1994), 78–87.

57. Trachtenberg, *The Incorporation of America*, 14, 23. For a commentary on the Canadian preoccupation with and interpretation of the concept of the 'Frontier', see J.M.S. Careless, 'Frontierism, Metropolitanism, and Canadian History', in Careless, *Approaches to Canadian History*, Introduction by Carl Berger (Toronto, 1970), 63; E. Brian Titley and Peter J. Miller, eds, *Education in Canada: An Interpretation* (Edmonton, 1982), 9. For an illustration of the pervasive influence of the cowboy in Canada, see Fraser Sutherland, *The Monthly Epic: A History of Canadian Magazines* (Markham, Ont., 1989), 80.

58. Jane Tompkins, *West of Everything: The Inner Life of Westerns* (New York, 1992), 4.

59. Mary Vipond, 'Best Sellers in English Canada, 1899–1918', *Journal of Canadian Fiction*: 106.

60. Tompkins, *West of Everything*, 145.

61. Among the many works that discuss this sad episode that has been cloaked by popular culture representations are Daniel Francis, *The Imaginary Indian* (Vancouver, 1992), 7–8; Patricia Nelson Limerick, *The Legacy of Conquest* (New York, 1987), 19; Robert F. Berkhofer Jr, *The White Man's Indian* (New York, 1979), 29, 71, 98.

62. Richard Hofstadter, *Social Darwinism in American Thought* (New York, 1965), 175.

63. Karen Calvert, *Children in the House: The Material Culture of Early Childhood, 1600–1900* (Boston, 1992), 4. Calvert's comment can be expanded to encompass Hector St John Crevecour's observation that 'The easiest way of becoming acquainted with the mode of thinking, the rules of conduct, and the prevailing manners of any people is to examine what sort of education they give their children, how they treat them at home, and what they are taught in their places of worship.' *Letters from an American Farmer*, H.L. Bourding, R.H. Gabriel, and S.T. Williams, eds (New Haven, 1963), 121, quoted in Thomas J. Schlereth, 'The Material Culture of Childhood: Problems and Potential in Historical Explanation', *Material History Bulletin* 21 (Spring 1985): 1.

64. Schlereth, 'The Material Culture of Childhood', 2.

65. Calvert, *Children in the House*, 110–12, 118.

66. See Miriam Formanek-Brunell, *Made To Play House: Dolls and the Commercialization of American Girlhood, 1830–1930* (New Haven, 1993), 39. On this point, Angus McLaren writes, 'Late-nineteenth-century social observers of youth worried more about boys than about girls. Young women, it was assumed, simply had to be prepared for marriage whereas young men had to be trained for more important and

complex roles in the worlds of labor, the military, and politics.' McLaren, *The Trials of Masculinity: Policing Sexual Boundaries, 1870–1930* (Chicago, 1997), 30–1.

67. Bernard Mergen, 'Made, Bought, and Stolen: Toys and the Culture of Childhood', in Elliott West and Paula Petrik, eds, *Small Worlds: Children and Adolescents in America, 1850–1950* (Lawrence, Kans., 1992), 94; Calvert, *Children in the House*, 118.

68. Thomas E. Jordan, *Victorian Childhood: Themes and Variations* (Albany, 1987), 196; Erik H. Erikson, *Toys and Reasons* (New York, 1977), 30; Brian Sutton-Smith, *Toys As Culture* (New York, 1986), 25.

69. See Lesley Gordon, *Peepshow into Paradise: A History of Children's Toys* (London, 1953), 135; Richard O'Brien, *The Story of American Toys* (New York, 1990), 61; Dan Foley, *Toys Through the Ages* (Philadelphia, 1962), 62; Gwen White, *Antique Toys and Their Backgrounds* (London, 1971), 193; Antonia Fraser, *A History of Toys* (London, 1966), 60, 61.

70. Kenneth D. Brown, 'Modelling for War? Toy Soldiers in Late Victorian and Edwardian Britain', *Journal of Social History* 24, 2 (Winter 1990): 238.

71. See Janet Holmes, 'Economic Choices and Popular Toys in the Nineteenth Century', *Material History Bulletin* 21 (Spring 1985): 51; Bernard Mergen, 'Toys and American Culture: Objects as Hypotheses', in Edith Mayo, ed., *American Material Culture: The Shape of Things Around Us* (Bowling Green, Ohio, 1984), 150.

72. Roland Barthes, *Mythologies* (New York, 1972), 53.

73. Dan Fleming, *Powerplay: Toys as Popular Culture* (Manchester, UK, 1996), 85.

74. George L. Mosse, *Fallen Soldiers* (New York, 1990), 141, 143.

75. Jane Pettigrew, *An Edwardian Childhood* (Boston, 1993), 89, 117–19. For a brief discussion of the popularity and influence of British toys in Canada, see *Playthings of Yesterday*, intro. H.L. Symons (Toronto, 1963).

76. Gary Cross, *Kid's Stuff: Toys and the Changing World of American Childhood* (Cambridge, Mass., 1997), 110, 111.

77. G. de T. Glazebrook, Katherine B. Brett, and Judith McErvel, *A Shopper's View of Canada's Past* (Toronto, 1968), 75, 128.

78. See Lesley Gordon, *Peepshow Into Paradise* (London, 1963) 133; Mosse, *Fallen Soldiers*, 141; Sutton-Smith, *Toys As Culture*, 120; Kline, *Out of the Garden*, 4.

79. Cecelia Tichi, *Shifting Gears: Technology, Literature, Culture in Modernist America* (Chapel Hill, NC, 1987), 4.

80. Mihaly Csikszentmihali and Eugene Rochberg-Halton, *The Meaning of Things: Domestic Symbols and the Self* (Cambridge, 1981), 92. Also see Donald W. Ball, 'Towards a Sociology of Toys: Inanimate Objects,

Socialization and the Demography of the Doll World', *Sociological Quarterly* 8 (1967): 450.

81. H.G. Wells, *Floor Games* (1911), quoted in Fraser, *A History of Toys*, 180.

82. Mary Tivy, 'Nineteenth-Century Canadian Children's Games', *Material History Bulletin* 21 (Spring 1985): 60, 63.

83. Bill Bryson, *Made in America: An Informal History of the English Language in the United States* (New York, 1994), 270. Also see David Wallace Adams and Victor Edmonds, 'Making Your Move: The Educational Significance of the American Board Game, 1832 to 1904', *History of Education Quarterly* 17 (Winter 1977): 377; Cross, *Kid's Stuff*, 87.

84. R.C. Bell, *The Board Game Book* (Los Angeles, 1979), 67.

85. Sally Sugerman, 'Children on Board: Images from Candy Lands', in Harry Eiss, ed., *Images of the Child* (Bowling Green, Ohio, 1994), 323, 324.

86. Kenneth D. Brown, 'Modelling for War?', *Journal of Social History*: 244.

87. Kimmel, *Manhood in America*, 161. Also see Cross, *Kid's Stuff*, 51, 52.

88. K. Rubin, 'Early Play Theories Revisited: Contributions to Contemporary Research and Theory', in D. Pepler and Rubin, eds, *The Play of Children: Current Theory and Research* (Basel, 1982), cited in Kline, *Out of the Garden*, 152.

89. David Cohen, *The Development of Play* (London, 1993), 16, 31.

90. Roberta J. Park, 'Too Important to Trust to the Children: The Search for Freedom and "Order" in Children's Play, 1900–1917', in John W. Loy, ed., *The Paradoxes of Play* (West Point, NY, 1982), 96, 97.

91. James Foster Scott, *The Sexual Instinct: Its Use and Dangers as Affecting Heredity and Morals* (New York, 1899), 64, quoted in Calvert, *Children in the House*, 114, 118.

92. Mergen, 'Made, Bought, and Stolen', 97.

93. See Dorothy Ross, *G. Stanley Hall: The Psychologist As Prophet* (Chicago, 1972); Gail Bederman, *Manliness and Civilization* (Chicago, 1995), 77–100.

94. See G. Stanley Hall, *Adolescence and Aspects of Child Life and Education*, cited in Donald J. Mrozek, 'The Nature and Limits of Unstructured Play, 1880–1914', in *Hard at Play*, 211.

95. Varda Burstyn, *The Rites of Men* (Toronto, 1999), 56, 57.

96. See Bruce N. Carter, 'James L. Hughes and the Gospel of Education', 357; Brown and Cook, *Canada 1896–1921*, 102. Carter (p. 358) writes: 'Hughes emphasized the value of supervised playgrounds for city children quite outside school hours, especially during vacations.'

97. Dominick Cavallo, *Muscles and Morals* (Philadelphia, 1981), 1–2. Also see Bernard Mergen, 'The Discovery of Play', in Mergen, *Play and Playthings* (Westport, Conn., 1982), 57.

98. George A. Dickinson, MD, *Your Boy: His Nature and Nurture* (Toronto, 1909), 53.

99. Cavallo, *Muscles and Morals*, 2.

100. Thomas M. Balliet, Ph.D., 'The Nature and Function of Play in Education', *Proceedings of the Forty-Ninth Annual Convention of the Ontario Education Association*, 29–31 Mar. 1910 (Toronto, 1910), 116.

101. See Burstyn, *The Rites of Men*, 66, 67; Donald Mrozek, *Sport and American Mentality, 1880–1910* (Knoxville, Tenn., 1985), 30, 22, 61.

102. See Peter McIntosh, *Fair Play* (London, 1979), 34.

103. Quoted in Cavallo, *Muscles and Morals*, 83.

104. Ibid., 22, 81.

105. Mergen, *Play and Playthings*, 58.

106. Ibid., 65, 106.

107. Dickinson, *Your Boy: His Nature and Nurture*, 38, 61, 62.

108. Ibid., 62, 63.

109. Christina Hardyment, *Dream Babies: Child Care from Lock to Spock* (London, 1983), 143.

Chapter 8

1. Robert Bothwell, Ian Drummond, and John English, *Canada 1900–1945* (Toronto, 1990), 155.

2. John S. Moir, 'Religion', in J.M.S. Careless and R.C. Brown, eds, *The Canadians: 1867–1967* (Toronto, 1967), 597.

3. Sandra Gwyn, *Tapestry of War* (Toronto, 1992), 50.

4. Thomas P. Socknat, *Witness Against War: Pacifism in Canada 1900–1945* (Toronto, 1987), 11–20.

5. J.M.S. Careless, *Toronto to 1918* (Toronto, 1984), 128.

6. Socknat, *Witness Against War*, 23.

7. Ibid., 30–42.

8. Kathryn M. Bindon, *More Than Patriotism: Canada at War 1914–1918* (Toronto, 1979), 7–8.

9. Jonathan F. Vance, *Death So Noble: Memory, Meaning and the First World War* (Vancouver, 1997), 16.

10. David D. Gilmore, *Manhood in the Making: Cultural Concepts of Masculinity* (New Haven, 1990), 4–5.

11. In the words of Graham Dawson: 'If masculinity has had a role in imagining the nation, then so too has the nation played its part in constituting preferred forms of masculinity. Those forms of manliness that have proved efficacious for nationalist endeavour have been approvingly recognized and furthered with all the power at the disposal of the state, while other subversive or non-functional forms (notably the effeminate

man or the homosexual) have met with the disapprobation and repression in explicitly national terms. A dominant conception of masculine identity—the true "Englishman"—was both required and underpinned by the dominant version of British national identity in such a way that each reinforced the other.' Dawson, *Soldier Heroes*, 1–2.

12. George L. Mosse, *The Image of Man* (New York, 1996), 107.
13. Samuel Hynes, *The Soldier's Tale* (New York, 1997), 45, 30.
14. Ibid., 47–8.
15. Banks, *A Manly Boy*, 82.
16. George Sterling Ryerson, *Looking Backward* (Toronto, 1924), 193.
17. Lieut.-Col. E.W. Hagarty, 'History of the Cadet Movement', in *Proceedings of the Fifty-Fourth Annual Convention of the Ontario Educational Association* (Toronto, 1915), 158–9.
18. Mosse, *The Image of Man*, 114. Mosse is talking specifically of the interwar popularity of T.E. Lawrence's *The Seven Pillars of Wisdom*, which was a favourite of English schoolboys. Lawrence's work equates masculinity with adventure.

Index

THE CANADIAN SOCIAL HISTORY SERIES

Terry Copp,
The Anatomy of Poverty:
The Condition of the Working Class
in Montreal, 1897–1929, 1974.
ISBN 0–7710–2252–2

Alison Prentice,
The School Promoters:
Education and Social Class in
Mid-Nineteenth Century
Upper Canada, 1977.
ISBN 0–7710–7181–7

John Herd Thompson,
The Harvests of War:
The Prairie West, 1914–1918, 1978.
ISBN 0–19–541402–0

Joy Parr, Editor,
Childhood and Family in Canadian History, 1982.
ISBN 0–7710–6938–3

Alison Prentice and
Susan Mann Trofimenkoff, Editors,
The Neglected Majority:
Essays in Canadian Women's History,
Volume 2, 1985.
ISBN 0–7710–8583–4

Ruth Roach Pierson,
'They're Still Women After All':
The Second World War and
Canadian Womanhood, 1986.
ISBN 0–7710–6958–8

Bryan D. Palmer,
The Character of Class Struggle:
Essays in Canadian Working-Class
History, 1850–1985, 1986.
ISBN 0–7710–6946–4

Alan Metcalfe,
Canada Learns to Play:
The Emergence of Organized Sport,
1807–1914, 1987.
ISBN 0–19–541304–0

Marta Danylewycz,
Taking the Veil:
An Alternative to Marriage,
Motherhood, and Spinsterhood in
Quebec, 1840–1920, 1987.
ISBN 0–19–541472–1

Craig Heron,
Working in Steel: The Early Years in
Canada, 1883–1935, 1988.
ISBN 0–7710–4086–5

Wendy Mitchinson and
Janice Dickin McGinnis, Editors,
Essays in the History of
Canadian Medicine, 1988.
ISBN 0–7710–6063–7

Joan Sangster,
Dreams of Equality: Women on the
Canadian Left, 1920–1950, 1989.
ISBN 0–7710–7946–X

Angus McLaren,
Our Own Master Race: Eugenics in
Canada, 1885–1945, 1990.
ISBN 0–19–541365–2

Bruno Ramirez,
On the Move:
French-Canadian and Italian Migrants
in the North Atlantic Economy,
1860–1914, 1991.
ISBN 0–19–541419–5

Mariana Valverde,
The Age of Light, Soap, and Water:
Moral Reform in English Canada,
1885–1925, 1991.
ISBN 0–7710–8689–X

Bettina Bradbury,
Working Families:
Age, Gender, and Daily Survival in
Industrializing Montreal, 1993.
ISBN 0–19–541211–7

Andrée Lévesque,
Making and Breaking the Rules:
Women in Quebec, 1919–1939, 1994.
ISBN 0–7710–5283–9

Cecilia Danysk,
Hired Hands: Labour and the
Development of Prairie Agriculture,
1880–1930, 1995.
ISBN 0–7710–2552–1

Kathryn McPherson,
Bedside Matters: The Transformation
of Canadian Nursing, 1900–1990, 1996.
ISBN 0–19–541219–2

Edith Burley,
Servants of the Honourable Company:
Work, Discipline, and Conflict in the
Hudson's Bay Company, 1770–1870,
1997.
ISBN 0–19–541296–6

Mercedes Steedman,
Angels of the Workplace: Women and the
Construction of Gender Relations in the
Canadian Clothing Industry, 1890–1940,
1997.
ISBN 0–19–541308–3

Angus McLaren and
Arlene Tigar McLaren,
The Bedroom and the State: The Chang-
ing Practices and Politics of Contracep-
tion and Abortion in Canada,
1880–1997, 1997.
ISBN 0–19–541318–0

Kathryn McPherson, Cecilia Morgan,
and Nancy M. Forestell, Editors,
Gendered Pasts: Historical Essays in
Femininity and Masculinity in Canada,
1999.
ISBN 0–19–541449–7

Gillian Creese,
Contracting Masculinity: Gender, Class,
and Race in a White-Collar Union,
1944–1994, 1999.
ISBN 0–19–541454–3

Geoffrey Reaume,
Remembrance of Patients Past: Patient
Life at the Toronto Hospital for the
Insane, 1870–1940, 2000.
ISBN 0–19–541538–8

Miriam Wright,
A Fishery for Modern Times: The State
and the Industrialization of the New-
foundland Fishery, 1934–1968, 2001.
ISBN 0–19–541620–1

Judy Fudge and Eric Tucker,
Labour Before the Law: The Regulation
of Workers' Collective Action in Canada,
1900–1948, 2001.
ISBN 0–19–541633–3

Mark Moss,
Manliness and Militarism: Educating
Young Boys in Ontario for War, 2001.
ISBN 0–19–541594–9